Advance Praise for *Two Coots in a Canoe:*

"Fans of Dave Morine will be delighted and not at all surprised that his newest work, *Two Coots In a Canoe,* is—nearly to the end—a book of laughter, an account of the comic misadventures of two old friends as they float down the sunlit Connecticut River. And then come the final pages: The two friends' dark destination will surprise and shock all readers, even those with the wits of a wood tick. This remarkable book should be bought and read. Those who do will remember it for a long time."
> —Bil Gilbert, author of *God Gave Us This Country*
> and winner of the National Magazine Award

"A great story about the mystery of friends and comfort of strangers. Dave is not just the supreme conversationalist but also the original conservationist; he virtually defined the art and practice of private land conservation in the 70's and 80's. No one engages people the way he does. His journeys are always worth sharing. John McPhee's birchbark canoe has nothing over two coots' canoe."
> —Spencer B. Beebe, President, Ecotrust

"Dave 'Bugsy' Morine has once again given us a great book—an adventure story that I would have published when editor of *National Geographic Magazine.*"
> —Bill Garrett

"This is the story of two men in one canoe, but on two different journeys. One sees endless opportunities while the other knows his fate is sealed before he ever picks up his paddle. Fresh and honest, light and dark, terminal yet hopeful—these are the undercurrents of a gifted storyteller who undertakes a modern adventure down a storied river valley. Enjoy Dave Morine's tale: he is a wonderful raconteur."

—Howard Corwin, M.D.,
psychiatrist, conservationist

"Dave Morine has done it again, proving that it is often what you do when you aren't striving to get ahead that is most important. When you finish this book, you'll want to drop everything, grab a canoe, and explore your own river."

—George H. Fenwick, President,
American Bird Conservancy

"It has been said Dave Morine never let truth get in the way of a good story, that this is all true makes it that much better a story—about a friendship and a river. The river conservation message is inspiring."

—Rebecca R. Wodder, President,
American Rivers

"I just finished my journey down the Connecticut River with Dave Morine and Ramsay Peard, and couldn't wait to share this recommendation with armchair adventurers everywhere. . . . I found good reading (and fascinating people) around every bend in the river. The ending makes all the more poignant their happy, revealing reliance on the kindness of strangers."

—Doug Wheeler, former Executive Director,
Sierra Club

Two Coots in a Canoe

An Unusual Story of Friendship

DAVID E. MORINE

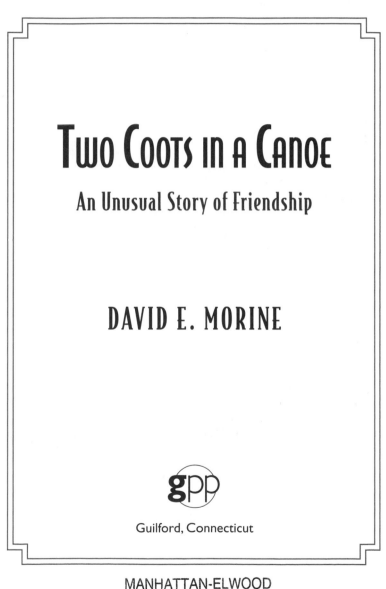

gpp

Guilford, Connecticut

Project editor: Jessica Haberman
Text design: Sheryl P. Kober
Layout artist: Kim Burdick
Maps: Mary Ann Dubé © Morris Book Publishing, LLC

Library of Congress Cataloging-in-Publication Data

Morine, David E.
  Two coots in a canoe : an unusual story of friendship / David E. Morine.
    p. cm.
  ISBN 978-0-7627-5459-5
  1. Connecticut River Valley Region—Description and travel. 2. Morine,
David E.—Travel—Connecticut River Valley Region. 3. Peard, Ramsay,
1942-2003—Travel—Connecticut River Valley Region. 4. Canoes and canoeing—Connecticut River. 5. Friendship—United States. I. Title.
  F12.C7M67 2009
  917.404'44—dc22

                                                           2009010719

Printed in the United States of America

10 9 8 7 6 5 4 3 2 1

To Ramsay,
you damn fool, our trip wasn't over yet.

Disclaimer: I tried my best to correctly recount the conversations we had with our strangers, but it has been six years since our journey began. If anybody at any time takes issue with anything I've quoted them as saying, I'm sure their recollection is absolutely correct, and I offer my sincere apologies. Hey, coots aren't known for their memories.

—D.M.

ACKNOWLEDGMENTS

Thanks to Mary Norris, Jessica Haberman, and the rest of the crew at Globe Pequot Press for their thoughtful presentation of our trip and their high tolerance of coots; to Jim Levine, my agent and every writer's best friend; to Charlie Taylor for keeping me technologically unchallenged and legally correct; to Sophie Sisler, Susan Flint, and Ruth Morine for catching grammatical errors and pointing out dumb, insensitive remarks; to Paul Flint for making everything I write readable; and, of course, to all the strangers who offered us hot showers, wined us, dined us, and tucked us into nice soft beds after long hard days on the river. It was their kindness that made our trip so enjoyable and gave Ramsay his greatest adventure, notwithstanding the blue marlin he caught off Los Cabos, the two holes in one, and his shaking hands with Ted Kennedy in the men's room at the Manchester airport.

PEARD: H. Ramsay Peard passed away unexpectedly on November 4, 2003. Mr. Peard was 61 years old. Born and raised in Baltimore, Mr. Peard attended the Hotchkiss School and from there went to Princeton University where he was a well-liked and much-respected member of Cottage Club. Mr. Peard graduated from Princeton in 1964. He worked for several years in Baltimore, first at Maryland National Bank, then, the Sheet Metal Coating & Litho Company. He enlisted in the Coast Guard Reserves in 1966. In the fall of 1967, he enrolled at the Darden Graduate School of Business Administration at the University of Virginia. During his two years at Darden, Mr. Peard was known as an unorthodox thinker with a brilliant mind for business. Continually at the top of his class, he received his MBA in 1969 and accepted a position with the Boston Consulting Group in Boston, MA. From BCG, Mr. Peard worked as a senior executive at ATE Management in Cincinnati, a transportation management company. Then he returned to Baltimore to become president of the Sheet Metal Coating & Litho Company. In 1983, he returned to Cincinnati to become senior VP of operations of ATE Support Services, Inc. Mr. Peard joined Jung Futuro, a medical products company, as an executive VP. Prior to his retirement in 2000, Mr. Peard had a successful career in real estate. Despite his many successes in business, Mr. Peard refused to take himself and other people too seriously. He figured that since he'd caught a blue marlin off of Cabo San Lucas, had two holes in one, and once met Ted Kennedy in the men's room of the Manchester, NH, airport, his next great adventure was to canoe down the entire length of the Connecticut River (which he accomplished the summer of this year). Mr. Peard is survived by his wife, Theresa J. Peard of Cincinnati; his daughter, Kimberly F. Coccoluto of Wakefield, MA; his brother, Trevor P. Peard of Wallingford, CT; three grandchildren and five nieces and nephews. Donations in his memory may be made to the American Cancer Society, 30 Speen St., Framingham, MA 01701. Services will be private.

Dave Morine and Ramsay Peard

Claire Lynch photo. the News and Sentinel, *Colebrook, New Hampshire*

FOREWORD

BUGSY

His name is not Dave Morine. Let's get that straight right off the bat.

"Dave" and I met at the University of Virginia. We were both students at the Graduate School of Business Administration, class of '69. Imagine, if you will, that environment. First, you have the preppy, ultracool aura of UVA. Then, add in the hyper-aggressive, take-it-all-too-seriously attitude of the hundred or so members of our class, eagerly seeking MBA degrees.

It was inevitable that some in the group, including Dave and myself, would have difficulty achieving assimilation. We weren't rebels or iconoclasts. That would have been too risky. We just felt somewhat uncomfortable, and that discomfort soon expressed itself in the form of a mocking irreverence. Our targets were the school, the faculty, our classmates, and each other. It was in this spirit that Dave became "Bugsy," after the notorious gangster George "Bugsy" Moran of *Untouchables* fame.

Dave abandoned the name Bugsy immediately upon graduating. MBAs migrating north to New York and Boston much prefer to be known as Dave, David, or even David E. This would have been an effective strategy except for the fact that some of us stayed in touch. As far as we are concerned, Bugsy will always be Bugsy.

The reason this is important is because Bugsy has an endearing propensity for getting involved in schemes, adventures, and escapades that someone should have realized at the outset were not very good ideas. At UVA one of his ambitions was to enter the university's boxing competition. I know because he needed a "second," and that was supposed to be me. Well, it never happened because try as he might, Bugsy was never able to convince me that there was absolutely no way the second could ever end up in the ring.

Bugsy grew up around Boston, and his family vacationed in the White Mountains of Maine. I grew up in Baltimore, and my family vacationed in the White Mountains of New Hampshire. With such family traditions, after B-school, Bugsy and I would sometimes cross paths. On one such occasion, we were fishing late at night on a little pond near Bugsy's place in Maine when an owl attacked my lure and got hooked. There we were in moonless darkness in a canoe on a deserted pond with a large, angry bird of prey thrashing around on the end of my line. Bugsy yelled at me to reel it in. Realizing at the outset that this was not a good idea, I cut the line.

In the darkness, we could hear the owl crashing around in the woods. Bugsy insisted we paddle ashore where he found the bird and captured it. From head to tail, the owl had to be at least thirty inches long. One look left no doubt that it could do big-time damage to anyone attempting unwanted surgery. Undaunted, Bugsy pulled out his Swiss Army knife and began cutting the hooks from the fearsome creature's talons and beak. Miraculously, the bird never moved the whole time. When Bugsy finally released it, the bird flew off into the darkness, apparently no worse for wear, but that doesn't alter the fact that Bugsy had a propensity.

On another occasion, Bugsy and another fishing buddy from B-school, neither of whom had a fishing license, attempted to outrun a game warden—this despite the fact that the warden was in a powerboat and they were paddling a canoe. The concept was to land, lug the canoe across a narrow peninsula, and escape to the other side of the lake before the warden could motor around. They didn't make it. The would-be fugitives only paid a modest fine, so not much harm was done, but shouldn't one of them have known at the outset that this was not a good idea?

Today, I live in Cincinnati and Bugsy lives in Northern Virginia. We both still summer in Maine and New Hampshire. Most years we talk long distance about getting together, but it never happens.

This past Christmas my wife, Theresa, asked me if she should write a brief note on the Christmas card we were sending to Bugsy and Ruth. "Sure," I said, "tell them we hope to see them this summer," meaning it's kind of a shame we never get together. That put Bugsy in mind, and since it was Christmastime, I decided to give him a call. Bugsy mentioned that he was just finishing another book. His books, no surprise here, are largely about him getting in and out of trouble, and they're always very humorous.

In addition to having become an old guy, now sixty, I no longer work, and I have too much time on my hands, so a few days later, I called Bugsy again. "Bugsy," I said, "I've got your next book. We're going to canoe the Connecticut River."

For those of you who don't already know, the Connecticut River starts at the Canadian border, travels south forming the boundary between Vermont and New Hampshire, flows through Western Massachusetts by Springfield, passes through Hartford, and empties into Long Island Sound at Old Saybrook, Connecticut. It's about four hundred miles long, and as canoe rivers go, not particularly difficult, but as Bugsy and I have proven in the past, we can make even the simplest river difficult.

Years ago, we tried a short trip on the Saco River in Maine. The Saco runs near Bugsy's cabin and is a very popular canoeing river because it's so easy. My most vivid memory of that trip is scrambling up onto a boulder with my wallet in my mouth watching our empty canoe float downstream through a minor riffle while listening to Bugsy laugh, flopping around in the water.

"Great, let's do it," cried Bugsy, after hearing my idea for canoeing the Connecticut. That's part of his propensity; Bugsy says "great" to almost anything. "But no camping out. I'm not sleeping on the ground, cooking over an open fire, or crapping in the woods. God didn't put me on this earth to have a lousy time."

It was too much to hope that this remark in any way signified that over the years Bugsy had gained wisdom. No, it's just that he has also become an old guy. But he's still Bugsy.

"What are we going to do?" I said.

"We'll rely on the kindness of strangers, like Blanche DuBois in *A Streetcar Named Desire*."

"Let me think about it," I said, and I did, for a couple of days. Canoeing four hundred miles relying on the kindness of strangers was not a good idea, like cutting hooks out of owls and trying to outrun wardens, but then I thought, why not, I wasn't getting any younger. I called Bugsy back. "Okay," I said, sealing the deal, and perhaps our fate.

"Great," Bugsy said.

One last introductory caution, and then I'll turn the reader over to Bugsy. And I admit right up front that this is more than a little self-serving.

Catching the owl in Maine was the basis for one of Bugsy's short stories, "One Over Our Limit." That's fine, it's a true story, and Bugsy's entitled to use it for his own purposes.

The problem is that in his story, I am portrayed as a slow-witted, fearful, clumsy guy whose one redeeming quality is his unwavering confidence in and admiration of the super-hero, David E. Morine. Furthermore, there is simply no end to the qualities possessed by "Dave."

In one of our conversations about the trip and the possibility of a book, I discussed this fact with Bugsy. He was unapologetic and justified his treatment of me as well founded in the traditions of great literature. "Look, Ramsay," he said, "Don Quixote had Sancho Panza, Holmes had Watson, Steinbeck had Charlie, Bryson had Katz: somebody's got to make the protagonist look good. That's what sells books."

Well, maybe so. I'm an MBA, I don't know literature from a hot rock, but I do ask the reader to consider the possibility that maybe I'm not the complete dolt Bugsy presents. If you'll do that, I can live with it, even though I know by now, some of you have to be asking yourselves, "Ramsay, shouldn't you have realized at the outset that this was not a very good idea."

—Ramsay Peard
Cincinnati
January 2003

PART I

THE NORTH COUNTRY

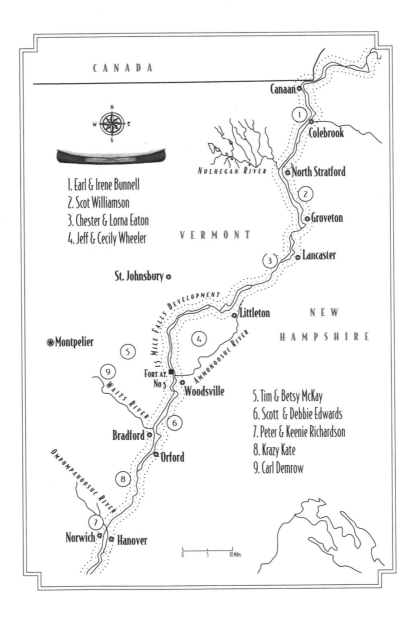

CANADA

Canaan

① Colebrook

NULHEGAN RIVER

North Stratford

②

Groveton

VERMONT

③ Lancaster

St. Johnsbury

1. Earl & Irene Bunnell
2. Scot Williamson
3. Chester & Lorna Eaton
4. Jeff & Cecily Wheeler

N
W   E
S

15 MILE FALLS DEVELOPMENT

Littleton

NEW

HAMPSHIRE

Montpelier

⑤

④

AMMONOOSUC RIVER

⑨

WAITS RIVER

FORT AT. No 5

Woodsville

5. Tim & Betsy McKay
6. Scott & Debbie Edwards
7. Peter & Keenie Richardson
8. Krazy Kate
9. Carl Demrow

⑥

Bradford

Orford

OMPOMPANOOSUC RIVER

⑧

⑦

Norwich   Hanover

0   5   10 Miles

1

MAY 28
CANAAN, VERMONT

Live Free or Die

It was raining, a cold steady drizzle that belied the coming of spring. Claire, a reporter, probably the only reporter, for the *News and Sentinel*, Colebrook, New Hampshire's "independent but not neutral" newspaper, sat on a rock looking very bored. Who could blame her? We weren't going to win Claire any Pulitzer Prize, but in Colebrook, New Hampshire, we were news. In Colebrook, two coots setting out to canoe the entire length of the Connecticut River was front-page news, especially since we had a hook.

When Ramsay asked me if I'd make this trip, I said I'd do it under one condition: no camping. "I'm too old to be sleeping on the ground, cooking over an open campfire, and crapping in the woods," I told him, "and so are you."

"But Bugsy," he'd said, "where will we stay?"

I'd been watching the movie *A Streetcar Named Desire* with Marlon Brando and Vivian Leigh, so I said, "We'll rely on the kindness of strangers, like Blanche Dubois."

"What the hell does that mean?"

"It means at the end of the day, instead of putting up a tent and getting eaten by black flies and mosquitoes, we'll find some stranger who'll offer us a hot shower, wine us, dine us, and then tuck us into a couple of nice soft beds."

"Well, I hope you and Blanche have a good time," Ramsay said, and hung up.

I thought that was the end of our trip, but after a couple of days, Ramsay called back. "Okay," he said, "let's do it."

In his retirement, Ramsay had become hooked on a TV reality show called *Beg, Borrow, and Deal*. I'd never seen the show, but as Ramsay explained it, the idea behind *Beg, Borrow, and Deal* was that three couples would race from New York to San Francisco relying solely on their wits. In addition to finding room, board, and transportation, they'd have to complete ten of twenty assigned tasks. The three examples Ramsay gave were score a goal on a NHL goalie, beat an NBA player in a game of H-O-R-S-E, and have your picture taken with an Olympic gold medalist wearing the medal. "Hot damn," he said, "if these kids can talk their way into those types of things, surely we can find somebody to put us up for a night."

Not wanting to dampen Ramsay's newfound enthusiasm, I didn't tell him I had no intention of begging, borrowing, and dealing my way down the Connecticut River. The strangers we'd be staying with weren't going to be strangers at all. They'd be people I'd met through Deerfield, Amherst, and working thirty years in conservation. Sure, there'd be nights we couldn't find anybody, but when that happened, we'd pull out some plastic and check into the nearest motel, hotel, or reputable bed-and-breakfast. Nothing begs, borrows or deals better than an American Express card, and I wasn't leaving home without it.

Then a funny thing happened. Ramsay's an organizational freak. He likes to plan things down to the minutest detail, so once we decided we'd make the trip, he began reading everything he could divine on canoeing the Connecticut. One of the books he found was *The Complete Boating Guide to the Connecticut River* (the *Guide*), published by the Connecticut River Watershed Council (CRWC). When Ramsay called CRWC to order a copy, he began talking with Whitty Sanford, CRWC's associate director. During their conversation, Ramsay mentioned we were planning to paddle the entire river relying solely on the kindness of strangers. That piqued Whitty's interest. "Maybe we can help," she said. "If you'll prepare a press release describing your trip, we'll e-mail it to our members. You guys sound nutty enough that some of them might be willing to put you up."

On Good Friday, 2003, the Connecticut River Watershed Council sent the following press release to its fifteen hundred members:

NEWS ... NEWS ... NEWS ...

For Immediate Release—April 4, 2003

GREY HAIRED RIVER PAD-DLERS SEEKING "THE KIND-NESS OF STRANGERS"

Connecticut River Watershed—Starting at the Canadian border in late May, two 60-year-old optimists will climb into a canoe and begin the 400+ mile trek down the Connecticut River to Old Saybrook, CT. Having no interest in carrying any equipment and sleeping outdoors, these carefree canoers plan to paddle ashore each evening to seek food, drink, and shelter from "the kindness of strangers." They hope to reach Old Saybrook on July 4.

"They assure me they're very affable company and would be good house guests," says Whitty Sanford, Associate Director of the Connecticut River Watershed Council, which is assisting the pair in planning this leap of faith. "We are hoping that others along the river will be willing to take them in for a night. My husband and I are looking forward to hosting them in mid to late June."

The bowman is Dave Morine, a native of Arlington, MA and a graduate of Deerfield Academy and Amherst College. During the '70s and '80s, Dave was the head of land acquisition for The Nature Conservancy. For the last twelve years, he's been a professional writer who's written several humorous books including *GOOD DIRT: Confessions of a Conservationist* and *VACATIONLAND: A Half Century Summering in Maine.* Dave's latest book, *SMALL CLAIMS: My Little Trials in Life* will come out in June while he is on the river. Will he be writing about this trip? "That'll depend on the kindness of the strangers," Dave says. "At our age, there's nothing humorous about drinking alone and sleeping on the ground."

In the stern, doing all the heavy lifting, will be Ramsay Peard, formerly of Baltimore, MD and a graduate of Princeton. Peard started his working career with The Boston Consulting Group and ended as the CEO of a medical products company in Cincinnati. Says Peard,

"I've caught a blue marlin off Los Cabos, had two holes in one, and met Teddy Kennedy at the Manchester, New Hampshire airport; other than that, this trip will be my greatest adventure. By the way, what's a black fly?"

When asked if their wives approve of them taking off for a month, both men reflected that, "they seem absolutely jubilant."

Strangers within easy drive of the River who are interested in perhaps hosting these two grey haired beggars should contact the Watershed Council.

Ramsay called me the first thing Saturday morning. He was very upset. "Bugsy," he said, "Whitty screwed us. Our press release said I'd met Ted Kennedy at the Manchester airport, but Whitty felt it was politically incorrect to say I'd met him in the men's room so she left it out. Hell, that was my best line."

It was his best line, but given the senator's checkered past, Whitty was right to leave it out, not that it mattered. On Easter Monday morning, CRWC had fifty-five responses from strangers all up and down the river offering to put us up. Ramsay was ecstatic. "Bugsy," he said when he called, "Whitty just e-mailed me the list. I'm going to start calling tonight, but we've got a problem."

"What's that?"

"A lot of them appear to be single women."

"Ramsay, don't flatter yourself. Nobody's going to mistake us for Newman and Redford."

"Hell, Bugsy, after a long cold winter, they might."

One of the strangers who'd responded was John Harrigan, the owner and editor emeritus of the *News and Sentinel*. When Ramsay called, John sounded genuinely enthused about our trip. He told Ramsay he was going to throw us a barbeque when we got to Canaan, the little town in the northeast corner of Vermont where we planned to shove off. That got Ramsay all excited. He was thrilled with the way the trip had caught fire and was looking forward to a big send-off.

Ruth, my wife, was driving us to Canaan. Just before we reached the bridge where we'd put in, Ramsay told Ruth and me he'd come up with a great bit. "When we shove off," he said, "we'll start paddling upstream. Then, when everybody starts yelling we're going the wrong way, we'll paddle back to shore, get out, and say, 'Hell, what's for lunch.' "

When we got to the bridge, Claire, the reporter, was the only one there. "Where's John?" Ramsay said, looking around for the crowd and the barbeque.

"He went fishing," Claire said, "but he told me to take your picture and give you this."

She handed Ramsay a brown paper bag. Ramsay took the bag and pulled out a six-pack of Pabst Blue Ribbon beer. Grudgingly, he popped one open. He was mad. Ramsay didn't like being stood up, but that wasn't Claire's problem. Having delivered John's gift, she sat on the rock in the rain and watched while we unloaded the car and packed the canoe.

Once we were set, Claire asked if we'd stand on the bank with our paddles so she could take our picture. It was then I noticed how odd Ramsay looked. He'd switched his regular tortoiseshell glasses for a pair of prescription sunglasses with dark lenses and heavy black frames, like Roy Orbison used to wear. In addition to the glasses, he'd donned a floppy, wide-brim boonie hat, the kind the army wore in Desert Storm, and for some reason, he'd put his life vest on under his sweatshirt. "Ramsay," I said, "why's your life vest under your sweatshirt? It makes you look like the Incredible Hulk."

"If we tip over," he said, "you'll want to get the heavy stuff off fast, and you can't do that if you have your life vest over it."

From past experience, we stood a good chance of tipping over. Still, I preferred wearing my life vest on the outside. I wasn't going to end up on the front page of the *News and Sentinel* looking like the Incredible Hulk.

With our picture taken, Ramsay chugged what was left of his Pabst, handed Claire the empty can, and said, "Here. Tell John he can keep his five-cent deposit."

I kissed Ruth goodbye and steadied the canoe while the Hulk lumbered into the stern. Once he was settled, I picked up my paddle and eased into the bow. "Okay," I said to Ruth, "you can push us off."

She did, and for a moment we hung suspended in an eddy. Then the current grabbed us and the river quickly proved who was boss. It swirled us sideways and whisked us downstream toward a long set of riffles. "Hot damn, Bugsy," Ramsay yelled, "Give me some speed!"

I started paddling knowing if we hit the riffles sideways, we were sure to flip over, but Ramsay got us straightened out just in time. Through the crisp, clear water, I could see a carpet of green moss flying along below us. Ramsay kept yelling and I kept paddling as the canoe kept bobbing its way down the Connecticut.

After a frantic half-mile, the river flattened and the water calmed. I stopped paddling to catch my breath and heard Ruth calling from what seemed very far away. I looked up and through the steady rain saw her standing high on a bluff on the New Hampshire side. She had both arms over her head waving, but before I could lift my paddle to wave back, we rounded a bend, and Ruth was gone.

It was then it hit me. What in the world had I done? Here I was, alone on a river paddling four hundred miles with a guy I hadn't seen in twenty years. Neither of us knew squat about canoeing, and if by some miracle we made it through the days, we'd be spending the nights with complete strangers. Why had I ever agreed to go on this trip? I must have been out of my mind.

After a few miles, it become obvious we had a problem. The upper Connecticut meanders through a series of seemingly never-ending oxbows. Paddling around them was literally a pain in the ass unless you let the current work for you, but Ramsay kept cutting every corner, which meant we were constantly losing the current and running aground.

"Whoa," he'd say as the stern of the Mad River suddenly spun sideways. "I don't understand what's happening here. Every now and then, the canoe just turns for no reason."

"That's because you keep moving us out of the current. Keep to the far bank, then we'll stay with it."

"No way, Bugsy. That would add a quarter of a mile to every turn."

Some genius at Princeton must have impressed on Ramsay that the shortest distance between two points was a straight line. However, the river, unencumbered by a Princeton education, didn't care about the shortest distance. It was looking for the path of least resistance, which meant the current kept weaving back and forth. When the river turned, the greatest speed was always on the outside bank, like the horses on the outside of a merry-go-round or the last skater in a pinwheel. But Ramsay wouldn't accept that fact. "Water's water," he maintained. "Why go around the outside of the loop when we can go right through it?" He kept cutting every corner, and we kept losing the current and running aground.

As bowman, it was up to me to get out and pull us free. The water was freezing and the riverbed was covered with slippery, fist-size stones that hurt my feet. Every time I got out, my feet were getting bruised and cold. After Ramsay put us aground for about the fifth time, I'd had it. As I took off my shoes and socks, I was about to tell him if he couldn't stay with the current he'd have to give up the stern, but I bit my tongue.

During our planning, I'd discovered Ramsay didn't take criticism very well. This fact came to light when Whitty Sanford told him she wanted a photo of us to send out with our press release. When Ramsay called to tell me we needed a picture, I told him not to worry, I'd send one to Whitty that very day. "No, no," he said, "you don't understand. It has to be of us together."

"Together? Ramsay, in case you've forgotten, we haven't seen each other in twenty years."

"No problem. I've got a buddy down the street who's got a digital camera. He's going to take a head and shoulders shot of me standing ten feet in front of a pine tree. You get a guy to do the same and e-mail the picture to my buddy. Then he'll merge them and e-mail the result to Whitty."

"You've got to be kidding. That would take all day, and I don't have a day to waste on some picture."

There was a long, stony silence at the other end of the line. Finally, Ramsay said, "Bugsy, it's no big deal. All you have to do is get your picture taken and e-mail it to my buddy. I'll take care of the rest."

"It may not be a big deal for you, but it's a big deal for me. Assuming I could find someone who has a digital camera, I wouldn't want to ask them to give up the time to take a picture of me standing ten feet in front of a pine tree, then e-mailing it to your buddy. What do you say I just send your buddy some pictures of me and he can use one of them? If that doesn't work, send Whitty a picture of you. Believe me, my feelings won't be hurt if I'm not in it."

Ramsay had been calling me every day for two months. Now, for four days, I didn't hear a word. On the fifth, he called. He was very serious. "Bugsy," he said. "I once dated a girl who wanted me to go out on a boat with her for the weekend. When I told a buddy what I was doing, he said, 'Don't you know the rule about boats? Every day you spend on a boat with someone, the boat gets a foot shorter.' Well, I figure we just lost about five feet of canoe on this picture deal."

As my toes hit the water, I kept biting my tongue. I didn't need to be losing five feet of a sixteen-foot canoe, not on our first day. Besides, what did I care. It was Ramsay's trip. If he wanted to cut corners, let him cut corners. Now that I was on the river, it wasn't like I had anything better to do. Still, as the rocks chewed at my feet, I could feel the canoe shrinking.

By the time I worked us free and climbed back into the bow, my feet were too numb to feel the cuts and bruises. But I didn't say a word. Having resolved not to confront Ramsay, I developed a private protest. The seats of the Mad River were attached to the gunnels with wooden pegs. When I leaned hard into the paddle, the pressure on the seat would make the pegs squeak. For the next 398 miles, making the pegs squeak was my way of telling Ramsay he was being an asshole. If Ramsay ever broke the code, he never let on, but hearing the squeaks always made me feel better. On the bright side, I was gaining new respect for our canoe. All the crunching and scraping didn't seem to bother it one bit. This despite the fact it was a cheap, bottom-of-the-line "second" that Mad River Canoes had given to CRWC and Whitty had lent to us.

On this, our first day, we'd planned to go from Canaan to Colebrook, a distance of ten miles. Not being experienced paddlers, we had no idea how long it would take us, but somewhere in his research, Ramsay had read that the current in this part of the river ranged from two to three miles per hour. Even with Ramsay constantly running us aground, we'd probably make it to Colebrook in less than four hours, so having nothing better to do, I decided to sit back and enjoy the ride.

In truth, there wasn't much to enjoy. For the most part, the ride was cold, rainy, and boring. The *Guide* said to watch for deer, moose, bear, mink, muskrat, fox, and turkey, but a flock of eight common mergansers had assumed the role as our advance party. Every time we got to within a hundred yards of them, they'd take off downstream, quacking and beating their wings on the water. Thanks to the mergansers, there was no chance we were going to surprise any wildlife.

"Bugsy," Ramsay said, "have you noticed all those trails coming down to the water? What do you think formed them? Cattle?"

I looked up and saw he was pointing to a muddy slide on the bank. "No, those are moose slides. Pull over and I'll show you the tracks."

Sure enough, when we pulled over the shoreline was covered with tracks. Moose tracks were the most obvious, but on closer inspection I found evidence of turkeys, foxes, raccoons, even a bear. Ramsay was duly impressed, as well he should have been. "Bugsy, how do you know all this stuff?"

"Well, I've been working in conservation for thirty years. During that time, you figure I had to learn something."

Actually, I knew very little about nature. My time with The Nature Conservancy was spent saving land, not studying flora and fauna, but I wasn't going to tell Ramsay that. Better he thought I was some great outdoorsman. That way, he might listen to me when I told him to stay with the current. But he didn't. As we came to the next bend, he started to cut the corner. "Ramsay," I said, "stay to the far bank. That way, you'll keep the current."

"No way. I'm taking it close. Just keep paddling."

Squeak! Squeak! Squeak! CRUNCH!

Earl Bunnell was our first "stranger." We were going to meet Earl at the Colebrook Bridge. The plan Ramsay had worked out with all our strangers was that he'd call them two nights before we were going to arrive to see if they were still willing to put us up. If they were, he'd call again the night before we arrived and tell them where to meet us. Finally, he'd call a third time when we got to the meeting spot.

Ramsay had called Earl Bunnell just before he'd left Cincinnati, then again the night before from Cornish, Vermont, where we'd stayed with Claire Porter, one of Ruth's college roommates. Now, as we pulled in under the Colebrook Bridge, he'd have to go find a phone to tell Earl we'd arrived. We'd made a conscious decision not to bring a cell phone. Time on a river's meant to be quiet and peaceful, not yapping on some cell phone.

The sun had come out, so Ramsay had taken off his sweatshirt. That left him wearing his life vest over a T-shirt. Before the trip, I'd gone to Wal-Mart and bought a snazzy BassMaster aquamarine life vest with gray lining and black trim. It looked manly. Ramsay, on the other hand, had gone into his basement and found a little kid's life vest that had long ago belonged to his daughter. It was candy-apple red with blue lining and white trim. It looked girlie. I hoped Ramsay wouldn't have to go too far to find a phone. Dressed in his dark Roy Orbison sunglasses, Desert Storm boonie hat, and red, white, and blue little girlie life vest, he was one weird-looking dude.

After about half an hour, Ramsay came running back down the embankment. "Bugsy," he gasped, "I've got to get my cards. There's a cop helping me out. He's waiting in a squad car on top of the bridge."

"A cop's driving you around?" That didn't sound good.

"Yeah, I had to walk all the way into town before I found a phone. While I was looking up Earl's number, this cop came by and asked me what I was doing. I told him I was trying to find Earl Bunnell, but there were two Earl Bunnells in the book, and I only had enough change for one call. When I mentioned I had the number back at my canoe, he said, 'Get in. I'll drive you out there.' Pretty neat, huh?" Pretty strange was more like it, but maybe small-town cops had nothing better to do than drive weird-looking guys around.

Ramsay dove into his duffel and found the waterproof plastic bag where he kept his maps, the 3 x 5 index cards he made for all of our potential hosts, and his copy of the *Guide*. He opened the waterproof plastic bag, found Earl's card, scribbled down the number, and carefully put the card back in the bag and the bag back in the duffel. I would have just taken the card with me, but Ramsay had a rule: His cards never left his duffel. That done, he ran back up the bank.

Typical of Ramsay's anal attention to detail, each card contained the name, address, telephone number, and a short first impression based on his initial call. Earl's card read, "Old New Englander." When I'd asked Ramsay how he'd formed his opinions, he said, "Easy, I chat 'em up and see how they react to my lines."

"Lines? What lines?" Nobody was going to mistake Ramsay for Groucho Marx.

"I'd start them off with, 'Hi, this is Ramsay Peard with the Kindness of Strangers Expedition. Your mother asked me to call and tell you you're not exercising very good judgment.' If that got a laugh, I'd tell them my golfing buddies said I must be crazy to spend a month in a canoe with a guy I hadn't seen in twenty years, but after thinking about it, I figured, 'What the hell, Bugsy couldn't have gotten any worse.' Finally, when they asked what we'd like for dinner, I'd say, 'If the beer's cold, who cares?' That was to make sure we didn't get stuck with anybody who didn't drink."

The bulk of Ramsay's notations were factual, such as "Has car-top canoe capability," or "Will be in Wyoming from 6/21 to 6/28." The most self-serving was "Doesn't drink, but will buy us beer." The least complimentary, "Very dull!" The most enthusiastic, "Super guy!"

Ramsay only gave out two "Super guys!" John Harrigan, the newspaperman, was one. John got his rating because when Ramsay called, John told him he raised sheep and didn't want to hear any sheep jokes. Ramsay said not to worry, he didn't know any sheep jokes, which was true. Except for some very old golf stories, Ramsay didn't know *any* jokes, sheep or otherwise. When John told Ramsay to take down his 800 number, Ramsay said, "Hold on, I've got to find a pen," to which John said, "Hey, watch it, that's a sheep joke." Bingo, that and the fact he was going to throw us a barbeque made John a "Super guy!" At least until he stiffed us and went fishing.

Ramsay's other "Super guy!" was Bill Webster, a Dartmouth grad who owned a home on Fenwick Island, a swishy enclave in Old Saybrook right at the mouth of the river. Fenwick Island would be our last stop. When Bill asked Ramsay what date he thought we'd be getting there, Ramsay said he wasn't sure, but figured it'd probably be around July Fourth. Bill said that would be perfect because he always had a big Fourth of July party, and we could be the honored guests. "To be honest," Ramsay said, "don't get carried away on our account. There's a chance we might crap out before we ever reach the Sound."

"Nonsense," Bill said. "I've got a thirty-two-foot cabin cruiser. You get to Hartford, and I'll come get you. Then, for the party, I'll let you off a half-mile upstream. While we set off some fireworks, you can paddle in. It'll be a real show."

Somewhere during the conversation, Bill mentioned his next-door neighbor on Fenwick Island was Katharine Hepburn, and somehow, Ramsay got the impression Katharine would be at the party. For Ramsay, a thirty-two-foot cabin cruiser, fireworks, and Katharine Hepburn were more than enough to rate Bill Webster a "Super guy!"

Ramsay hadn't been gone more than few minutes when a rosy-cheeked octogenarian dressed in a coat and tie appeared under the Colebrook bridge. "You one of those guys canoeing the river?" he said.

"Guilty as charged," I said. "You must be Earl Bunnell."

"Where's the other guy?"

"A cop just drove him into town. He's trying to call you."

"That guy's always calling me," said Earl, clearly exasperated with Ramsay's three-call system. "I told him I had to go to a friend's funeral this afternoon and would meet you here at four. I'm going home to get my truck. You all right sitting here?"

"Just fine."

"Okay, I'll be back in about fifteen minutes."

"What about Ramsay?"

"If the cops got him, serves him right. All he had to do was wait until four."

Right at four, Earl and I were loading the Mad River into the back of Earl's pickup truck, when I saw Ramsay trudging our way. His little girlie vest was unzipped in the front and the brim of his boonie hat was stained with sweat. Behind his dark sunglasses, I could see he was pissed. Ramsay didn't like glitches, and not being able to get a hold of Earl was a definite glitch. "Ramsay," I said, when he reached the truck, "meet Earl Bunnell."

I was sure Ramsay was going to quiz Earl on why he hadn't waited for his call, but Earl beat him to the punch. "Ramsay," he said, "it's about time you showed up. While you were out sightseeing, Dave and I were doing all the work."

That immediately defused Ramsay. "Earl," he said, "if you got Bugsy to do some work, you'd be the first."

On the way to Earl's house, Ramsay told us the cop had driven him back to the police station and let him use their phone. While Ramsay was talking to Earl's wife, Irene, the cop got called out on a case, so Ramsay had to hoof it all the way back to the bridge. "Earl, people aren't too friendly up here," he said. "I tried bumming, but nobody would pick me up. I swear a few guys actually sped up when they passed me."

Seeing Ramsay in his boonie hat, dark sunglasses, and little girlie vest, I couldn't blame them. I sure as hell wouldn't have stopped for him.

Earl lived out in the country a few miles north of the Colebrook Bridge. His modest but comfortable two-story wooden house sat back in a field off of Route 102, the main road running along the Vermont side of the river. Earl pulled into the driveway, parked his truck, and after we left our shoes by the door, (which is the custom in the North Country), he ushered us in. After introducing us to Irene, Earl asked us if we'd like a drink. Surveying Earl's well-stocked bar, I said, "Sure, how about a Myers's Rum and tonic."

"I can do that," Earl said "How about you, Ramsay?"

"I'll have a cold beer, if you've got one."

Earl got Ramsay a beer from the refrigerator, then went over to the bar to fix drinks for me, Irene, and himself. While Irene started dinner, Ramsay went outside for a smoke, and I wandered into a small den off of the kitchen. The den was full of family photos. I immediately was taken by a black-and-white picture of an attractive, middle-aged woman sitting on a rock holding an English setter puppy. "Who's this?" I said to Earl.

"Oh, that's Vicki, our daughter," Earl said, handing me my rum and tonic.

"Vicki's an attractive woman. Where's she now?"

"Vicki's dead. She was murdered six years ago."

I almost dropped my drink. "I'm awfully sorry," I said, not knowing what else to say.

"You might have read about it." Earl said, studying the picture. "It was national news. The guy who murdered her killed two state troopers, the editor of the paper, and wounded three other people before they finally got him."

I might have remembered something about a mass murder in northern New England, but with so many mass murders in the news, I wasn't sure. I took a gulp of my drink hoping Ramsay would come in, but he was still outside having his smoke. Earl took his bourbon and water and sat down at the kitchen table. I joined him while Irene kept cooking. There was a long, awkward silence.

Now what? I could ask more about Vicki, or I could change the subject. Changing the subject seemed like the polite thing to do, only I didn't want to change the subject. If Earl and Irene wanted to talk about Vicki, that was their call. Why ignore it? "Earl," I said, "I think I remember something about a mass murder up here, but I don't know the details. If you want to talk about it, that's fine, if not, we can move on to something else."

"The guy was trouble," Earl said. "Always had been."

"Vicki called him a time bomb," Irene added, not looking up from the stove.

"Vicki had a gun, but it wasn't loaded," Earl said. "She kept the clip locked in a drawer. When she saw Drega drive up—that was his name, Carl Drega—she couldn't find the key. Vicki never had a chance. He shot her in the back as she was running to her car."

At that moment, Ramsay came in. "Ramsay, Earl and Irene are telling me about their daughter, Vicki. She was murdered six years ago."

Ramsay took a sip of his beer and sat down without saying a word. For the next hour, neither of us said much. Instead we listened to Earl and Irene tell us about Vicki and how she'd come to be murdered by Carl Drega, the time bomb that finally went off.

Earl and Irene had two children, Earl and Vicki. After finishing school, Earl Jr. got a job with the New Hampshire Registry of Motor Vehicles and moved to Colebrook. He still lived there, which was why Ramsay had found two Earl Bunnells in the phone book. Vicki had gone to Plymouth State College and then to the University of Puget Sound Law School in Tacoma. "Graduated with honors," Earl said.

Vicki came home after law school, worked for a while with a lawyer in Colebrook, then hung out her own shingle. Over the years, she established a practice that dealt mostly with child custody cases, adoption, family abuse, and the environment. She never married and lived with her English setter in Columbia, a little town on the New Hampshire side of the river just south of Colebrook.

"In 1990, Vicki was elected a selectman for Columbia," Earl said. "That's when she got drawn into a long-running fight the town was having with Drega, an ex-Army MP who moved up here in the early seventies. Drega built a house down on the river, but in order to reduce his taxes, he never finished it. After a while, the neighbors started complaining his tar-paper siding was an eyesore, so the town hit him with a zoning violation. From then on, it was one battle after another."

"Did Drega have a family?" I said.

"Naw, he was a loner, and a real nut. He had a bunch of guns and was always shooting them off. He never went anywhere unarmed. He'd strap a pistol on just to walk out for the mail. People were scared to death of him."

"The neighbors all thought he was weirder than a three-dollar bill," Irene said.

"Vicki got crossways with Drega one night in 1991," Earl said. "She was working late in the selectmen's office when he showed up and began rummaging through the property files trying to find out what other people were paying in taxes. Vicki told him the town hall was closed and he'd have to leave. Drega said he wouldn't go so she called the state police. When they came, Drega still wouldn't leave so they cuffed him and physically lugged him out. He was madder than a wet hen. After that, Vicki was on his hit list, and she knew it. Drega told her point blank he was going to kill her. Then he started sending her notes saying the same thing."

"Damn, Earl," Ramsay said, "couldn't she get a restraining order against him?"

"She had all that stuff, but it didn't do any good. Drega had a whole list of people he said he was going to kill. Everybody knew it, but nobody would do anything about it. That's why Vicki got a gun."

On August 19, 1997, at 2:45 p.m., Drega exploded. According to clippings Earl had from the *News and Sentinel*, two state troopers pulled Drega over after he'd run a red light in downtown Colebrook. As they approached his pickup, Drega, who was 67 at the time, pulled out an automatic rifle and shot both of them. Leslie Lord, 45, died instantly, but Scott Phillips, 32, managed to stagger into an adjacent field before he collapsed. While a number of people watched in horror,

Drega, who was wearing a bulletproof vest, got out of his pickup, calmly walked over to where Phillips was lying, and shot him four times. Then he got into the police cruiser and headed for the building that housed Vicki's law office and the *News and Sentinel*, John Harrigan's newspaper.

"Someone had the presence of mind to call Vicki and tell her Drega was coming," Earl said, "but before Vicki could find the key to the drawer where she kept the clip to her gun, he pulled up in the squad car. When she saw him get out, she ran back to the *News and Sentinel* and told everybody to get out, Drega was coming and he had a gun."

It was too late. Dennis Joos, editor of the *News and Sentinel*, tried to tackle Drega as he came through the door chasing Vicki, but Drega shot him dead. Then Drega followed Vicki out into the parking lot and shot her once in the back with the assault rifle as she was getting into her car. That was enough. Vicki, one of the North Country's brightest stars, had been murdered by some wacko everybody knew was a nutcase who should have been put away years ago. Having killed four people in Colebrook, Drega got back in the police cruiser and raced over the Colebrook Bridge, the same bridge where Earl had picked us up, into Vermont. By that time, every enforcement officer, local, state, or federal, in the North Country was after him.

"Drega ended up wounding a game and fish officer, a border patrol agent, and another state trooper before they finally got him," Earl said. "Shot him dead in a lumberyard just south of here in North Stratford, which was good. At least we had closure the same day. We'd never have made it through a long, drawn-out trial."

Irene nodded.

Later that night, as I lay in bed, it occurred to me why the cop had given Ramsay a ride back to the bridge. After what happened to Vicki, some oddball wandering around Colebrook dressed in dark sunglasses, a boonie hat, and what could have been a bulletproof vest looking for Earl Bunnell would have raised a few eyebrows.

I also realized I'd met Vicki. In the summer of '83, Champion International, the big paper company, gave Fourth Connecticut Lake, a small bog just 300 yards south of the Canadian border that is the headwaters of the Connecticut, to The Nature Conservancy. At the time, Ramsay had just divorced his first wife and was visiting Ruth and me at our cabin in Maine. Champion International was having a big dedication ceremony at Fourth Connecticut Lake, and as the head of land acquisition for the Conservancy, I'd driven over to accept the deed. It turned out Vicki was the local attorney we'd hired to record it. I remembered her because she came to the ceremony with an English setter, probably the mother of the puppy in the picture. When I got back from the ceremony that night, I mentioned to Ramsay how the Connecticut was truly a New England river in that it started right at the Canadian border and ran all the way to Long Island Sound. That's when he got the idea that someday we should canoe it. Now, twenty years later, here we were spending the first night of our trip with Vicki's parents in Vicki's house, maybe even in Vicki's bed. Amazing.

2

Nobody Gets Lost on a River

Over breakfast, Ramsay asked Earl if he would mind driving us down to North Stratford so we could avoid fooling with the dam at Lyman Falls. Putting in at North Stratford meant we'd skip fourteen miles of river, or a whole day's paddling, but I was in full agreement. According to the *Guide,* "The breached Lyman Falls Dam can offer fun whitewater for the experienced paddler. However, numerous hazards must be watched for, including some steel rods sticking out of the dam. Proceed with caution, and don't plan on running the dam unless you're prepared to swim." We were not experienced paddlers, and we weren't prepared to swim, especially through steel rods.

"That's a good decision," Earl said. "There's not much warning before you reach the falls, and once you're there, there's no easy take out. If you boys didn't see the dam in time, you'd be in a heap of trouble."

After a stop at a convenience store so Ramsay could buy a six-pack of Bud Light and a pack of Carltons, Earl drove us to a put-in just south of North Stratford. As we settled into the Mad River, Earl said, "You boys keep those life jackets on all the time?"

"You bet," I said, remembering Earl had mentioned he was a member of the Colebrook Volunteer Rescue Squad.

"Good," Earl said. "I never pulled anybody from the bottom of a river who was wearing a life jacket."

As we pushed off, we saw a look in Earl's eyes that we would see over and over. Earl wished he was coming with us, and who could blame him. While he was left standing on shore dealing with the realities of life, we were like Tom Sawyer and Huck Finn setting off on a new adventure.

Earl gave us a push and once again, the Mad River hesitated, then caught the current. This time, we were prepared. I started paddling and Ramsay pointed us downstream. We'd barely gone a mile when the river split. The main course swung far to the right around an island. A smaller channel kept going straight. "Ramsay," I said, "stay with the current. Go right."

"No way, Bugsy. That channel has to be shorter."

I was sure taking the channel meant I'd be spending the rest of the morning pulling us off sandbars, but for the first few hundred yards it was flat and calm. We soon discovered why. Somebody, probably a fisherman wanting to create a pool, had built a dam between the shore and the island. "Ramsay," I said, "pull over. This dam could be trouble."

Both banks of the channel were high and steep. To get ashore, I tied the Mad River to a tree hanging over the water. Then, using the trunk, we climbed up onto the island. From above, we could see the dam was formed by a wall of rocks a couple of feet high. Below the dam, the current picked up, but it was nothing we couldn't handle.

"Piece of cake," Ramsay said. "Let's shoot it."

"Are you nuts?" I said, surprised Ramsay would be so aggressive. "Look at the flow. There's not enough water to make it over the dam. We'll have to portage it."

"Bugsy, just give me some speed. We'll be fine."

"Look, if we tip over, we're going to be cold and wet the whole day. Why take the chance? We can portage it in twenty minutes."

"Look at that bank. How are we going to lug the canoe up that? Hell, let's just go for it."

"I'll tell you what: Let's portage the bags. That way if we go over, at least we'll have some dry clothes. And taking the bags out will make the canoe lighter."

Ramsay agreed, albeit reluctantly. With the duffels safely downstream, we got back into the Mad River and pushed off. "Give me speed, Bugsy," Ramsay yelled. "*Speed!*" I did, and he pointed the Mad River for the dead center of the dam. We hit it perfectly, and much to my surprise, there was plenty of water. We bobbed over, whisked through the riffles, and pulled into the beach where we'd left the bags. Neither of us said a thing. Neither of us had to. We both knew Ramsay had been right. Now, no matter how many times he ran us aground, he'd earned the stern for the rest of the trip.

Our goal for the day was to reach Maidstone Bridge, which, according to the *Guide,* was twelve miles from North Stratford. Scot Williamson, our host for the evening, lived in Stratford, just up from the bridge. Except for the weather, which once again was cool and rainy, it looked like we were in for an easy day. We'd gone from Canaan to Colebrook, a distance of ten miles, in about four hours so we should be able to do the twelve miles from North Stratford to Stratford in no more than five. That would put us at Maidstone Bridge around three.

As we meandered mile after mile through a broad floodplain, we saw nothing of real interest. The banks were high, and even without our advance party of mergansers, we surprised no wildlife. One thing we were glad to miss was the black flies. Everyone had assured us we were going to get eaten alive, but so far, we hadn't seen a black fly, or any other bugs.

Ramsay liked to pull ashore every couple of miles for a smoke and a beer. During these breaks, I'd get out the snack bag Ruth had given me. The snack bag, which took up a good third of my duffel, was supposed to be for both of us, but Ramsay wasn't a snacker. He was a beer and butt man. That left all the Nature Valley granola bars, Hershey Kisses, Nestlé Crunch Bites, Snickers bars, Tom's peanut butter crackers (cheese and regular), Blue Diamond salted almonds, See's Krispy Mints, and Starbucks chocolate-covered cherries for me. It was Halloween every stop. After one day, I'd become addicted to breaks.

Around mid-afternoon, Ramsay said, "Bugsy, start looking for the bridge. We have to be getting close," but we never saw it.

The only thing that crossed the river was a trestle of rusty steel girders covered with rotting wooden planks. "What the hell's that?" Ramsay said.

"Looks like an old railroad bridge." I said, peering up through the holes in the planks.

At that point Ramsay stopped paddling, unzipped his duffle, and pulled out the *Guide*. "Bugsy, what does it mean when they say twelve miles? Is that river miles or road miles?"

"Well, since we're on the river, I'd assume it's river miles." Just then, a school bus came rumbling along south on Route

102. "You know, while I was waiting for you and Earl under the Colebrook Bridge, I noticed the school buses came by at around three-thirty. If that school bus is any indicator, it must be about three-thirty, which means we've gone at least twelve river miles." As with cell phones, we'd both agreed that watches have no place on a river; rivers should be timeless.

Ramsay kept looking at the *Guide*. "This map shows a road going across the river between Stratford, New Hampshire, and Maidstone, Vermont. We haven't seen any road crossing the river. Hell, we haven't seen any town."

"So, where the hell is this Maidstone Bridge?"

"It has to be up ahead. Keep paddling."

The Connecticut kept weaving back and forth, and we kept paddling and paddling. At one turn, a forty-foot-long, ten-foot-high metal bulkhead was driven into the bank. Ramsay pulled in just past the bulkhead. While he lit up a Carlton and popped a Bud Light, I got out and climbed to the top of the bulkhead. On the other side, not a hundred yards away, there was the river. Left to its own devices, the Connecticut would have breached that hundred yards, but due to the bulkhead it was forced to stay the course. That meant we were going to have to paddle a mile to the west, make the loop, and paddle a mile back to the east, all for a hundred yards.

"Damn," I said as I climbed back into the canoe and gave Ramsay the bad news. "The maps must be in road miles."

"Either that, or we're lost."

"Lost! How can we be lost? Nobody gets lost on a river. It only goes one way."

After a while, another yellow-and-black school bus rumbled by, but this one was empty. It had dropped off all its students and was heading back to the barn. We'd been paddling for at least six hours. During that time, we hadn't seen a soul. Ramsay kept pulling out the *Guide* and saying Maidstone Bridge had to be around the next bend, but after a half dozen next bends, neither of us believed it. As impossible as it might seem, we were lost.

I'd picked a mountain to try to monitor our progress, but it wasn't getting any closer. As the river kept weaving, the mountain kept moving slowly back and forth like a cat's tail. Finally, I saw what looked like a sizable tributary coming in from the left. "Ramsay," I said, "Give me the map. That river's got to be on the map."

Ramsay zipped open his duffel, took out his waterproof bag, and handed me the *Guide*. I opened it to the map for North Stratford to Guildhall, a span of twenty-three miles. "Ramsay, if I'm reading this map right, that river up ahead is the Upper Ammonoosuc, and that mountain is Cape Horn. If that's the case, the next takeout is about four miles downriver at Northumberland."

"Northumberland? Impossible. That's where we're stopping tomorrow. Plus, we can't get there without going under the Maidstone Bridge. It has to be around the next bend."

Three bends and four miles later, we saw a bridge. "Thank God," Ramsay said. "I thought we'd never make it."

"Those look like rapids on the other side of the bridge. Are you sure that's Maidstone?"

"Has to be. According to the *Guide,* there's no rapids after Maidstone. Just give me some speed. Shooting them will be a piece of cake." With that, Ramsay headed the Mad River right for the center of the bridge.

At that moment, three kids came out of the brush on top of the bank. They were the first people we'd seen on the river. "Hey, is that Maidstone Bridge?" I shouted.

They looked at each other, not knowing if they should talk to two coots in a canoe. "Bugsy, ask them what town it is."

"What town is this?"

"Northumberland," one of the kids shouted.

"Shit!" Ramsay said, abruptly turning the Mad River towards shore. "Start paddling. If that's the Northumberland dam, it's more dangerous than Lyman Falls."

When we reached the shore, there was no place to land. The bank was too steep. Realizing we were in trouble, and probably deciding we were harmless, the three kids scrambled down and held the bow while we climbed out. Once we'd caught our breath, Ramsay said, "Hot damn, you kids saved our asses. Now, could you help us get our bags up the bank?"

To us the bank looked like Mt. Everest, but the kids, boys in their early teens, had no trouble. They grabbed our duffels and like little Tenzing Norgays scooted to the top. Unfortunately, Ramsay and I were no Edmund Hillarys. When we tried to pull the Mad River up onto the bank, we promptly fell in the mud. "We're never going to get this canoe up there," Ramsay said. "We'll be lucky to get ourselves up. Leave it here. We'll worry about it later."

"Where?" I said, looking around for something to tie the Mad River onto. There was nothing. The bank was all mud. The best we could do was wrap the bow line around a little bush. That done, we crawled on our hands and knees up the bank. Once on top, I dug out three dollar bills and gave each kid one. A small price for saving us, but then again, I'm not known as a big tipper.

When Ramsay asked where he could find a phone, one of the kids said he lived just down the street and volunteered his house. While Ramsay went off with the kids to call Scot

Williamson, I sat with the gear. I was looking forward to meeting Scot. I'd seen Ramsay's card on Scot and it said he worked for the Wildlife Management Institute, a conservation organization headquartered in Washington. I'd done some deals with WMI while I was at the Conservancy and liked the people. They were committed to saving wildlife habitats, so I figured Scot could bring us up to date on conservation efforts along the river.

Ramsay came back with the kid's father in tow. The father worked the second shift at the James River Paper Mill in Groveton. He had a few minutes to kill before he had to go and was using them to bend Ramsay's ear about the river. He couldn't believe we'd paddled from North Stratford to Guildhall in one day. "With all those bends," he said, "that's a hell of a long way."

"How long?" I said.

"At least twenty-three miles, maybe more, and let me tell you, you were smart not to run that dam. Most people who try it, even the good ones, get busted up, some of 'em pretty bad."

We were still chatting with the father when Scot Williamson drove up. Scot was a big, outdoorsy type with broad shoulders bulging under a plaid work shirt. After a crushing handshake, he took a quick inventory of our equipment. "Where's your canoe?"

We pointed down to the river.

"That current's pretty strong," he said. "We better bring it up."

Before we could tell Scot we'd tried and fallen on our faces, he slid down the bank, grabbed the bow of the Mad River, with one hand, and pulled it up. We liked Scot immediately.

On the way to Scot's house, he stopped to show us the Maidstone Bridge. It turned out to be the rusted metal trusses and rotting planks I thought were a deserted railroad bridge. "Damn," I said, "we were here three hours ago."

"I guess I should have told you the bridge was closed," Scot said, "but I figured you'd see it on your maps."

"I pack the maps in my bag to keep them dry," Ramsay said. "Once we're on the river, we could be in Montana for all we know."

"Here's what you need," Scot said, removing a couple of slim, green pamphlets from the glove compartment of his pickup. "You can keep these right in your life vests."

The pamphlet, entitled *Boating on the Connecticut River in Vermont and New Hampshire,* was published by the Connecticut River Joint Commissions, an advisory body created by the states of New Hampshire and Vermont to help guide growth and protect the resources of the Connecticut River Valley.

Like CRWC's *The Complete Boating Guide to the Connecticut River,* the Joint Commissions' pamphlet contained a series of maps buffered by a running narrative, only the Joint Commissions' narrative was not as detailed as CRWC's. The pamphlet just covered Vermont and New Hampshire, which is why it was small enough to slip into a life vest. "Scot," I said, studying the series of bends we'd just traversed, "we saw some real expensive bulkheading on one of these turns. Why would anybody spend all that money to keep the river from breaching? Why not let it follow its natural course?"

"Property taxes," Scot said. "The river's the boundary between New Hampshire and Vermont. If a piece of land moves from one state to the other it's going to be reassessed, and that could mean higher taxes; so if a farmer sees the river's getting ready to breach, he might figure in the long run it'd be cheaper to put in a bulkhead."

I was glad I asked. I wouldn't have thought of that in a hundred years.

In the 1880s North Stratford, New Hampshire, was the timber capital of New England. With America's industrial revolution in full swing, sawmills and paper mills in western Massachusetts were starving for timber. The Connecticut River provided a natural highway to the timber rich North Country, and young men seeking their fortune moved upriver to tap into it. In 1879, they organized the first major log drive, which sent three million board feet of timber to the mills in Massachusetts. By 1890, the annual spring drive was up to fifty million board feet. The men who controlled that timber quickly became rich and built lavish homes along banks of the Connecticut in the little village of Stratford, ten miles to the south of North Stratford. From there, they could sit on their porches and watch the source of their tremendous wealth come floating by.

When the timber industry moved west during the thirties, forties, and fifties, the town of Stratford died with it. Today, only a handful of the grand houses survive. Scot, his wife Bonnie, and their daughter Molly, lived in one of them, a big, rambling farmhouse built by Andrew Jackson Ockington, one of the men who'd come upriver from Connecticut in the late 1800s to make his fortune. The Ockington house had been deserted for ten years and was in terrible shape when the Williamsons purchased it in 1995. After eight years of loving restoration, Scot and Bonnie had recaptured much of the Ockington grandeur. In fact, the kitchen exceeded anything Ockington ever could have imagined.

That was because Bonnie had been a professional chef when Scot suggested they move to Stratford. Bonnie said she'd make the move, but under one condition: she could take her kitchen with her. The big Viking stove, industrial refrigerator, granite counters, and racks of whisks, graters, grinders, presses, shears, ladles, and spoons testified to Scot's total capitulation.

Unfortunately, Bonnie wasn't there to cook for us. She and Molly had driven to Wisconsin to visit Bonnie's parents. Sensing our disappointment, Scot told us not to worry, he was right at home in the kitchen. "While you guys get cleaned up," he said, "I'll start dinner."

A cold rain had moved back into the valley while we were showering, so Scot had fired up the big woodstove that sat just off the kitchen. Ramsay and I immediately claimed two comfortable wing chairs facing the fire. It was then I noticed an old English setter asleep in front of the stove. "Who's this old girl?" I asked Scot.

"That's Talak. She was Vickie Bunnell's dog. We adopted her after Vicki died." Talak must have been the puppy in the picture with Vickie.

"Earl and Irene told us about that," Ramsay said. "Not a pretty story."

"That's for sure," Scot said, leaving it at that. "Say, would you guys like a drink?"

Ramsay opted for his usual beer while I asked for a rum and tonic. Scot got Ramsay his beer, then opened his liquor cabinet and began rummaging around for some rum. After a thorough search, he pulled out a bottle of Captain Morgan's. "Is Captain Morgan all right?" he said. "It's all I've got."

"Aye, matey, start pouring."

While Ramsay and I sat by the fire nursing our drinks, Scot proved he was true to his word. Beside a big juicy steak, which was Ramsay's favorite meal, he'd fried up some asparagus he'd just picked from his garden. I'm not a big fan of asparagus, but these were hot, crispy, and tasted more like french fries than asparagus. Delicious.

After dinner Ramsay went outside for a smoke while I poured myself another Captain Morgan. By the time he came back, Scot and I were talking conservation. Scot was telling me about a conservation easement program he'd helped design to protect the bottomlands along the upper part of the river. Under this program, conservation groups would pay farmers $200 per acre for an easement over their bottomlands. The easements would allow traditional farming practices, but would forbid any other forms of development. Ramsay immediately excused himself and went to bed. He had little interest in conservation.

By the time Scot and I called it quits, the Captain Morgan was gone. I was sleeping in Molly's room, and like many girls her age, Molly was into horses. Pictures of palominos and paints were hanging all over her walls. When I lay down on the bed, a herd of mustangs was running wild on the ceiling above me. I blinked once, then twice, trying to rein them in, but the Captain kept them spinning round and round. It was then I realized I was in for a rocky morning and that I'd been over-served.

3

MAY 30
STRATFORD, NEW HAMPSHIRE

Cows and People

I woke up feeling a little fuzzy, but a hot shower, a couple of cups of coffee, and Scot's big country breakfast straightened me out. After we'd eaten and packed up, Scot took us on a tour of the bottomlands he was helping to protect. They were part of five farms in a section of the river known as the Coos, an Abenaki Indian word meaning "place of the curved river." These rich bottomlands were first farmed by the Indians, then the white man. They're still farmed today, and conservationists hoped to keep it that way by buying conservation easements that would restrict development forever.

"Scot," Ramsay said, after we'd seen the five farms, "why would you waste your money buying easements over this land? Who's going to develop it? It looks like the highest and best use is farming."

It was a good question, and Ramsay knew what he was talking about. After he quit managing companies, he'd made a bunch of money convincing farmers around Cincinnati they should sell their land for development, but that land was high and dry, and right in the growth path of Cincinnati. This land was low and wet, and from what we could see, no growth was coming this way. So what was the threat?

In answer to Ramsay's question, Scot listed all the usual suspects: dumps, sand pits, sod farms, and on some of the higher ground, second homes, then ended with the most dreaded of all developments, a trailer park. "But Scot, can't all those things be controlled by zoning?"

"They can, but in many cases, they aren't, and even if they were, zoning can be changed. After 9/11, we're feeling the pressure of people wanting to get out of the city. Who knows what they'll do? For two hundred bucks an acre, it's easier just to buy an easement and be done with it."

Neither Ramsay nor I knew enough about the demand to debate Scot's reasoning, but to us it sounded like a sweet deal for the farmers. If somebody came along and offered me two hundred bucks an acre to keep doing what I already was doing, especially on land that was subject to flooding, I'd be signing up every acre I had. I must have been missing something.

When we got to the Mad River, Ramsay took a look at the rapids below the Northumberland Bridge and said, "Bugsy, I've been thinking. Let's run that dam."

"Are you nuts?" I said, pulling out the pamphlet Scot had given me. "It says here Wyoming Dam is more dangerous than Lyman Falls. We'd be out of our minds to try and run it." I didn't mean to curb Ramsay's enthusiasm, but successfully shooting that little dam the day before must have gone to his head.

"Ramsay, I have to agree with Dave," Scot said. "You don't want to be messing with that dam. There's a real nice put-in just a mile down the road. That's where you want to be."

Reluctantly, Ramsay agreed.

Scot's put-in was a small, pretty stream that flowed under a high granite arch into the Connecticut. At one time, the arch must have been the crossing for a carriage road or railway line, but judging from the trees growing over it, that had been long, long ago. While Ramsay and I picked up our own duffles, Scot hefted the Mad River out of the truck and, with one quick and seemingly effortless move, centered it on his broad shoulders and walked it down to the stream. What a guy.

"Is there anything else I can do for you?" he said, plopping the canoe into the water.

Scot already had done everything he could for us, including offering to pick us up the next morning at the farm where we were staying that night and driving us around Moore Reservoir, a long impoundment we had no interest in paddling. Still, as a joke, I said, "Yeah, Scot, if you have a minute, could you pick me up a bottle of rum?"

"Captain Morgan?" he said.

"Hell no, my head still hurts from the Captain. Make it Myers's."

We only had eight miles to go that day, but that was plenty. Between the Captain and the twenty-three miles we'd done the day before, I was sore all over. When we came to the first bend, Ramsay, of course, cut the corner, but by now, a sixth of the Connecticut's 148 tributaries had found their way into the river so we had plenty of water. Of course, we lost the current, only this time Ramsay's stupidity was rewarded. By cutting the corner, we surprised a big fox standing on a log. When it saw us, it seemed more annoyed than threatened. It wasn't until we were about fifteen yards away that it reluctantly hopped off of the log and pranced into the woods.

"I wonder if that fox was about to swim the river?" I said.

"Maybe," Ramsay said, "I know for a fact fox can swim."

"How do you know that?"

"That's how they get rid of fleas."

"Get rid of fleas? What are you talking about?"

"One of my golfing buddies told me when a fox wants to get rid of fleas, it puts a stick in its mouth, and jumps into the water. Then, rather than drown, all the fleas jump onto the stick and the fox swims away."

"Ramsay, that's the craziest thing I ever heard. The guy had to be pulling your leg."

"Bugsy, think about it. It makes sense."

I did, and had to admit it did make some sense. Fleas can't breathe under water. They'd have to do something. But why a stick? Why wouldn't the fox just let them drown? Ramsay had to be kidding. After thirty years in conservation, I'd never heard of anything that strange.

The bluffs along the river just north of Lancaster, New Hampshire, were high and steep. To hold them in place, the banks were riprapped with hundreds of old, pre-World War II cars. In some places, the cars were stacked three, four, even five high. Over the years, many of them had sunk deep into the mud. The effect was eerie. With the hoods as yawning mouths, the old split windshields as empty eyes, and the round tops as craniums, they looked like huge human skulls peering out from the bank.

"God, does that look weird," I said. "It reminds me of the killing fields in Cambodia."

"But Bugsy, you have to admit, it works. After all these years, there's hardly any erosion."

"Yeah, only I'm going to bet the genius who came up with the idea of using old cars to stabilize the banks forgot to remove the batteries, gas, and oil before chucking them in. Those cars probably are still polluting the river."

In September of 1960, John Steinbeck and his dog, Charley, stopped at the bridge in Lancaster, New Hampshire. In *Travels with Charley,* Steinbeck described how he'd swung Rocinante, the custom-made camper he named after Don Quixote's horse, into a motor court "of neat little white houses on the green meadow by the river." I was looking for the motor court when Ramsay said, "Bugsy, what's that over there?"

I looked to the Vermont side and saw three fox kits frolicking on the bank. They were all orange and fuzzy and couldn't have been more than a month old. "Let's take a look," Ramsay said, steering the Mad River right at them.

Having just seen the big fox on the log, I wasn't so sure that was a good idea. We couldn't see over the bank, and for all we knew, momma fox could be up there just waiting to pounce on two coots harassing her cubs. "Ramsay, be careful," I said. "Don't get too close to the bank. The mother might be right up there."

"Hell, Bugsy, this is the neatest thing we've seen so far." He paddled even closer.

The kits were having such a good time rolling around they didn't see us coming. When they did, they froze, then, realizing we might be trouble, let loose a chorus of yips. They were still yipping as they scampered up the bank into their den, which was just under the lip. Once safely inside, the barking stopped and three little heads popped out to look at us.

While Ramsay fumbled through his duffel looking for his camera, I backed the canoe far enough from the shore so momma couldn't reach us if she came flying over the bank. Ramsay was still fumbling around for his camera when the current began sweeping us right toward the bridge. "Ramsay, forget about your camera and start steering. We're about to hit the bridge."

Ramsay quickly straightened us out then said, "What the hell's that hanging from the bridge?"

I looked up and saw a string dangling from one of the girders. A brown paper bag was tied to the end. I got out my knife and as Ramsay guided us under the bridge, cut the bag free from the string. "Ramsay, you're not going to believe this," I said, opening the bag. "It's a bottle of Myers's Rum."

When I was a kid, Vermont's trademark slogan was MORE COWS THAN PEOPLE. It stayed that way until 1957 when the state's bovine population of 386,075 cows was overtaken by 386,500 people. In 2003, the cows were all the way down to 147,000 and the people had grown to 617,000, almost double. (Figures courtesy of the Vermont Department of Libraries in Montpelier.)

Chester and Lorna Eaton, our hosts for the third night, milked 170 of the 147,000 cows left in Vermont. That made the Eaton's Auburn Star Farm one of the largest family-owned and -operated dairy farms left in New England. That was one of the reasons we were looking forward to staying with the Eatons. The other was Ramsay had marked Lorna Eaton down as "very accommodating."

When Ramsay had called to feel out the Eatons, he'd talked with Lorna. During their conversation, she asked him what we'd like for dinner. Ramsay, of course, had given her his stock line, "We don't care, just so long as the beer's cold," to which Lorna said, "You should know, we don't drink," to which Ramsay replied, "Well, I guess we won't be staying with you," to which Lorna said, "Don't worry, I'll buy you some beer."

Lorna *was* very accommodating. I would have told Ramsay to go to hell.

We'd no sooner passed under the Lancaster Bridge when Ramsay said, "Okay, Bugsy, start looking for a flag. Lorna told me that's how they'd mark the farm."

"What type of flag?" I said.

"Panamanian."

"Panamanian? What's the Panamanian flag look like?"

"Blue with white stars. Keep your eyes open."

It seemed a bit strange the Eatons would fly a Panamanian flag, but just having found a bottle of rum hanging from the Lancaster Bridge, I was ready for anything.

Less than a mile beyond the bridge, Ramsay started getting antsy. "Hell, Bugsy, we must have missed it. Lorna said the farm was right after the bridge, and we've already gone a couple of miles."

Of course, we hadn't. Now that I had my own set of maps, I'd come to realize Ramsay was cartographically impaired. He never knew where we were. Still, given our experience with Maidstone Bridge, I figured we'd better stop and find out just where the Eaton's farm was before we went too much farther. If we missed it, we'd be too sore and too discouraged to paddle back.

We'd been running parallel to Route 2 ever since Lancaster, but according to my map, the river was about to make a big loop. It would be at least two miles before we saw the road again so if we were going to find somebody to ask where the Eatons lived, we had better do it now. "Ramsay, pull over up here where the river turns. Let's find out where the Eatons live before we get too far from the road."

Dressed as always in his dark sunglasses, boonie hat, and little girlie vest, Ramsay climbed the bank and set off down Route 2 looking for somebody who knew the Eatons. I fully expected him to come back in another cop car, but about twenty minutes later, he returned by himself. "We're in luck. A guy at the gas station told me this loop in the river *is* the Eaton farm. Now, all we have to do is find the flag."

After another half-mile we saw an American flag flying from the smokestack of an old tractor parked on the bank. "That's it," Ramsay said.

"But that flag's American, not Panamanian."

"Gotcha!" And he had, which was good for Ramsay. As anal as he was, it wasn't like Ramsay to fool with the facts. First the fleas, now the flag. Maybe he was becoming Groucho Marx.

We were looking for a place to land when a lean, wiry man about our age appeared on the bank next to the tractor. We figured he must be Chester Eaton. "Go round the bend," he yelled, "you'll see a place to pull in. I'll meet ya there."

Chester Eaton was a throwback to the old-time New England farmer. His rosy-red cheeks, wire-rimmed glasses, trimmed white beard, Auburn Star baseball cap (tipped slightly askew), and work shirt with AUBURN STAR FARM embroidered over one pocket and CHESTER over the other left no question as to who he was and what he did. That was good because Chester wasn't much of a talker. After he'd showed us where to stow the Mad River and told us to throw our duffels in the back of his pickup, the most we got out of him on the drive to the house were a few "ayuhs."

There was a big group waiting for us on the porch. It was headed by Lorna, who was every bit as talkative as Chester was laconic. "Ramsay, I got that beer you wanted," she said, proudly holding up a six-pack of Michelob.

"Hot damn, Lorna," Ramsay said, "pop me a cool one."

In addition to a half-dozen Eatons and two dogs, Eileen Alexander, a reporter for the *Coos County Democrat,* was there too. Eileen wanted to know how we'd come up with the idea for the trip and how it was going. Ramsay, of course, gave her his spiel on *Beg, Borrow, and Deal,* and I told her how we'd just found a bottle of rum hanging from the Lancaster Bridge. Eileen took a picture of us with Chester and Lorna, then asked the question I'd been wondering about. "Lorna," she said, "whatever prompted you to offer these two freeloaders a room?"

"We're always taking in strays," Lorna said, "and after reading their press release, they seemed pretty harmless."

"Harmless," Ramsay snorted. "Hell, Lorna, we're the coolest thing you'll ever see come down this river."

With four generations of Eatons gathered around the table, dinner seemed like something out of a Norman Rockwell painting. Besides Chester and Lorna, there was Conan, their oldest son; Conan's wife, Maureen; their three children, Samantha, Shane, and Luke; Samantha's fiancé, Steve Russo; and Steve's little daughter, Julianna. The Eatons weren't putting on any airs for us. Their dress was work clothes, mostly sweatshirts and jeans, and for good reason. Dinner on a dairy farm didn't mark the end of the work day. It was just a refueling. The evening milking still had to be done.

As a big bowl of mashed potatoes, a platter of pork loin, a dish of peas, and a basket of bread made their way around the table, the conversation focused on the weather, which was great for Ramsay. For most people, talking about the weather was an ice breaker. For Ramsay, it was a core conversation. He was addicted to the Weather Channel and knew all about jet streams, high and low pressure fronts, tropical depressions, and seasonal temperatures.

Conan was itching to start haying, but with all the rain, he said the grass was too wet. "It'll take at least one sunny day over 75 degrees before it's dry enough to cut," he griped. "This is getting to be one of the wettest springs on record, and I'm getting sick of waiting for it to turn."

"You won't have to wait long," Ramsay said. "The clouds are circling counterclockwise, which means this low is moving east."

"You sure?" Conan said, willing to grasp at any straw.

"You can take it to the bank."

The only thing to drink on the table was a big pitcher of water. When Lorna asked if she could pour me a glass, I said I'd like to try some Eaton milk. That got a laugh. The Eatons had no milk. "Everything's automated," Conan said. "We'd disrupt the whole process if we tried to pull some milk off for personal use. For what we drink, it's easier to buy it."

After dinner, Conan and Samantha were going back to the barn for the evening milking. When I asked if we could tag along, Conan said sure, but added there wasn't much to see. "You coming?" I said to Ramsay. "You're always talking about how much pull you have. Here's your chance to prove it."

"No, I'm going to make my calls for tomorrow and check the weather." Ramsay was funny like that. He was delighted to be staying on a real farm, but he had no interest in farming. He'd rather sit and watch the Weather Channel.

Conan was wrong about there not being much to see. A modern milking parlor is a complex manufacturing operation. The control center was a four-foot wide by three-foot deep concrete trench running down the middle of the parlor. Ten stalls made of heavy metal gates lined each side of the trench. A black box with four black hoses attached to it hung at the end of each stall. These were the milking machines. (Note to all city slickers, a cow has four teats.)

Samantha placed me at the top of the trench. "You'll be okay here," she said. "Just don't make any sudden moves. Cows are curious. A few may come up and sniff you, but they won't bite."

With me set, Samantha and Conan jumped into the trench and went to work. Once they'd rinsed out all twenty of the milking machines, Conan pushed a button and the heavy metal gates started moving: some up, some down, some to one side, some to the other. There was nothing Norman Rockwell about the milking parlor; it looked more like something out of a George Lucas movie. "Whatever happened to the three-legged milking stool?" I said. "This is pretty high-tech."

"I designed and built the whole thing myself," Conan said. "Welded the gates, set up the hydraulics, installed the machines." He paused to look at his creation. "Not bad for a guy who never went to college."

The herd, all 170 of them, lived in sheds attached to the rear of the parlor. Conan told me cows no longer grazed free in the fields. They were kept in sheds and the feed was brought to them. That way, farmers could control what they ate, they were insulated from accidents and disease, and they had more energy to produce milk. As the gates opened, cows started lumbering in. They were huge. Seeing them, I felt like I was on the streets of Pamplona for the running of the bulls, but I had no place to run. "It's okay," Samantha said, sensing my uneasiness. "Just remember, no sudden moves."

The first thing I noticed was that every cow's tail had been bobbed. It made them look very strange, like a huge Vizsla or Weimaraner. "What happened to their tails?" I said, trying to sound blasé as a cow four times the size of Dick Butkus waddled by me.

"I was sick of them swishing in my face," Conan said. "Besides, they don't need tails anymore. They don't go outside."

I could see his point. Standing in the trench, Conan and Samantha were eye-to-udder with each cow. Having their dung-encrusted tails swishing in your face six hours a day would tend to be annoying.

The ladies knew their routine. They moseyed into their usual spots and when all twenty stalls were filled, Conan pushed the button that started the gates moving so each cow was fenced into place. Once they were set, Conan and Samantha began milking. First they wiped down each teat with a rag soaked in disinfectant. Then they placed the teat into a silver suction cup attached to the end of each milking machine hose. A rhythmic pumping began. Soon, the parlor felt like a discotheque pulsating to the beat of eighty teats.

Conan and Samantha no sooner had gotten to one end of the line when the cups started popping off teats at the other. "That's amazing," I said. "How do the machines know when to stop?"

"It's all computerized," Conan said, pointing to a small gray control box connected to each milker. "There's a sensor in each cup. When the suction hits a certain pressure, it blows itself off."

Having a calf is what causes a cow to produce milk so there's a constant crop of newborn calves. The Eatons kept their newborns in pens along one side of the parlor. After the cows had been milked, most of them would saunter over to look at the calves like mothers looking at babies in the maternity ward. "How many calves do you have a year?" I asked Samantha.

"It depends on how many twins we have, but it averages around 225."

"What do you do with them?"

"All the bulls are sold, but we keep most of the heifers as herd replacements."

"How much do you get for a calf?"

"Depends on the market, but usually about a hundred and fifty."

There was a huge cistern in the corner opposite the pens. After the cows had inspected the newborn calves, they ambled over to the cistern for a drink. They reminded me of employees hanging around a water cooler not wanting to go back to work. When I mentioned this to Conan, he said, "Milk's ninety-five percent water. As far as I'm concerned, they can stay there as long as they want."

"They all seem to get along," I said. "Do you ever have any problems?"

"You ever tried managing a hundred and seventy women? You bet we have problems. Most of the time, they work it out, but I had to sell one the other day. She was a real bitch."

"But a good milker," Samantha said. "I would have kept her, but Dad just couldn't take it anymore."

While Conan and Samantha kept milking, I kept asking questions. What I learned was that milk is measured by weight, not quantity, and the standard measure is a hundred pounds, or "hundred weight." In addition to letting the computer know when to stop milking, the sensors recorded exactly how many pounds each cow produced at each milking. Those figures ranged from thirty-five to fifty-four pounds per cow depending on age, breeding, and when she was last "freshened" (or impregnated in order to produce milk). Based on those figures, the Eatons' herd was producing about 140 hundred weight a day, or just over five million pounds of milk a year.

According to Conan, the New England Dairy Compact used to guarantee New England farmers a minimum of $15 per hundred weight, but after Senator Jim Jeffords quit the Republican Party in the fall of 2002, a vindictive Republican-controlled Congress refused to renew the compact. Instead, it voted New England dairy farmers a temporary subsidy reimbursement of $.02 a pound, or $2 per hundred weight. The current price of milk was $11 per hundred weight, so with the subsidy reimbursement, the Eatons were selling their milk for $13 a hundred weight. Conan told me his banker figured it was costing the Eatons $13.56 to produce a hundred weight. That meant they were losing $.56 on every hundred pounds of milk they produced, but as Conan said, "What can we do? It's not like a factory. We can't turn off the herd and send everybody home. We just have to keep milking and hope things get better."

If you threw in the sale of the calves, the Eaton family was working twelve hours a day, 365 days a year, just to break even. I asked Conan if there was any way to increase production without raising costs. He said Steve was working on boosting the overall production of the herd, and Samantha was upgrading the breeding, plus he'd just bought thirty-three acres of pretty good pastureland about fifteen miles to the north. Since it took one acre of pastureland to support a cow, the Eatons could increase the herd to two hundred, which would give them more milk without a pro rata increase in costs. Still, that would just allow the Eatons to hang on until the price of milk went up.

Most of the Eatons' pastures were prime bottomland, the kind of land Scot Williamson was trying to protect. At two hundred bucks an acre, that would give the Eatons a big chunk of dough to buy more land, so I asked Conan if he'd ever thought of selling a conservation easement. "We looked at it," Conan said, "but it's not worth the trouble. The conservationists want to retain the right to tell you when and where you can cut. When a field's ready, we've got to get in there and cut it. We can't be waiting for some bird to get through nesting or some flower to bloom, not for two hundred bucks an acre."

That was the point I'd been missing when we were talking to Scot about his easement program. If you're managing a business that's operating right on the edge, the last thing you want is somebody who's in a different business telling you what you can and cannot do.

All the time we were talking, new waves of cows kept rolling in, and Samantha and Conan kept milking. "What do you do with the tails?" I said, still not used to seeing a cow without a tail.

"We throw them out."

"You know, Conan, I have a great idea for you. You should cure the tails and sell them as 'Original Vermont Fly Swatters.' They'd be the rage of New York. I bet you could get a hundred bucks a tail, minimum."

Neither Conan nor Samantha jumped at my idea. They were dairy farmers, plain and simple. They didn't have the time to be fooling with anything that didn't have to do with producing milk. That's why they were one of the last family-owned and -operated dairy farms in New England.

4

MAY 31
LUNENBURG, VERMONT

The Village Bookstore

As we'd agreed, Scot Williamson arrived at Auburn Star Farm at ten the next morning. We introduced Scot to Chester and Lorna, then started kidding him about the bottle of Myers's he'd left hanging under the bridge. "You should have seen the looks I was getting from cars that went by," Scot said. "The country's operating under a Code Orange, and here I am tying a brown paper bag under the bridge. I'm surprised I didn't get arrested."

"Hot damn, Scot," Ramsay said, "it would have been worth it. This is the kind of stuff that'll get you in Bugsy's next book."

Before we left, I told Lorna and Chester I'd like to see Luke's machine shop. Luke was Conan and Maureen's third and youngest child. During the milking, Conan had told me Luke would eventually take over all the mechanical work on the farm. "In fact," Conan said, "Luke's so good with machines, we just built him his own machine shop. He can fix anything on this farm, and fix it fast. When you're racing the weather, that's real important."

Over breakfast, Lorna had given us another story. She was worried about Luke making it through the eighth grade. The root of Luke's academic struggles was simple. He was a gifted mechanic who already had a full-time job on the farm.

To Luke, school seemed like a waste of time, a feeling that was reinforced by his father. According to Lorna, Conan was content to have Luke working on the farm.

"Luke's only fourteen," she said. "I'd like to see him finish high school, then go to Vermont Technical College for a couple of years. That's what Samantha and Steve did, and it was good for them. Luke's got his whole life to spend on the farm."

With that background, we figured it wouldn't hurt to look at Luke's machine shop, and maybe give him some moral support. What fourteen-year-old kid couldn't use a little praise? The shop was on the other side of the farm so Chester suggested we all drive over in his pickup. While Chester and Lorna got in the cab, Scot, Ramsay, and I piled into the back. As we climbed in, we noticed a sticker stuck to the rear window that read KILL THE PARADIGM.

"Chester," Ramsay said, leaning into the cab window, "what's this sticker mean?"

"We have to break down the old models," Chester said. "People become entrenched in their attitudes. Take one group and teach them about oxygen and another group and teach them about hydrogen, then put them together, and no one will talk about water. They'll still be fixed on oxygen and hydrogen. Kill the paradigm, that's the only way to move ahead."

Still water runs deep. Who'd expect one of the last traditional family farmers in New England to be talking about killing paradigms?

Luke's machine shop was a 30-foot by 30-foot metal prefab building on a cement slab. As we walked around the parts of an old tractor Luke was in the process of rebuilding, he proudly showed us his lifts, jacks, compressor, wrench sets, and whatever else was in his big red metal twelve-drawer rolling tool chest. Then he unveiled his next project: a very fast, but very beat-up stock car he was planning to fix up. "Hot damn, Luke," Ramsay said, running his hand over the hood, "you got some work to do on this baby."

"I've got a couple of years to fool with it," Luke said. "I can't drive off the farm till I'm sixteen."

"Luke" I said, looking around at the bare walls, "This is nice, but I hate to tell you, it's not a real machine shop."

Luke look confused, and a little hurt. "How's that?" he said.

"Every machine shop I've ever been in has a girlie calendar hanging on the wall, but don't worry, I'll see if I can get you one."

"Don't you go corrupting my grandson," Lorna said. "Luke, your shop looks just fine."

Scot crossed the covered bridge at South Lancaster and drove us twelve miles south on Route 135 to Moore Dam, the largest structure on the river. Built in 1956, Moore Dam creates Moore Reservoir, a twelve-mile-long water-storage area for Moore Station, the largest conventional hydroelectric power plant in New England. The dam, reservoir, and station all were named after Samuel C. Moore, a former president of New England Power.

Immediately below Moore Dam was the start of Comerford Reservoir, which was created by Comerford Dam, an eight-mile water-storage area for Comerford Station. This dam, reservoir, and station was built in 1930 and named for Frank D. Comerford, former president of New England Power Association, the predecessor of New England Electric

System. Six miles downriver was McIndoe Dam. It formed McIndoe Reservoir, which supplied the water for McIndoe Powerhouse. Built in 1931, McIndoe, the smallest of the three power plants, was deemed too insignificant to bear the name of a former president. Instead, New England Power just kept the name of the falls it had obliterated.

Moore, Comerford, and McIndoe make up what New England Power proudly refers to as the Fifteen Miles Falls Development. Before 1930, this same section of the river was known as Fifteen Miles Falls, which was the longest, steepest stretch of whitewater in the Northeast. Today, it's two big, boring lakes and one small, boring lake, with a four-mile stretch of river in the middle. According to the *Guide,* this stretch can provide the most challenging canoeing along the Connecticut—and some of the most dangerous. Depending on Comerford Dam's output, "the water level can fluctuate as much as six feet. DO NOT CAMP on any of the islands in the river, or near the river banks. In the past, several campers have been swept away by the sudden rise in water levels."

To make matters worse, this part of the river is, for all practical purposes, dead. For years the towns above Moore Dam and the paper mill in Groteton dumped their wastewater directly into the river. After the development, this waste was no longer flushed downriver. Instead, it sunk to the bottom of the reservoirs. As a result, their bottoms are covered with organic sediment that sucks all the oxygen out of the water as it decomposes. Ten feet below the surface of these lakes, no living thing can survive. Improvements are being made, but it'll be years before the Fifteen Miles Falls Development will ever be able to support any form of aquatic life. Dead rivers are the price we pay for cheap power and paper.

"Where do you want to leave the canoe?" Scot said.

Originally, we'd planned to leave the canoe just below Moore Dam, but watching the whitecaps being kicked up by a strong headwind whipping across the reservoir, Ramsay said "Bugsy, the hell with this crap. Let's put in below McIndoe and be done with it." That was fine by me. I wanted nothing to do with the development. I'd signed on to paddle a river, not a series of man-made lakes.

At McIndoe Falls, Ramsay and I watched Scot, his muscles bulging, stash the Mad River back in the woods above the put-in. Then we headed for Littleton, where we were going to meet up with Jeff Wheeler, our stranger for the evening. Jeff was the brother of Doug Wheeler, one of America's great conservationists and a good friend of mine. I'd met Jeff once twelve years earlier at Doug's fiftieth birthday party. Although I hadn't seen him since then, I knew he'd recently bought the Village Book Store and moved to Littleton. When Ramsay agreed we'd rely on the kindness of strangers, Jeff had been the first stranger I called. He couldn't have been nicer. He told me his wife and his youngest daughter hadn't moved north yet and he'd welcome the company.

On this sunny spring Saturday afternoon, downtown Littleton was alive and hopping. Traffic was bumper to bumper, the sidewalks were crowded with shoppers, stores on both sides of the quarter-mile main drag bustled with activity. Scot found a parking spot, and we walked a few hundred yards up to the very center of town and the Village Book Store. We were impressed. We'd been expecting a snug little hole in the wall typical of village bookstores. Instead, we were looking at the keystone to downtown Littleton, the store that held Main Street together. Inside, we found a large, spacious emporium that would rival any of the major chains, and that was just the half of it. Downstairs was a children's section complete with games, toys, and books, as well as a gallery selling arts and crafts certified by the League of New Hampshire craftsmen. All in all, the Village Book Store was quite an operation for little Littleton.

Ever the consultant, Ramsay saw a way for Jeff to increase the store's traffic. "Jeff," he said, "this place is neat, but you should install some comfortable chairs and serve free coffee. That would draw more people into the store and get them to stay longer."

"I thought about it," Jeff said, "but there's a few homeless people who hang around town. If we put in comfortable chairs and served free coffee, that would encourage them to come in. In New York, that's not a problem. You ask them to leave and they move a couple of blocks. In Littleton, there's no place to go, and they're part of the community."

When we got to Jeff's house, a small eighteenth-century cape on a hill looking straight into the White Mountains, Ramsay said he was going to take a nap. I decided to go for a jog. David Bloom, a reporter embedded with American troops in Iraq, recently had died from a pulmonary embolism he'd developed from sitting all night in a tank. I'd been getting cramps in my legs from sitting in the canoe and figured a jog would be good for my circulation. Jeff said if I ran down the road in front of his house and kept bearing left at every turn, I'd complete a circle of about two and a half miles, just the distance I was looking for.

As I left, Ramsay was asleep in the den and Jeff was happily guiding his big, brand-new Swisher industrial mower around the house. When I got back a half-hour later, Ramsay was still asleep and Jeff was standing at the end of a line of neatly cut grass leaning over the Swisher. "What's wrong?" I said.

"The belt's gotten loose, but to tighten it, it looks like I have to take the whole cover off."

I watched Jeff attack a nut with a wrench that was entirely too small for the job. "You got a bigger wrench?" I said.

"No, this is it."

At that moment, Ramsay came out for a smoke. "Ramsay," I said, "you know anything about mowers?"

Ramsay lit up a Carlton and strolled down to where we were standing. After Jeff had given him his diagnosis, Ramsay performed his own examination of the Swisher. "It doesn't seem right you'd have to remove the whole cover to get to the belt," he said. "Where're the directions?"

"Up at the house," Jeff said, "but the dealer's just down the road." He looked at his watch. "It's not quite five. If they're still open, maybe I can get somebody to come up."

We all knew that was a pipe dream. Nobody was coming out at five o'clock on a Saturday night to fix a lawnmower. The three of us stood there staring at the Swisher: Jeff, a graduate of Dartmouth with a Ph.D. in Latin American Studies from Columbia; Ramsay, a graduate of Princeton with an MBA from UVA; me, a graduate of Amherst with an MBA from UVA. Together, at today's prices, we represented close to a million dollars of education, and we didn't have the slightest clue how to fix that machine. And to think Lorna Eaton was worried about Luke making it through the eighth grade. I would have bet the entire million that Luke could have fixed the Swisher in less than ten minutes, and I would have won.

Over dinner that night, we were joined by Cecily, Jeff's oldest daughter. She'd graduated from Hamilton the previous spring and moved to Littleton to help her dad run the store. The store was our main topic of conversation. Jeff and Ramsay, both former business consultants, did most of the talking while Cecily and I listened. Ramsay and Jeff were a lot alike: quiet, somewhat aloof, and cerebral. It was only when the conversation turned to business that they perked up. Ramsay's main concern was what would happen to Jeff's business if somebody big like Wal-Mart moved in.

"I looked pretty carefully at that," Jeff said, "and came to the conclusion the demographics wouldn't support a big-box store. But even if one did move in, I think we'd be all right. Our customers, for the most part, aren't big-box customers, at least when it comes to books. They want service and selection. Plus, a huge part of our business comes from tourism— the fall foliage, skiers, fishermen, summer folk—and they didn't come all the way up here to go to some mall to shop at Wal-Mart. They like walking around town, coming into a real bookstore, talking with our people, getting a flavor of the place. We're the only ones who provide that, especially now with the local arts and crafts. "

I was beginning to see that. The Village Book Store's market went well beyond Littleton, and Jeff seemed to be trying to capitalize on the store's regional reputation to make it a must-stop for people visiting the North Country, like Wall Drug in South Dakota, or even Pedro's South of the Border in South Carolina. Ramsay was almost won over, but not quite. "Let's hope you're right," he said. "The crafts are a good addition, but it's too bad you can't figure out a way to get rid of the vagrants. I still feel some comfortable chairs, coffee, and maybe something to eat would help pull more people in."

5

JUNE 1
LYMAN, NEW HAMPSHIRE

Baccalaureate

Sunday was a short day. After a nice breakfast at Polly's Pancake Parlor in Sugar Hill, New Hampshire, Cecily drove us to McIndoe Falls, where we'd stashed the canoe. From McIndoe Falls, we were going to the bridge at Woodsville, New Hampshire, a distance of eight miles. The only difficult part was going to be the portage around Ryegate Dam, our first of the trip. Without any camping gear, the portage proved to be a nonevent. We were able to make it in two trips, one with the duffels, the other with the canoe.

Rain was our nemesis. Contrary to Ramsay's prediction, Saturday's sunny, warm afternoon had given way to more clouds and rain. "Ramsay, I thought you said today was going to be nice," I said, as we relaunched the Mad River below Ryegate Dam.

"It's a new low. The jet stream took a dip south pushing this front down from Hudson Bay. According to the Weather Channel, it'll be gone by tomorrow."

The river from Ryegate Dam to the Woodsville bridge was flat and easy. The only tricky part was just before Woodsville. Here the river made a sharp turn left, then narrowed and made a sharp turn right between some ledges. Fortunately, Scot Williamson had told us the best way through them was to stay to the left. We did, and safely pulled the Mad River into a landing just beyond the Woodsville Bridge.

The town of Woodsville was located right next to the bridge, so Ramsay didn't have to go far to find a phone to call Tim and Betsy McKay, our strangers for the night. Ramsay's note on Tim was, "Claims Bugsy's book, *Good Dirt,* is the best he's ever read." Naturally, I was looking forward to meeting Tim.

The McKays lived in Peacham, Vermont, a good forty minutes west of the river. As we drove up into the hills, Tim told us he was the U.S. Soil Conservation Service's agent for northern Vermont. He and Betsy had been living in Peacham for twenty-five years. Through the fog and rain, we couldn't see much of the countryside, but mile after mile of dirt road confirmed we were in rural Vermont.

Tim and Betsy's house was a meticulously restored cape set in a field surrounded by stately maples and well-maintained fieldstone walls. Tim pulled into a spacious two-car garage, and led us into the mud room. By now, like the Japanese, we automatically removed our shoes before entering a house. While I was storing my shoes under the bench, I noticed a well-oiled baseball glove hanging on the wall. "Who's the ballplayer?" I said.

"I play for a senior's team," Tim said.

Taking a shot, I said, "You ever play against the Spaceman?" The Spaceman was Bill Lee, a free spirit who pitched for the Red Sox back in the seventies. *Yankee Magazine* had done an article on the Spaceman a few years back that mentioned he'd moved to Vermont and was playing in a senior's league.

"As a matter of fact, we've got a game with his team this summer," Tim said. "I'm looking forward to getting up against him." I could understand why. The Spaceman was a legend.

Getting a hit off the Spaceman would give a guy bragging rights in any bar in New England.

Tim and Betsy had two daughters. Both girls were home when we arrived. Jessica, the McKays' oldest, was twenty and had just finished her sophomore year at the University of Vermont. Sarah, almost eighteen, was graduating from St. Johnsbury Academy the next morning. We still had an hour before dinner, so I said I'd like to stretch my legs. Despite a cold rain, Tim and Betsy offered to take us on a tour of their property.

Betsy was a superb gardener, Tim a master mason. Together they'd built a path lined with neatly tended flower beds and meticulously constructed fieldstone walls that meandered from the house down to a pond. Even Ramsay, who didn't mind the walk since it gave him a chance to smoke, was impressed. The pond, which wasn't much bigger than an Olympic-size swimming pool, was crystal clear with a white sandy bottom. Tim told us he'd designed it. I wasn't surprised. During my years in conservation, I'd learned nobody designed a better pond than the Soil Conservation Service.

At dinner, we sensed some tension. It revolved around Sarah. She was going to Simmons College in the fall, but on a visit to the school earlier that spring, she'd met a guy, found an apartment, and gotten a summer job, all without consulting her parents. She was leaving for Boston right after graduation, and Tim and Betsy didn't seem too happy about it. Who would? But the battle of Boston already had been fought and lost. The tension we were feeling was the two sides negotiating an uneasy truce over what Sarah should take with her, and who'd drive her to the bus. Having nothing to contribute, Ramsay and I focused on Betsy's chicken casserole, which was delicious. Still, watching kids leave the nest ain't easy, even under the best of conditions, and these conditions didn't sound too good.

After dinner, Betsy, Jessica, and Sarah were going to the baccalaureate service at St. Johnsbury Academy. Tim had elected to stay home with Ramsay and me. He set a fire in the family room and while Ramsay and Tim watched the Weather Channel, I browsed through Sarah's copy of *The Lamp,* the Academy's yearbook. *The Lamp* was an interesting insight into education in the North Country. Of the two hundred–plus students in the graduating class, thirty different Vermont towns, eighteen states, and fifteen countries were represented. Roughly twenty percent of the students were foreign, and eighty percent of the class was going to college. Not bad. To me, those numbers indicated St. Johnsbury Academy was a good school with a diverse student body.

I was deep in *The Lamp* when Tim announced he was doing a load of laundry. He asked if we had anything we wanted washed. Ramsay said he was fine, but I jumped on the offer. I hate doing laundry. Once Tim had the laundry under way, he brought out his copy of *Good Dirt,* a hardcover no less, and asked me to sign it. In the inscription, I referenced Ramsay catching an owl when we were fishing in Maine. Since Ramsay and I have different versions of that story, there was much banter back and forth over what really happened. Ramsay, of course, had to have everything just right while I, on the other hand, have been accused of never letting the facts get in the way of a good story. It was a dumb discussion, but Tim didn't seem to mind. Being outnumbered by three women for most of his adult life, he seemed to enjoy spending a night with the boys.

6

JUNE 2
PEACHAM, VERMONT

The Annual Sports Banquet

The first rays of light came streaming into my room at 4:57 a.m. This time Ramsay was right. After five days of rain, it was good to see the sun. So good, I got up, showered, shaved, dressed, and went for a long walk. As beads of sweat began to form on my brow, I thought of the Eatons. This was the day Conan had been waiting for, and another day Luke would be AWOL from the eighth grade.

When I got back to the house, Tim was serving up a big pancake breakfast. It was Polly's all over again, only Tim's syrup was a lot thicker and better than Polly's. It seemed everybody in the North Country had a gallon of the "good stuff" they brought out only on special occasions. We would have been flattered to be a special occasion, but in fact, the "good stuff" was in honor of Sarah's graduation.

The plan was for Tim to drop us off back in Woodsville while Betsy and Jessica held a seat for him. A big crowd was expected and this being Betsy's last high school graduation, she was determined to be right up front. Before we went our separate ways, Ramsay insisted the McKays pose for a picture. He'd decided he was going to take a picture of each of our hosts. It wasn't a bad idea. It would be nice to have a permanent memory of our strangers.

Betsy had planted a very pretty bush, a Bird's Nest Spruce, in front of the house. I thought the Bird's Nest Spruce would provide a distinctive background, but Ramsay wouldn't hear of it. He wanted something more traditional. He lined the McKays up in front of an old maple set among one of Tim's fieldstone walls. "Smile," he said, squinting into his cheap little yellow throwaway camera, "this could be your Christmas card." And it could have been. The McKays, with Sarah in her cap and gown, looked good all dressed up standing in the morning sun high in the hills of Vermont.

On our way back to the river, I gave Tim what I thought was some good advice. "Tim," I said, "I've been thinking about your first at-bat against the Spaceman. What you want to do is wait for the third pitch. The first will be a major league fastball because the Spaceman will want to show you who's boss. The second probably will be a curve or a slider, something to prove what a real pitcher can do with a baseball. Then, having made his point, rather than just strike you out, the Spaceman will thank you for playing the game by serving you up a meatball. That's the pitch you have to hit."

"Hot damn, Tim," Ramsay said, "Bugsy doesn't know his ass from second base. Listen to him and you'll be riding the pines for the rest of the season."

It was nine by the time Tim dropped us off. If he wanted to make Sarah's graduation by ten, he had to keep moving only he seemed reluctant to leave, like maybe we'd ask him to come with us instead. "Tim," I said, worried he'd be late and Betsy would be stuck trying to hold his seat, "you better get going. We've got to run some errands so we won't be leaving for a while."

"Well," Tim said, getting back into his car, "you're sure you're okay?"

"Yeah, we'll be fine, and forget about Ramsay. You wait for that third pitch."

As we watched Tim drive away, I hoped I was right. You never know about the Spaceman.

From 1879, which marked the first major log drive down the Connecticut, until 1915, the year of the last drive, Woodsville, New Hampshire, was known as the liveliest town in the North Country. That's because it was home to the biggest and best red-light district north of New York City. Rivermen, trainmen, lumbermen, and salesmen all loved stopping over in Woodsville. That was then. Now, on a Monday morning, Woodsville looked old and tired, like an aging call girl in need of a serious face-lift. A burned-out motel sitting at the east end of town was the prominent blemish. The fire appeared to have happened some time ago, and nothing had been done to clean it up. Whereas Littleton was making an obvious effort to rejuvenate itself, Woodsville seemed content to be dying.

The errands I told Tim we had to run were Ramsay's daily purchase of beer and butts, but as soon as Tim had left, Ramsay pulled out his dirty laundry. "You think this place has a Laundromat?" he said.

"A Laundromat? Why didn't you let Tim do your laundry last night?"

"I like a cold wash. If you use warm water, your T-shirts shrink."

What the hell was he talking about? "I'm pretty sure Ruth washes my T-shirts in warm water, and they never shrink."

"Bugsy, believe me, they shrink."

After asking around, we found the only Laundromat in Woodsville was down by the burned-out motel at the other end of town. "I'll walk that way with you," I said. "While you're doing your laundry, I'm going to get a haircut, buy some stamps, and see if I can find an automotive store where I can buy Luke Eaton a girlie calendar."

"How about picking up a sponge while you're at it. That sand in the canoe is really starting to bother me."

"Why don't we just flip it over?"

"Just flipping it over wouldn't get it all. I need a sponge."

One good thing about old, dying towns is that they have old, dying barbershops, the kind with a red-and-white spinning pole out front. Seeing the spinning pole means you know you're not going to end up in some unisex shop sitting next to a garrulous gossip with curlers that make her head look like the inside of an old radio. We hadn't gone two blocks when I spied a spinning pole. "There's my barbershop," I said to Ramsay. "I'll meet you back at the canoe."

The place was Paul's, a one-chair operation right out of the fifties: bright fluorescent lights, green linoleum floor, mirrored walls, waiting chairs with chrome frames and vinyl seats. Paul was working on a UPS guy. What looked like an old woodsman in red suspenders, a drab olive green chino shirt, and matching drab olive green chino pants was waiting. The place was like a morgue. The UPS guy and Paul weren't saying anything and the old woodsman was asleep. I picked up a copy of *Outdoor Life* and waited my turn.

During my cut, about all I got out of Paul was that there were three auto shops in Woodsville. Back outside, I tried all three and was disappointed to learn that none of them sold girlie calendars. "We used to carry them," one guy told me, "but with all this women's liberation stuff, the companies won't make 'em anymore. They don't want to piss off the ladies, and I can't blame 'em. These women are tough."

I found the post office, bought some stamps, and was almost back to the canoe when I remembered Ramsay's sponge. There was a small supermarket just up from the Woodsville Bridge. I went in and bought a twin pack: one for me, one for Ramsay. If he was cleaning the stern, I'd have to do something about the bow.

When I got back to the Mad River, Ramsay was sitting under a tree drinking a beer and having a smoke. "Here's your sponge," I said, unwrapping the twin pack and throwing him one. He finished his beer, stubbed out his Carlton, and went to work. I started to sponge the bow, but what was the use? The minute we got back in, we'd bring some more sand with us.

Instead, I got out the *Guide*, and started thumbing through the section on Woodsville to South Newbury, our next stop, and found a blurb describing Major Robert Rogers's raid on the Indian village of St. Francis in Quebec on October 5, 1759. This raid and Rogers's subsequent retreat down the Connecticut was the basis for Kenneth Roberts's historical novel, *Northwest Passage*, the book that got me hooked on reading.

According to the *Guide,* the Fort at No. 5 had been located directly across from where we were standing. I was looking at the exact spot where 244 years earlier, Rogers and his Rangers had met their greatest disappointment. "You know, Ramsay," I said, "the Fort at No. 5 was located right across the river. That's where Rogers's Rangers were supposed to get resupplied after their raid on the St. Francis Indians, but by the time they made it here they were so beat up and disheveled the lieutenant in charge of resupplying them thought they must be a pack of wild French and Indians and took off with all the food and clothing. We should paddle over and take a look. There must be a plaque or something marking the spot."

"Bugsy," Ramsay said, carefully placing his sponge under his seat, "I've seen enough of Woodsville. We're out of here."

Doing his laundry and getting the sand out of the canoe were important to Ramsay. Taking ten minutes to see the spot where Major Robert Rogers faced his greatest disappointment was a waste of time. What was he thinking? As we pushed off, I started paddling. Hard. Squeak! Squeak! Squeak!

After a mile or so, Ramsay said, "Bugsy, how much did you pay for that haircut?"

"Eight bucks, plus a two-buck tip. How much do you pay in Cincinnati?"

"I don't pay anything. I cut my own hair."

"You cut your own hair? You've got to be kidding."

"No, I've been doing it for thirty years, ever since some barber stopped in the middle of my haircut, looked in the mirror, and trimmed his nose hairs with the same scissors he was using on me."

Unbelievable. During the last thirty years, Ramsay had been the CEO of a number of good-size companies. Whoever heard of a CEO cutting his own hair? "How'd you learn?" I said.

"Right after I caught the guy trimming his nose, *Esquire* had an article on how to cut your own hair. The key is getting a pair of scissors with rounded points on the end."

"What about the back?"

"You get an extension mirror. It's easy once you get the hang of it."

"You must have looked like hell the first time you tried."

"Naw, I asked the girls at work how I looked, and they said fine. They didn't know I'd done it myself. There was a barber's school down the street that gave cheap haircuts. They probably figured I'd tried to save a couple of bucks and gone there."

Between flossing his teeth, washing his clothes, cleaning the canoe, and cutting his own hair, Ramsay was one fastidious dude. I never remembered him being like that. He was beginning to remind me of Howard Hughes: an unorthodox thinker with a brilliant mind for business who'd become consumed with personal fetishes.

After almost a week of paddling, we hadn't seen a soul on the river. I didn't mind, I kind of enjoyed having the river to ourselves, but Ramsay was terribly disappointed. After the response we'd received from the press release, he figured we'd be bumping into all kinds of neat people. Ramsay claimed bumping into people was why he bought a six-pack of Bud Light every morning. He said beer was a good icebreaker. "When we see somebody who looks interesting, we'll paddle over, offer 'em a beer, and chat 'em up."

Since Ramsay wasn't much of a schmoozer, his desire to chat people up seemed a bit insincere, and since we never saw anybody, he was drinking the entire six-pack all by himself. Every day, by the time the first school bus came rumbling by, I'd hear the empties rattling around in his otherwise meticulously clean stern. Although he never got sloppy, or even high, I was beginning to wonder if Ramsay was a closet alcoholic. Like anybody who has reached the age of sixty, I'd known my share of alcoholics, and drinking during the day was one thing they all had in common. That might also help explain some of Ramsay's idiosyncrasies: how he withdrew into himself, his intransigence, his compulsive neatness.

About ten miles south of Woodsville, we spotted two paddles flashing in the sunlight. "Hot damn, Bugsy! There's a canoe. Quick, pick up the pace, don't let them get away."

"Take it easy, Ramsay. I think they're coming our way."

The heavy granite shores around Woodsville had reverted back to a broad floodplain, but now, thanks to the change in geology, instead of mud, the river was bordered by long stretches of sandy beach. We watched the canoe pull into a wide spit of sand and two people got out. As we got closer, we could see it was a man and a woman roughly our age, dressed like they could have stepped out of the Orvis catalogue. "How you doing?" Ramsay said, guiding the Mad River into shore.

"Fine, it's good to see the sun again," the woman replied. "You out for the day?"

"We're out for the month," Ramsay said. "We started in Canaan last Wednesday, and we're going all the way to Long Island Sound." He held up a can of Bud Light. "How about a beer?"

"I think we'll wait a while," the guy said, "but thanks anyway." I could see that he was eyeing our bags, somewhat suspiciously. "For two guys going all the way to the Sound, you're traveling pretty light."

"That's the beauty of it," Ramsay said. "We're not doing any camping. We're relying solely on the kindness of strangers."

That sparked the woman's memory. "I remember reading something about two old guys going down the river staying with different people every night. So, how's it going?"

"Fine," I said, "except this is our sixth day out, and you're the first people we've seen on the river. Where is everybody?"

"It's been a cold, wet spring," the man said. "This is really the first nice day we've had. I imagine you'll be seeing lots of people from here on, especially when school lets out."

Even without the beer, we began chatting them up. They were Dave and Anne Stephens, and Anne was the headmistress of the Mountain School, a former commune in Vershire, Vermont, that Milton Academy had taken over and turned into an off-campus facility where kids from Milton and other prep schools could go to learn about farming.

I'd heard about the Mountain School but never quite understood the concept. Why would parents who were paying $40,000 a year to send their kid to a fancy prep school want them taking off a semester to learn about farming? For that much money, you'd think they'd want them studying their asses off so they could get into a good college and become doctors, lawyers, or captains of industry. If they wanted to learn about farming, it would be cheaper to send them to Vermont Technical College like the Eaton kids, or better yet, work on a real farm for the summer where they might actually make some money.

When the Stephenses said they'd be happy to put us up that night, I was ready to take them up on their kind offer. I would liked to have seen the Mountain School, met some of the kids, and found out more about the program, but Ramsay, of course, already had us booked for the night, and there was no changing his plans. However, meeting the Stephenses definitely had revived his spirit. He was sure the ice had been broken and from now on we'd be running into all kinds of neat people. For my part, I was relieved to know he really was buying the Bud Lights so he could give them away. I didn't need to be stuck on a river with an alcoholic.

We were spending the night with Scott Edwards in North Haverhill, New Hampshire. Ramsay's notes on Scott said he was a teacher at Woodsville High. Ramsay had designated Bedell Bridge State Park, which was just south of North Haverhill, as our takeout. That would give us thirteen miles for the day. As we paddled up to the boat ramp, we could see that the park was deserted: no cars, no people, no phone, and contrary to the park's name, no bridge. A stone pier on each side of the river marked where the bridge had been, but the bridge itself was long gone. The only vehicular access to the park was a dirt road that ended in the parking lot just above where the bridge used to be.

"What the hell?" I said, fishing out Scot Williamson's pamphlet. I turned to Map 5, Woodsville/Wells River, and began reading to Ramsay. "'Bedell Bridge State Park commemorates a long-loved covered bridge, whose stone piers remain in the river. Rebuilt in 1979, the bridge was lost in a sudden windstorm only two months later.' Hell, Ramsay, what kind of a windstorm blows a whole bridge away?"

"A big fuckin' windstorm, that's what."

"So, what do you want to do?"

"I want to find a phone, call Scott Edwards, and get the hell out of here. This place gives me the creeps."

"Well, it's Monday afternoon. There's not much chance of anybody showing up here." I looked down the dirt road. It seemed to go on forever. "We could paddle down to the next takeout, but that's close to eight miles. If you want to call Scott Edwards, I guess you'd better start walking."

Ramsay wasn't too pleased with that suggestion. He lit up a Carlton and started weighing our options. At that moment, we saw a cloud of dust heading our way down the dirt road. A minute later, a white van pulled into the parking lot. "Quick, Bugsy, run up and see if that guy's got a cell phone."

I was sprinting toward the parking lot when the side door of the van slid open and six little kids tumbled out, four girls and two boys. Dressed in white bonnets and wide-brimmed black hats, smock dresses and wool britches, home spun socks, and black leather boots, they must have been Amish, which was too bad for Ramsay. What were the odds of the Amish having a cell phone?

Seeing our canoe, the kids made a beeline for the river. Their father and mother, dressed in the same attire, tried without luck to corral them. "Excuse me," I said, as the father chased the kids past me, "you wouldn't happen to have a cell phone, would you?"

"Yes, but it's back in the van," he said, stopping. "Where do you want to call?"

"It's a local call, to the guy who's supposed to pick us up."

"Come then," he said, forgetting the kids and turning back to the van.

"Ramsay, bring the number," I yelled. "This guy's got a phone."

While Ramsay walked up to make his call, I walked down to join the mother and kids, who'd gathered around the Mad River. The mother was painfully shy, but the kids couldn't have been more outgoing. The girls took off their shoes and socks, hiked up their dresses, and began wading into the river. They were laughing and squealing about the cold while peppering me with questions: "Is this your canoe?" "Where are you from?" "Where are you going?" "Where do you stay at night?"

I dug out Ruth's snack bag and asked the mother if I could give them each a piece of candy. She agreed, and I became the kids' new best friend—and was glad of it. These kids were fun. As we watched their parents herd them back into the van, I asked Ramsay, "What are the Amish doing with a cell phone? I thought that was a no-no?"

"They must be Mennonites. I think they can have cell phones."

"I wonder why they're moving to New Hampshire."

The guy told me the kids have allergies and he thinks this'll be a better climate for them. He said he had a commercial window-washing business in Pennsylvania and plans to start one up here. He must be out of his mind. What's the demand for a commercial window washer around here? I couldn't argue with that. It looked like my new little friends were in for a rough time.

Scott Edwards was middle-aged, tall, athletic, and very outgoing. As we were driving to his house in North Haverhill, Ramsay asked Scott how he'd gotten into teaching. "I kind of backed into it," Scott said. "For twenty years, I was the head of sales for a local sawmill. When it went out of business a couple of years ago, we had to decide whether to move or stay here. We like living in North Haverhill, and my wife has a good job at Dartmouth, so we decided to stay. While I was figuring out what I was going to do, I volunteered to teach woodworking at the high school. I liked teaching, so when they offered me a job, I took it."

Scott lived with his wife, Debbie, and their two sons in a little subdivision about ten minutes from Bedell Bridge Park. His mother-in-law, Noel, so named because she was born on Christmas day, lived next door. Scott told us Noel had been widowed a few years earlier, and rather than move her into a retirement community, they bought the lot next door and built her a house. "It's the best of both worlds," Scott said. "Unlike the stereotype, I love my mother-in-law."

In addition to teaching, Scott was the local distributor for We-no-nah Canoes. When we got to his house, he immediately showed us six We-no-nahs stored in his garage. Since we were paddling the entire river, Scott must have assumed we were avid canoeists. As such, he figured we'd know all about We-no-nahs, the Cadillacs of canoes. Scott soon realized we knew nothing, but like any good salesman, he began to educate us.

"We-no-nahs are composite canoes," he said, tapping the hull of a sleek, yellow number. "By composite, I mean we use the most superior fibers and resins to create highly sophisticated hulls designed to give the best comfort and paddling pleasure for whatever you want to do: fishing, racing, touring, whitewater, or just paddling down a river like you guys."

"So what's it made of?" asked Ramsay, caressing the yellow hull.

"Kevlar. The same fiber they use to make bulletproof vests. We've been using it for twenty-five years. What makes it so unique is it's both light and strong. Here, feel this," he said, lifting the hull with one hand.

"What's one of these things cost?" I said, hefting the hull.

"Depends on what you're looking for, but figure somewhere between fifteen and twenty-five hundred."

That was about double the cost of a good Old Town or a Mad River. I knew what Ramsay was thinking because I was thinking the same thing: How many We-no-nahs could Scott sell? We-no-nahs were aimed at the high end of the market, and from what we could see, the North Country wasn't a high-end market.

Scott ended the tour by taking us behind the garage and showing us his pride and joy, a fully restored, twenty-five-foot, wood and canvas, 1949 Old Town war canoe. "Found it up in the Adirondacks," he said, removing the tarp and pausing so we could fully appreciate the beauty of the big canoe's highly polished honey-colored wooden interior. "It was in pretty bad shape so I was able to get it for a hundred and fifty bucks."

"What's it worth now?" I said.

"Probably around twelve five. Actually, the guy had two of them. I should have bought them both, but if I'd come home with two canoes, Debbie would have killed me."

After we got settled, Scott told us he had to go to the annual sports awards banquet at Woodsville High. He said Debbie got home about seven, but if we were hungry, there was a pasta salad in the refrigerator, and we should just make ourselves at home. "Of course, if you want to come along," he added, "you're more than welcome."

"Sure, I'll come," I said. I wanted to see firsthand what high-school kids in the North Country were like.

"What about you, Ramsay?" Scott said.

"Naw, I'll stay here." I could see Ramsay was eyeing Scott's big-screen TV. "I want to check on the weather and make my calls, but Scott, is there any chance I can get the Ducks game?"

"No problem," Scott said, handing Ramsay the remote. "It'll be on fifty-six."

The Anaheim Mighty Ducks were playing the New Jersey Devils for the Stanley Cup. Why Ramsay cared about the Anaheim Mighty Ducks or who won the Stanley Cup was way beyond me.

Woodsville High was just down the street from the burned-out motel and the Laundromat where Ramsay had washed his clothes. By car, it took us less than twenty minutes to get there. That's the trouble paddling a river that's bordered by roads. Your sense of accomplishment is continually compromised. We'd just spent the whole day paddling from Woodsville to Haverhill.

Woodsville High's sports teams are known as the Engineers, a carryover from the days when Woodsville/Wells was the hub for loading logs onto trains, which had replaced the river drives for the trip south to the mills in Massachusetts. The Engineers were holding their sports banquet in the gym, but before we went in, Scott gave me a tour of the woodworking shop. For the spring term, he'd broken his classes into teams and had each team make a wooden kayak. A dozen or so kayaks, all in the final phases of construction, were scattered around the shop. Clearly Scott was passing on his passion for wooden boats to his students. The painstakingly sanded, lacquered, and polished honey-colored wood glowed like the inside of his big war canoe.

According to the information sheet, 171 students representing eighteen different teams were at the banquet. I was impressed. Most of the boys wore ties, the girls skirts or slacks and blouses. Their haircuts and hair colors looked normal. From what I could see, there were no tattoos, and except for a few earrings, very little body piercing. While Woodsville looked like it was dying, its kids, at least its athletes, looked healthy and wholesome, which said a lot about the importance of not cutting back on school sports.

As they started giving out the awards, it became clear why Scott was so eager to attend the banquet. Nick, Scott and Debbie's second son, was one of the Engineers' top athletes. Only a sophomore, Nick had lettered in three sports: soccer, skiing, and track. By the time the evening was over, he'd been named MVP in soccer, most improved in track, and next year's captain of all three teams. Not too shabby for a junior.

Watching Nick pick up his letters and hardware cast a new light on Debbie's job at Dartmouth. With decent grades and respectable SATs, Nick might get into Dartmouth, and since Debbie worked there, might get a free ride. At $45,000 a year or whatever college costs these days, it was no wonder the Edwardses didn't want to move.

When we got home, Brad, the Edwards's older son, was lying on the couch watching the Ducks and the Devils. He'd just returned from his freshman year at the University of Maine. When I'd asked Scott what Brad was doing for the summer, he'd told me Brad would be out looking for a job first thing in the morning.

Ramsay and Debbie were in the kitchen talking. Ramsay was happy to see us. Talking to Debbie was keeping him from the game. I could see Debbie had opened a bottle of wine, so I was glad to relieve him.

It turned out Debbie worked in the development office at Dartmouth. Her job was writing grant proposals, which with the stock market down was tougher than ever. "It's much harder than in the past," Debbie said. "A lot of foundations that have supported us for years are either cutting back on their donations or not giving at all. We're under a lot of pressure to produce. No sooner do I finish one proposal then they give me another."

Having put in twenty years at The Nature Conservancy, I knew what Debbie was talking about. In good times, nonprofits build up a lot of overhead. When the market goes south, donations fall off, and they don't know how to cut expenses. This puts tremendous pressure on the development departments, which even in bad times are expected to keep raising more money.

Debbie liked talking to somebody who had a firsthand appreciation of what she was going through. Like Ramsay, Scott and the Edwards boys were more interested in watching the game than listening to Debbie's day at work. "With the market down," I told Debbie, "all nonprofits are having a tough time. You just have to hang in there until things turn around."

Debbie seemed more relaxed by the time we finished the bottle of wine. As for Ramsay, he and the Edwards boys had a swell time watching the game, especially when Ramsay's Mighty Ducks won by a goal. All in all, it had been an interesting evening, and having lent Debbie a sympathetic ear, we felt we'd given as good as we got.

7

JUNE 3
NORTH HAVERHILL, NEW HAMPSHIRE

Options for the Golden Years

All was quiet at the Edwards house when we got up the next morning. Debbie had left at 6:30 for another day of writing grant proposals. Scott and Nick had set off for Woodsville High at 7:00, and Brad, still on his college schedule, was in bed dreaming about a summer job.

Scott had left us a pot of coffee, some muffins, and a note saying Noel would drive us back to the river. We'd just poured our first cup when Noel came knocking on the door and asked if we'd like to come over to her place for breakfast. We did, and after finishing off a big platter of eggs, bacon, and home fries, we understood why Scott liked having Noel next door.

As we headed downstream, Ramsay and I dissected the Edwards's situation. We agreed it must have been a shock when the sawmill closed down. From what we'd seen, there weren't a lot of white-collar jobs in the North Country. "Is wood-working a real teaching job?" Ramsay wondered. "I thought in the public schools you needed a certificate to teach."

"I'm not sure, but I can tell you one thing: If it weren't for Debbie's job at Dartmouth, there's no way the Edwardses could have stayed in North Haverhill."

"Bugsy, that's the new paradigm. When both a husband and wife are both working, you have to go with whoever has the best job."

"I guess you're right, but don't tell Debbie that. Right now, I think she'd like to kill the paradigm."

It was another beautiful spring day: sunny, warm, with a nice breeze and still no bugs. The river was slow, but mostly straight with no portages, which was good since we were planning to make sixteen miles that day. "Ramsay," I said, as we paddled along, "I've been meaning to ask you, why in the world do you give a rat's ass about the Anaheim Mighty Ducks?"

"Come on, Bugsy, the Ducks are neat, and it's the Stanley Cup playoffs. Plus it gives me a chance to lose some money to my son-in-law."

"Hell, if you want to lose money, lose some to me. What's your son-in-law got that I haven't?"

"My daughter."

Ramsay liked his son-in-law, but he worked for a company that made fax machines. With all the technological advances sweeping over the communications industry, Ramsay figured fax machines were going the way of the buggy whip, and Kim and her husband had to be living on a tight budget. "I don't just want to give them money," he said, "but I do want them to have some discretionary income. My son-in-law's a sports junkie, so I came up with this betting scheme. I pick the games, he chooses the teams. I put up a hundred bucks, he puts up a dollar with the stipulation that if he wins, he has to take Kim out to dinner. As a stay-at-home mom with three kids, she needs a night out every now and then, and losing bets with my son-in-law is an easy way to give it to her."

Just after noon, we decided to stop for lunch in Bradford, a town on the Vermont side of the river about eight miles south of Bedell Bridge State Park. The takeout for Bradford was Bugbee Landing, a state ramp on the Waits River about a quarter-mile up from where the Waits flows into the Connecticut. A park, ball field, and a nice little nine-hole golf course adjoined the landing. With the exception of some senior citizen golfers, it was a quiet Tuesday in Bradford. We lugged the Mad River ashore, turned it over, stashed our duffels underneath, and walked into town. Among the stores lining old Route 5, the main drag, was a sandwich shop. We found a table overlooking the golf course and ordered a couple of pastrami sandwiches. As we sat there eating, we watched a couple of old duffers butcher the hole below us. "You know," I said, "that course looks just about my speed. What do you say we rent some clubs and play a quick nine?"

"No way, Bugsy. We don't have time for golf. I told Pete Richardson we'd meet him in Orford between three and four. We've got at least another six miles to go." Actually, it was closer to eight, but I wasn't going to tell that to Ramsay.

"Ramsay, we're not on any schedule. Call Pete and have him pick us up here. What does he care? By car, it's only another five minutes," but I was talking to a wall. Once Ramsay made his plans, there was no changing them.

A mile downstream from Bradford, we passed under the Route 25 bridge. Below the bridge, the river made a two mile jog to the east and back. To break the boredom Ramsay asked me about Donald. Donald was the foster child Ruth and I had adopted after we gave up trying to conceive. Like most adoptions from foster care, it hadn't worked, at least as we'd hoped. Before Don, I'd assumed a person's intelligence and personality were determined fifty percent by heredity and fifty percent by environment. After dealing with Don for thirteen years, I'd become convinced intelligence and personality are ninety percent set the moment the sperm introduces itself to the egg. Granted, Don was five when he came to live with us and had spent the bulk of his early life being shunted from one foster home to another, but still, Don was Don and nothing we were going to do was going to greatly change him. His past demons would never let him realize our unrealistic dreams. That was the gist of what I told Ramsay and ended with, "Don stays in touch, and much like you and your son-in-law, we try to think of ways to send him some money without him coming to expect it."

"Don't be too hard on yourself, Bugsy, but I thought Don was a pretty good athlete. How come you never traded up on that?"

"Don was a hell of an athlete. I honestly believe he had the physical ability to pitch professionally, but mentally, he didn't have the discipline. In many ways, Don reminds me of John Daly: a big, affable kid with great athletic ability and no mental discipline. In fact, one of my fantasies is to caddy for John Daly. After dealing with Don, I think I could straighten him out."

"I caddied for a pro once," Ramsay said.

"You did? When you were a kid?"

"No, just a couple of years ago. I read in the paper that the Nike Tour was coming to Dayton. It said if you wanted to caddy, you could sign up. Dayton's only an hour from Cincinnati so I figured, what the hell?"

"So, you drove to Dayton and signed up?"

"Why not? I had nothing better to do."

"Who'd you get?"

"A guy named J.C. Anderson from Plano, Texas. The first thing he said to me was, 'Are you the best caddy?' so the first thing I said to him was, 'Why, are you the best golfer?' I figured it was going to be a two-day affair, but damn if Ol' J.C. didn't make the cut, and I had to go back Saturday and Sunday."

"Did you like him?"

"Not particularly. One time I was having a smoke and forgot to pick up the cover to his driver. When I told him it was back on the tee, all he said was, 'That's not my problem.'

"Then he stiffed me. They pay fifty bucks a round, but when he made the cut, I should have gotten ten percent of his winnings. J.C. won thirty-five hundred, but he only gave me two hundred."

"Maybe he figured the cover was worth a hundred and fifty."

"Yeah, right, Bugsy. Keep paddling."

I did, all the way to Orford.

The public landing for Orford was a quarter-mile past town, which meant Ramsay would have to walk back to town to call Pete Richardson, our stranger for the evening. We'd had a long, hot day and Ramsay wasn't walking anywhere. He pulled the Mad River into a private landing right in the middle of town. The landing looked deserted so we decided to leave the Mad River there for the night. We chained it to a tree, grabbed our duffels, and walked up to Orford's quiet and very gracious common.

According to the *Guide,* Washington Irving, the author of *Rip Van Winkle* and the *Legend of Sleepy Hollow,* visited Orford in the 1830s and wrote, "In all my travels in this country and Europe, I have never seen any village more beautiful than Orford." We could see exactly what Irving meant. Orford was one of the original enclaves of wealth along the river, but unlike Stratford, which had let most of its old mansions fall to ruin, Orford looked perfectly preserved. This was especially true of the seven grand homes that faced the east side of the common. A plaque on the common identified them as "Bullfinch Row," so named after Boston's renowned architect, Charles Bullfinch, who reportedly designed the southernmost house on the "Row," and whose influence was reflected in the other six.

A little white post office sat facing the common, so while Ramsay went off to find a phone, I decided to send Dan Lufkin a postcard. Dan Lufkin, a founding partner of the investment firm Donaldson, Lufkin & Jenrette, is best known as a great businessman. What's not so widely known is that he's also a great conservationist. I first met Dan in 1975 when he came on the board of The Nature Conservancy. Over the next ten years, Dan used his business skills and contacts to help make the Conservancy one of the most successful private land conservation organization in the world.

About the time Ramsay and I decided to canoe the Connecticut, I'd heard Dan had gone on the board of a new foundation and was directing much of its giving to land conservation, so I wrote him a letter. In it, I described our trip and told Dan that since leaving the Conservancy, I'd kept my hand in conservation by volunteering for several little land trusts. I said I liked working with local trusts because, like Dumbo the baby elephant, they could fly, but often didn't know they could fly until somebody gave them a "Dumbo's feather." I ended the letter by telling Dan there were sixty-one small trusts working to save parts of the Connecticut River, and what they needed more than anything else was confidence, "the same confidence you gave us when you came on the board of The Nature Conservancy."

A couple of days later, Dan called. He said he was making me the foundation's one-month, unpaid project manager for the Connecticut River, and I had $50,000 to give to local land trusts. When I asked Dan how he wanted to handle the grants, he said the foundation was too thinly staffed to have people calling and sending in proposals. "When you find a project, drop me a note with the name and address of the organization, and we'll send them a check."

That night, I planned to meet with the Upper Valley Land Trust in Hanover, New Hampshire. Upper Valley had a program where it bought and maintained primitive camp sites along the river. We'd seen a half-dozen of these sites between McIndoe Falls and Orford. My thought was that by using these campsites as toeholds, maybe the land trust could start protecting larger sections of the river. The problem was, I hadn't talked with Dan since our initial conversation so before I made any commitments, I wanted him to know his one-month, unpaid project manager for the Connecticut River was alive, well, and ready to spend some of the foundation's money.

Having mailed my card to Dan, I walked back to the common, found a sunny spot, and lay down on the warm grass to wait for Ramsay. Within minutes, I was sound asleep. Paddling sixteen miles had done me in.

Pete Richardson lived in Norwich, Vermont, twenty miles south of Orford. When friends in conservation heard we were canoeing the Connecticut, they told me we had to spend a night with Pete. After retiring as director of admissions for MIT, Pete had become very active in the Appalachian Mountain Club and was one of the founding members of the Connecticut River Joint Commissions, the group that had published the booklet of maps Scot Williamson had given us. As such, he could tell us anything we wanted to know about the river.

Norwich was a swishy little town across the river from Hanover, New Hampshire, home of Dartmouth College. Pete and his wife, Keenie, lived just up from the main square. From their front steps we could see the Baker Library tower, the centerpiece of Dartmouth. Once we'd met Keenie and gotten settled, Keenie remembered she had a message for me. A woman from the Upper Valley Land Trust had called, and wanted me to call her back. "Pete," I said, "what do you know about the Upper Valley Land Trust?"

"They're a good group. Keenie and I are members. In fact, I think we have the latest copy of their newsletter right here."

Pete rummaged through a stack of magazines and came up with the newsletter. The lead article described how the land trust had just bought its own building. That was not good. When a nonprofit organization buys its own building, it's a sign that maintaining the organization has become more important than pursuing the cause.

It was a little after five when I called. A recording answered. "If you know your party's extension, you may dial it now. If not, you may choose from the following menu." When the recording reached the sixth person, I hung up. Upper Valley Land Trust was no struggling little Dumbo that needed a push from us. With its own building and a staff of at least seven, it already was flying.

After dinner, Pete asked if we'd like to take a ride over the river and see the college. I said I would, but assumed Ramsay would rather stay and make his calls. To my surprise, he seemed very interested in seeing Dartmouth. As we drove through Norwich, we got a taste of how wealthy this area was compared to the northern part of the river. A manicured common was surrounded by immaculately restored buildings housing boutiques and specialty shops selling high-end goods to people dressed in lime greens and pinks and driving fancy cars. "Pete, this place is a pretty upscale," I said. "I never pictured Norwich looking like this."

"A lot of professionals live here: professors, administrators, doctors. Norwich is a wealthy community."

The bridge over the Connecticut was nothing like the rusty wrecks we'd seen upriver. It was new and clean and had big cement balls perched on the railings. "This is Ledyard Bridge," Pete said. "It's where the Appalachian Trail crosses the Connecticut."

"Pete, what the hell are those cement balls?" Ramsay asked.

"Those are the Orbs of Knowledge. They've caused quite a controversy. Some people consider them art, others think they're a waste of taxpayer's money."

"I'll go with a waste of money," Ramsay said. "All of the bridges above here look like they're about to fall down, and this damn thing has the Orbs of Knowledge. Give me a break."

Once over the bridge, we drove up the hill to the main intersection of Hanover. The college was on the left, the town on the right. Pete turned left, drove us around the quad, past Baker Library, and through the medical center. I'd gone there thirty-seven years ago to get my lip sewn up after a rugby match. Then, it was just little Mary Hitchcock Hospital. Now, it was huge Dartmouth-Hitchcock Medical Center, an enormous complex.

From there, we went around the golf course, by the athletic fields, past Memorial Stadium, and back into town. Dartmouth had gotten a lot bigger than I remembered. New construction, most of it modern, was going up everywhere, especially around the medical center. "God," Ramsay said, as we watched the setting sun reflect off the buildings, "look at all those damn windows. Dave Yeager had it right. A commercial window washer up here could make a fortune."

"Dartmouth fuels the economy," Pete said, "and it's not just the college. The medical center creates a lot of jobs and helps draw retirees to the area."

"And every damn one of them has enough money to buy a We-no-nah canoe," Ramsay said. "Here's the market, Bugsy."

When we got back to the house, Keenie was sitting in the living room reading the *Wellesley* alumnae magazine. "Pete, here's a nice article on Hillary," she said, holding up the magazine. "Dave, you live around Washington. What do you hear about Hillary?"

"Nothing you don't," I said, "but my wife was in Hillary's class at Wellesley, and I've got a great story for you."

In the spring of '69, I decided I was going to marry Ruth Sisler. With that thought in mind, I skipped my own graduation from UVA business school and went to Ruth's graduation at Wellesley. That was the first year Wellesley had two commencement speakers: One was the traditional luminary, the other a member of the class. The luminary in '69 was Senator Edward Brooke, the first black person ever elected to the senate by popular vote. For the class, '69 had chosen Hillary Rodham, the head of Wellesley's student government. According to Ruth, Hillary took her graduation speech very seriously. She spent the entire spring meeting with the different groups on campus soliciting their thoughts on what she should say.

Senator Brooke spoke first. In essence, what he told the class of '69 was that Wellesley had given them a good education, and now it was time for them to go forth and use that education to make some man successful. Even though many of these women were at the vanguard of the feminist movement, the senator received a polite if somewhat reserved applause when he finished. Then Hillary stepped to the dais. She looked at the crowd through her heavy black-framed glasses, and said, "I had a prepared speech, but after hearing Senator Brooke, I feel I must respond on behalf of the class of '69."

For the next half hour, Hillary respectfully but forcefully explained how Wellesley hadn't prepared the class of '69 to help some man become a doctor, lawyer, or the CEO of a big corporation. Wellesley had prepared them to be doctors, lawyers, and the CEOs of big corporations, and that's what '69 was going to do no matter what a male-dominated society might think.

What made Hillary's speech so amazing was everyone knew it was right off the cuff. When she sat down, all the graduates, their families, their friends, and even Senator Brooke, jumped to their feet and gave her a standing ovation.

Keenie and Pete liked my story. Unfortunately, I didn't have an encore, and it was only eight-thirty. I wasn't sure if I could sit through another rendition of *Beg, Borrow, and Deal.* Luckily, just as Ramsay was getting warmed up, the back door opened and a middle-aged man walked in. He was Dr. Dennis McCullough, Pete and Keenie's next-door neighbor and the head of medical services for Kendall at Hanover, a three-hundred unit retirement community. When Pete mentioned Dennis was writing a book on how to treat senior citizens effectively and reasonably, Ramsay started grilling him. Who decided what procedures were really necessary? When were they necessary? Most important, when should they be terminated?

"Dennis," Ramsay said, "It seems to me a large part of geriatric medicine is just keeping people alive. For the last few years of their lives, my parents were just wasting their money taking up space."

"What we're trying to do is adopt a more interdisciplinary approach to understanding the diseases of elderly people," Dennis said. "That means providing patients with both the very best care and caring. Doctors have to listen more, discuss more, and work more to develop a partnership with their patients and the patients' families, but that's not easy. Many doctors, and many families, just don't have the time."

Dennis's more holistic approach to geriatric medicine did little to comfort Ramsay. No matter how good the care or the caring, he saw nothing propitious about getting old.

What Ramsay and I found interesting was how retirement communities had become a booming business. Pete and Keenie were right in the middle of deciding when they should sell their home and move into a retirement community.

Given the fact that living in a retirement community was more expensive than living on their own, Pete and Keenie wanted to remain on their own as long as possible, but there was a risk in that. "You can't wait too long," Pete said. "You have to go when you're healthy. If you come down with something like a stroke or Alzheimer's, they won't take you. Then you'll be stuck in a nursing home for the rest of your life.

I could see Ramsay wince at the thought of being stuck in a nursing home. I winced too. Who wouldn't? "So, what are you going to do?" Ramsay said.

"We've bought an option at Kendall at Hanover, and another in a retirement community in Exeter, New Hampshire. We staggered them a couple of years apart. If we're still doing okay when the Kendall option expires, we'll let it go and wait for the place in Exeter. The options cost ten thousand apiece, but it's worth it to have the flexibility."

"Buying a series of options is an interesting approach," I said. "Ramsay, that could be a new business for you, trading options on retirement communities. With the baby boomers coming on line, I bet there'd be a huge market for that type of thing. You could make a million."

"It's too capital intensive for me," Ramsay said, "but you can bet if the demand stays ahead of the supply, somebody's going to do it."

"From what I see," Dennis added, "the demand for space in retirement communities like Kendall of Hanover is going to stay well ahead of the supply, at least for the foreseeable future."

"Dennis," I said, "you should put a chapter in your book that explains how seniors can use options to guarantee a spot in a retirement community of their choosing."

Ramsay jumped on that idea. "Hot damn, Dennis, if you can show people how to stay out of a nursing home, I guarantee you'll have a best seller."

8

Krazy Kate

The next morning while showering, I discovered a tick embedded in my hip. It must have burrowed in there while I was asleep on the Orford common. I pulled it off and showed it to Ramsay. In preparing for the trip, Ramsay had read several articles about Lyme disease. Ramsay studied the tick. "It's too big to be a deer tick," he said. "That's good." Then he looked at the spot where the tick had bitten me. "You got the head out, and there's no rash. One sign of Lyme disease is a red rash around the bite. Keep an eye on it, but I think you're okay."

When we came downstairs, Pete was waiting for us. "Good morning, boys," he said, rubbing his hands together like he was anticipating the start of a great day. "How about some scrambled eggs?"

"Sure," we said, "scrambled eggs would be great."

Pete hustled off to the kitchen looking very pleased. A few minutes later, Keenie came down. When she went into the kitchen, all hell broke loose. "Pete, what are you doing?" she barked. "You know you're not allowed to have eggs."

"But Keenie, the boys wanted eggs. What was I supposed to do, say no?"

"Pete," we yelled from the dining room, "it's okay, we don't need eggs. Toast and coffee will be fine."

"Don't be silly. We're all having eggs, and that's that." And it was. Judging from the big smile on Pete's face, it was the most enjoyable breakfast he'd had in some time.

Pete decided to forgo Interstate 91 and drive us back up to Orford over old Route 5. This section of Route 5 was dotted with the little towns of East Thetford, North Thetford, and Ely. They had escaped the drive-through development and fast-food facades that proliferate around exits of the interstate. They still were classic New England villages: a few homes, a post office, a general store, a fire station, a library, and a white Congregational church. Where the road ran next to the river, we were able to get a feel for some of the stretch we'd be canoeing that day. We were planning to paddle from Orford to the confluence of the Ompompanoosuc River, a distance of about fourteen miles. Pete knew this section well and pointed out some of the natural features we'd see, like Hewes Brook, Childs Pond, and Reeds Marsh. For the most part, it appeared we were in for a straight, easy run. As he pushed us off into another beautiful spring day, Pete looked like he would have loved to come with us. "Have a good one," he said, "and if you need a place to stay tonight, you're always welcome."

We were sure he meant it. To Pete we were another batch of scrambled eggs.

By the time we pulled into the landing at North Thetford, we'd paddled off Pete's big breakfast and were ready for lunch. "Bugsy, you stay here with the bags," Ramsay said, lighting up a Carlton. "I'll walk into town and see what's available."

He was no sooner gone than he was back. "There's a post office, but not much else. The postmistress said there's a convenience store down in East Thetford, but that's about it. So what do you want to do?"

"Look," I said, knowing there was always Ruth's snack bag, "every time we've run into a problem, somebody's come along to bail us out. First it was the kids at the dam, then the Stephenses, then the Mennonites. Let's head downriver and see what happens."

We'd gone about a quarter-mile when Ramsay said, "Bugsy, what's that coming?"

I looked up and saw the oars of a shell flashing erratically in the sun. "I think it's somebody in a shell, but they're not going very straight."

The shell was jumping around like a water bug, going one way, then the other. The closer it got, the more clear it became that whoever was rowing had no idea where they were going. We were almost even with the shell when suddenly it veered and started coming right at us. "Hey, watch out," I yelled, "you're going to hit us."

The rower, a middle-aged woman with frizzy blond hair and John Lennon glasses, swung around in her seat totally surprised. Seeing us, she stopped rowing, and said, "Hey, you must be the two old geezers."

"That's us," Ramsay said, delighted with the recognition.

"We were going to put you up," she said, "but nobody ever called us back."

"Well, you're in luck," I said. "We're here, and we're looking for lunch."

The woman paused for a moment thinking it over, then said, "I can do that. My name's Kate. My house is about a mile downriver, first dock on the right." With two powerful strokes, Kate turned the shell around and began rowing downriver.

"Hot damn," Ramsay said. "Bugsy, start paddling. Don't let her get away. Kate's crazy."

Try as we might, we couldn't keep up with Kate. Rowing with the current had straightened her out. She was a good quarter of a mile ahead of us when she pulled up to her dock. In the distance, I could see her lift the shell from the water and carry it over her head into a small boathouse. Then Kate came back to the dock, took off all her clothes, and jumped into the river. "Ramsay," I said, "I think Kate just went skinny-dipping."

Ramsay stopped paddling and peered downriver. Kate was climbing back onto the dock. "My god, Bugsy, you're right. Kate's naked as a jaybird. That girl is crazy."

When we reached the dock, Kate, fully dressed, led us along a path across the railroad tracks and up a very steep embankment. Her slicked-back hair was the only sign she'd been swimming. An unpainted wooden house looking like something out of a thirty-year old *Whole Earth Catalog* was perched on top of the bluff. Kate stopped at the garden by the back door and filled a basket with lettuce, peas, carrots, and asparagus. "Here's your lunch," she said. "Come on in."

The inside of the house, like the outside, had lots of raw wood. Most of the seating was on pillows. What furniture there was appeared homemade. In the main living room, instead of a couch, a swing hung from a big beam. Kate took us upstairs to the kitchen. She set us on stools around a rough planked table and started rummaging around inside the refrigerator. She came out with a loaf of homemade bread, a big block of cheese, and an assortment of homemade dressings. "That's it," she said. "My husband and I are leaving for Idaho this afternoon, so I've kind of cleaned out the refrigerator."

As we ate, Kate asked us how our trip was going, and we told her we were surprised the Stephenses were the only people we'd seen on the river. "It's early yet," she said. "The water's still pretty cold. Wait till you get to Dartmouth. Things'll pick up."

"We stayed in Norwich last night," Ramsay said, "and I've got to tell you, Dartmouth's totally out of sync with the rest of region. Norwich and Hanover don't look like anything we've seen upriver."

"Yeah, things have gotten pretty yupped up down there," Kate said. "That's why Bill and I like living up here."

"Yupped up," Ramsay said. "You mean like the Orbs of Knowledge."

"You got it."

"What do you do up here?" I wondered out loud.

"Bill works for the Upper Valley Land Trust," Kate said. That was interesting. Having met Kate, I'd have to re-evaluate my initial assessment of the Upper Valley Land Trust. A free spirit like Kate would never put the organization before the cause.

"Is the trust buying any land?" I said.

"They're more into policy than land protection, but they're doing some pretty good things."

I would've liked to ask Kate more about the land trust, but she had to leave for Idaho and Ramsay was getting itchy. Talk about conservation always made him itchy. We thanked Kate for lunch and walked back down to the river. As we were about to get into the canoe, I looked around and seeing nobody said, "What the hell, if Krazy Kate can do it, so can I."

I stripped down, jumped in, and immediately wished I hadn't. Kate was krazy. The Connecticut was freezing.

Our strangers for that night were truly strange. When Ramsay called the night before, the guy who answered had no idea who he was or what he was calling about. When he put his wife on, all she said, "Oh, good, houseguests, won't that be fun," then proceeded to tell Ramsay that they had to go out for the evening, but a babysitter would be there with their two-year-old daughter, and we should just make ourselves at home. Who'd invite two perfect strangers to spend the evening with their two-year-old daughter and the babysitter?

The house, a run-down Cape that nobody was fixing up, was at the confluence of the Ompompanoosuc River and the Connecticut. A picnic table painted in psychedelic colors was standing out on the front yard. A kiddie pool with toys scattered all around it sat next to the table. From inside, we could hear the shouts of children playing. A young woman with a baby on her hip appeared at the screen. Ramsay told her who we were. "Come on in," she said. "Jean told me to put you in the back bedroom."

The house was a mess: dirty dishes piled up in the sink, toys strewn all over the floor, four little kids dressed only in Pampers running around blowing bubbles at each another. "Who are all these kids?" I said. "I thought there was only one daughter?"

"This is her play group," the woman said, leading us into a dark, dirty bedroom. "I guess one of you will sleep in the bed and the other on the mattress on the floor."

The bed was unmade, the mattress stained and bare. The play group jumped on the mattress and squealed with delight as they bounced up and down in their Pampers, which probably explained the stains. I followed Ramsay outside as he popped open a beer.

"So," I said, "what do you think?"

"I think we've gotta get the hell out of here. But how? Where will we go?"

"Call somebody else. Don't you have a bunch of names around Norwich?"

"It's four o'clock. We can't call anybody this late. I told everyone we'd give them at least a day's notice."

"We could call Pete and Keenie. I'm sure they'd take us back."

"Hell, Bugsy, we can't go back. That'd be admitting defeat." Ramsay paused to drain his Bud. "I'm out of beer. Let's go in and see if they've got any." That was all he could think of to do.

As soon as we entered, the play group swarmed around us. Apparently, two coots were more interesting than any of the toys lying around. I opened the refrigerator and looked in. It was packed with baby food, fruit, fruit drinks, milk, and vegetables. There was no meat, no beer, nothing for us. We walked back out to the picnic table. "Ramsay, I've got an idea. Let's call Carl Demrow and see if he can come pick us up."

Carl Demrow worked for the Conservation Fund, a national group run by my friend Pat Noonan. Pat had just hired Carl as the Conservation Fund's representative for northern Vermont. When I'd told Pat about our trip, he'd asked me if I could meet with Carl and look over some of the projects he was working on. Pat said Carl was a great naturalist, but hadn't had much experience buying land. Pat thought maybe I could help him out, but with Ramsay's inflexibility, I'd given up on meeting Carl. Now, I saw an opening. "So what do you say, Ramsay, should I call Carl?"

At that moment, the play group came streaming out the screen door. They jumped into a kiddy pool next to the picnic table. One of the kids had a load in her Pamper. It began to ooze into the water. Ramsay looked pale. The kids all squealed and began splashing him. "Oh, hell. Bugsy, call Carl."

9

JUNE 5
WAITS, VERMONT

Little Ramsay

Carl lived by himself in an old farmhouse on top of a hill above Waits, Vermont, about twenty miles west of the river. Carl's place was just ten miles up the Waits River from Claire Porter's, Ruth's college roommate, where we'd spent the first night on our way north. Carl was in the midst of a major renovation. Phase I was the kitchen. With new cabinets, counters, sink and matching stainless steel appliances, it looked pretty spiffy for an old farmhouse. When Ramsay complimented Carl on his taste, Carl said, "Yeah, I'm about Martha'd out." To which Ramsay replied, "You mean, yupped up." To which Carl said, "No, there's a difference. 'Yupped up' means new, expensive, and trendy. 'Martha'd out' means stylish, affordable, and functional." Ramsay was delighted to learn of this distinction. Now he had two new phrases to throw around.

Ramsay slept upstairs in the guest bedroom, I was on the sofa bed in the living room. When we went to bed, the stars were shining. When I woke up, it was to the sound of gurgling gutters. A low had moved in during the night bringing with it another day of cold rain. The smell of fresh coffee coming from Carl's new kitchen lured me out of my warm bed, but there was no one around. I poured myself a cup and settled in next to the toasty woodstove. I'd just poured my second cup when I heard Carl on the porch taking off his boots. He came in with six big, brown eggs resting in his Conservation Fund cap. "It's a mess out there," he said, shaking the water from his hair. "You wouldn't want to be on the river today."

"I wouldn't, but I don't know about Ramsay. When it comes to his schedule he's pretty inflexible."

"I told him if you wanted to stay another night, that would be fine with me and he was up for that."

I was glad to hear it. After three days of sun, I had no appetite for paddling in the rain, and being with Carl was easy. He was more like a kid brother than a stranger. "Where is Ramsay anyway?"

"Outside having a smoke. We've been gathering eggs." Ramsay gathering eggs? I couldn't picture that. Imagine a guy who cut his own hair, spent fifteen minutes every night flossing his teeth, and wouldn't trust anybody else to do his own laundry sticking his hand under a chicken's ass? That was like Howard Hughes visiting a leper colony.

Carl scrambled up the eggs and served them with a pound of maple-cured bacon and a stack of French toast smothered in homemade maple syrup from trees we could see out the window. While we ate, I asked Carl if he had any projects we could see. He said he had one right up the road, so after breakfast, the three of us climbed into the cab of Carl's four-wheel-drive pickup and went to have a look.

The project consisted of seven properties totaling just over 3,000 acres of forest. After an hour of cruising up and down a series of desolate dirt roads, Ramsay asked Carl the same question he'd asked Scot Williamson, "So Carl, what's the threat?"

"There are two," Carl said. "One's clear cutting, which kills sustainable forestry. The other's development. After

9/11, developers are nosing around looking for large tracts they can turn into gated communities. We don't need gated communities around here. We want to keep these lands as working forests. Hell, up here people don't even lock their doors."

"That's all well and good," I said, "but what's the cost and where's the money coming from?"

"The state has appraised the type of easement we've proposed at two hundred an acre. Most of that will come from a fund the state's set up to promote sustainable forestry. If we can buy easements over four of the properties, the other three owners have said they'll voluntarily restrict their land to sustainable forestry."

"So, what you're telling me is the project's going to be funded by state money matched by gifts of easements?"

"Mostly, but we're going to need some private funds to get the project going, and later on, to monitor the easements."

"Who'd hold the easements?"

"The Vermont Land Trust and Upper Valley Land Trust."

"Upper Valley Land Trust?" I said. "You work with them?"

"We've done some things with them," Carl said. "Their main focus is on developing guidelines for land use along the Connecticut, but since this project contains the headwaters of both the Waits and White Rivers, they'd like to be part of it."

"Carl, I'll tell you what. Draw me up a proposal, and we'll ask the foundation we're dealing with to make a grant of $10,000 to Upper Valley Land Trust for this project. You'll have to match it one-for-one with either dollars or gifts of easements, but with that you should be able to protect a hundred acres and get the project going."

Carl like that idea and wanted to show us more, but Ramsay was getting itchy and I'd seen enough. However, before we quit, Carl said it would really help him if we could meet with "the Dawg," a flower child of the seventies who owned six hundred acres that once had been a thriving commune and now was one of the key properties in Carl's project. He turned the pickup onto a rutted track that wound up the side of a mountain. At the top, the woods opened up exposing a big wooden farmhouse surrounded by lawns, gardens, and a couple of outbuildings. "Carl," Ramsay said, "this place looks pretty neat. I was expecting a couple of yurts and a teepee."

"The Dawg's son is getting married this weekend," Carl explained, "so he spruced up the place."

An old hippie with a ponytail tied in a red bandanna was standing in the driveway working on a front-end loader. The rain had stopped and through the clouds we could see a patch of blue sky. Carl pulled up next to the front-end loader, rolled down his window, and said, "The Dawg around?"

"In the house," Red Bandanna said, not bothering to look up.

At that moment, the Dawg came out. He probably was about our age, but his fuzzy grey beard, long grey hair, and faded Pittsburgh Pirates cap made him look much older. He greeted us suspiciously. It wasn't until Carl introduced me as a career conservationist that the Dawg perked up. Career conservationists either had money or knew where to find it.

"Hey, Dawg, I could use a hand over here," shouted Red Bandanna.

We all walked over to see what he needed. "The battery on the bushhog's dead, so I'm gonna use the battery from the front-end loader, but I can't get to the battery 'cause the arm of the bucket's in the way, and I can't raise the bucket 'cause there's a leak in the hydraulics. I guess we gotta lift it by hand."

Carl and the Dawg each grabbed a side of the bucket. Reluctantly, Ramsay and I joined in. We didn't know it at the time, but we were about to get a lesson in why communes fail. On the count of three, we all gave a heave, but the bucket didn't budge. Undaunted, Red pointed to a pile of cement blocks stacked next to one of the sheds. "Okay," he said, "each of you grab a couple of those blocks, and when I back up the loader, slip 'em under the bucket. That way, we'll force it up."

After a good half hour of lugging blocks and shoving them under the bucket, we'd built a pyramid that forced the bucket high enough for Red to get to the battery and out. During our labors, I heard Ramsay mumble, "Hell, given the time we've been screwing around here, we could've bought the Dawg a damn battery."

But we had gotten a feel for why the Dawg was supportive of Carl's project. At $200 an acre, he'd net about $100,000, and as Ramsay noted when we'd climbed back into Carl's pickup, "Hot damn, a hundred thousand would set the Dawg up for life."

When we got to Carl's, Ramsay was ready for a nap and Carl was going to work on his proposal for the foundation. I decided to jog down to the town of Waits River. Plodding along, it occurred to me that maybe I should fix Carl up with Claire Porter. At first blush they seemed like a natural fit. Both were single, both were attractive, both were bright, both lived alone in old farmhouses they were renovating, both were into animal husbandry, and they only lived ten miles apart. Then I realized Claire had a few years on Carl. But so what? A little May-November romance might be good for them, and who'd care? Hey, this was the North Country; you had to take what you could get.

With this idea fresh in my mind, I hustled back to the house. Carl and Ramsay were huddled over Carl's computer laughing and having a grand time. "What are you guys doing?" I said.

"Bugsy, you've got to see this. Carl lost his rooster to a coyote and his egg production's down because the hens are unhappy, so we're ordering a rooster online from Iowa."

"A rooster from Iowa? Why don't you just buy one from a farmer down the road?"

"No, no." Ramsay held up a mail-order catalog. The picture of a very studly rooster graced the cover. "This is a big business, very specialized." He handed me the catalog. It was from Murray McMurray, the world's largest rare breed hatchery. "We're getting a black sex link. If they ship him today, he'll be at the post office in Waits River by Saturday."

"I'm calling him Little Ramsay," Carl said, typing in the order.

"Well," I said, as Carl sent the order, "with six hens out there, Little Ramsay ought to be in for a good time."

"Not really," Carl said, "those hens got some years on them. Put a young rooster in with a seasoned hen, and she'll beat the hell out him. That's where the term 'henpecked' comes from."

Hmm. So much for fixing Carl up with Claire.

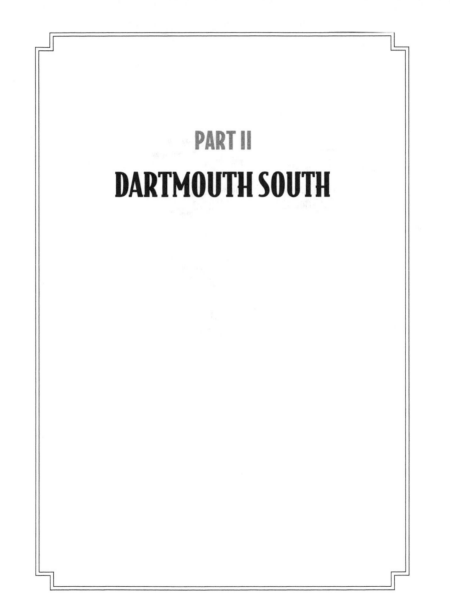

PART II

DARTMOUTH SOUTH

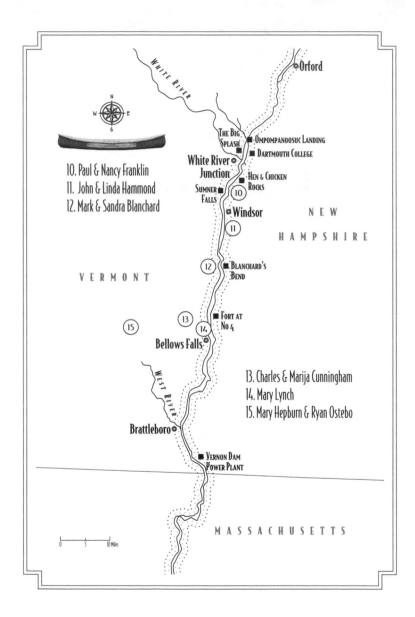

WHITE RIVER

Orford

THE BIG SPLASH
Ompompanoosuc Landing
Dartmouth College

White River Junction

Hen & Chicken Rocks

Sumner Falls

10

Windsor

11

NEW

HAMPSHIRE

10. Paul & Nancy Franklin
11. John & Linda Hammond
12. Mark & Sandra Blanchard

VERMONT

12 Blanchard's Bend

13 Fort at No 4

15 14

Bellows Falls

WEST RIVER

13. Charles & Marija Cunningham
14. Mary Lynch
15. Mary Hepburn & Ryan Ostebo

Brattleboro

Vernon Dam Power Plant

0 5 10 Miles

MASSACHUSETTS

10

JUNE 6
OMPOMPANOOSUC LANDING, VT

The Orbs of Knowledge

Hobbled by Wilder Dam nine miles below, from the confluence of the Ompompanoosuc to Hanover, the Connecticut
ran flat and slow. As we approached Dartmouth, we saw two
eight-man shells beating their way upriver. *Resolute* was
first. We could hear the coxswain barking up the beat into a
microphone attached to his headset. Even with the mike, his
face was red from yelling. "Bugsy," Ramsay said, "how'd you
like to have that little prick yelling at you?"

"I don't need him. I've got you."

W. H. Perry, Jr. '53' was two boat lengths behind *Resolute.*
Its coxswain was screaming into his mike too. Between them,
they were upsetting the harmony of the river. "Whatever
happened to megaphones?" Ramsay said. "They sound like
those damn kids with boom boxes."

The shells passed us, turned around, and started back.
Now they were neck and neck. In describing this part of the
river, the *Guide* suggested, "If you're in a canoe, try to give
the shells a run for their money."

"Ramsay," I said, accepting the *Guide*'s challenge, "let's
see if we can make it to that tree before they pass us."

"Forget the tree. Paddle for shore. Those assholes think
they own the river."

From the safety of shore, we watched *Resolute* and *W. H. Perry, Jr. '53'* race by. The rowers were soaked in sweat, their faces grimacing in pain. The sunlight beating off their oars reminded me of the common mergansers we'd seen on our first day. When I mentioned this to Ramsay, all he said was, "Yeah, only these are common Dartmouths."

Ledyard Canoe Club was located on the Hanover side of the river just a few hundred yards up from Ledyard Bridge, site of the Orbs of Knowledge and the point where the Appalachian Trail crosses the Connecticut. We decided to dock at the club and walk into Hanover for lunch, but we got sidetracked by Julie, the comely coed in charge of renting canoes.

Julie was sitting alone on the porch of the clubhouse in short shorts, her long, creamy legs stretched languidly toward the river. Like the sirens of Greek myth, they sang alluringly to us. When Ramsay offered Julie a Bud Light, it became clear she was bored and wouldn't mind being chatted up by two coots.

College towns have become popular spots for retirement communities because they offer a wide variety of cultural and athletic events. And, if there is a medical school like Dartmouth's, they also offer excellent health care. Chatting with Julie brought out another reason. Living in a college town gives old geezers like Ramsay and me a chance to interact with coeds, and that made us feel young again, like we were still in the game, at least until Ramsay started his spiel on *Beg, Borrow, and Deal*. That sent me into the Ledyard clubhouse.

The clubhouse looked like the inside of a fraternity. An empty tequila bottle lay on the stairs, beer cans filled the trash can, and paddles painted by students who'd made the annual spring run from Hanover to Long Island Sound hung on the walls. A bookcase was tucked in one corner. Browsing through it, I came across a long-neglected biography of John Ledyard. Knowing Ramsay would be chatting up Julie for at least one more Bud Light, I blew off the dust, found a comfortable chair, and started reading.

While Daniel Webster, class of 1804, is without question Dartmouth's most illustrious alumnus, John Ledyard, class of 1776, embodies the most spirit. John's mother, a devout Christian, wanted her son to become a missionary, and since Eleazar Wheelock, the founder of Dartmouth, was by all accounts a very pious man, Mrs. Ledyard was sure Dartmouth would be just the place for her son. But John, who was known in his native Long Island as something of a rake, was not taken with Wheelock's four-year-old college. For most of the fall of 1772, this twenty-year-old freshman wandered along the Canadian border soaking up the Indian culture and made no attempt to convert the tribes of the Six Nations to Christianity. With the coming of winter, he returned to Hanover where his only class consisted of chopping down a huge pine next to the river and hacking it into a fifty-foot canoe. When the ice broke in early April, John pushed his big canoe into the swirling waters of the Connecticut, climbed in, and waved goodbye to Dartmouth forever. With an "Incomplete" in Missionary 101, he was on his way to becoming the college's most famous voyager.

In what had to rank as a major miracle, John somehow navigated his big canoe through raging rapids and over cascading waterfalls 173 miles to Hartford. There he gained passage on a clipper ship to England and for the next fifteen years sailed and traipsed all over the globe. His most notable adventures were serving with Capt. James Cook from 1776 to 1778 on Cook's third and final voyage to the Pacific, and then in 1786, hatching a plan in Paris with Thomas Jefferson where John would walk across Siberia, cross the Bearing Strait to Alaska, and hike the breadth of North America to Jefferson's home in Virginia—only he never made it. That trek ended in Siberia when Catherine the Great had John arrested as a spy and banished him from Russia forever.

No matter, by the time John died from an overdose of vitriolic acid in Cairo in 1788, at the age of thirty-seven, he'd seen more of the world by land and sea than any man in history. That's why in the spring of 1920, when a group of alumni raised $1,600 to start a canoe club, they didn't name it for Daniel Webster. Instead they honored the memory of John Ledyard, Dartmouth's most beloved dropout.

I put the book back on the shelf and went outside to see how Ramsay was doing. He was doing just fine. He and Julie had been joined by Allison, another comely coed who happened to be vice president of Ledyard Canoe Club. When I mentioned to Ramsay we should get some lunch, Allison offered to give us a lift up the hill into town. We would have been better off walking. Cars were backed up all the way across Ledyard Bridge. Allison told us the traffic was due to the start of graduation and reunion weekend, which Dartmouth, unlike most colleges, held at the same time. As we crawled up the hill, we asked Allison where we should eat. "Lou's," she said, without hesitation. "It's an institution, but you might have to wait for a table."

Allison was right. When we walked into Lou's a long line of "common Dartmouths" were waiting to be seated. "God, I hate reunions," Ramsay said.

"Why's that?"

"Because the guys who come back to reunions are the ones you never want to see."

"That might be true at Princeton, but what about Virginia? Smyth, Patterson, Grimball, LaVine, Flint, Kiernan, me, we all go back to reunions."

"I don't have to go back to a reunion to see you guys."

"Ramsay, it's been twenty years since you've seen any of us."

"Yeah, but I haven't seen any of the guys I don't want to see either."

Given our time at the Ledyard Canoe Club, the lunch crowd was breaking up and we didn't have to wait long for a table. Ramsay, in his Roy sunglasses, boonie hat, and little girlie vest, was drawing a few stares, but none seemed disapproving, which was another good reason for retiring to a college town. There's a lot of odd ducks roaming around so you can be as daffy as you want.

I thought the food and atmosphere at Lou's was fine, but Ramsay wasn't happy. Lou's reaffirmed his feeling that Dartmouth was completely out of sync with the region. "Can you believe this crap," he said, pointing to the menu. "A dollar ten for a cup of coffee. That's ridiculous."

"Why's that?"

"Because in Woodsville, it would cost fifty cents."

"So, let me get this straight. You think Lou should charge fifty cents even though there's a line of people waiting to pay a dollar ten?"

"Bugsy, you're missing the point. It's a false economy. The only people who can afford to live here are the ones who made their money someplace else, or work for Dartmouth."

"It's the same with any small college town. Look at Charlottesville, Williamstown, Middlebury, hell, even Princeton. According to you, they're all false economies. And what about Washington? That's the most false economy of them all. All of Washington's money comes from someplace else."

Ramsay grunted and ordered a $1.10 cup of coffee.

To get back to the Canoe Club, we had to walk by Dartmouth's new rowing center. It was a grand facility. The back was a huge, well-lit garage full of shells, oars, and other equipment; the front, a beautiful new building with meeting rooms, weight rooms, dressing rooms, and a large party room with a solid glass wall overlooking the river. Debbie Edwards must have worn out a few pens writing grants for this place. It must have cost a boatload, and then some.

At the clubhouse, business was brisk. Julie was helping a rotund alumnus and his equally rotund wife into a canoe while their two overweight kids squeezed into kayaks. Two other families were pacing the porch waiting to be outfitted, and a van loaded with boisterous Indians, or to be politically correct, Big Greeners, was pulling into the parking lot. When Ramsay asked Julie if she wanted to chuck it all and come with us, she only smiled. With a big party weekend just getting on tap, Julie wasn't going anywhere.

As we passed under Ledyard Bridge, Ramsay looked up at the cars crawling past the Orbs of Knowledge and said, "Bugsy, just for the record, I don't like this bridge."

"Just for the record," I said, "except for Julie, you didn't like anything about Dartmouth."

"That's not true," he said. "I liked Allison."

After a couple of flat, easy miles, we came to Wilder Dam. Wilder was only our second portage. It took two round trips of a half-mile each to get the Mad River and the duffels around the dam. By the time we'd finished, we were hot, tired, and not looking forward to negotiating another seven miles of river. A sign on the bank by the put in said in big red letters, CAUTION: WATCH FOR RISING WATER LEVELS. We'd been watching for a rise during the portage, but had seen nothing. No rise meant no release so we figured we were set to go, but just as we were about to push off, a loudspeaker started bellowing, "Opening the Dam. Be prepared for a period of rapid water! Opening the Dam. Be prepared for a period of rapid water!"

"Bugsy," Ramsay said, "what the hell does that mean? How rapid is rapid? Do you think we can go?"

"Let's pull the canoe up to higher ground and go up to the office and find out."

The office was a small brick building at the end of the dam on the New Hampshire side. We'd walked past it four times during our portage. As we entered the office, the half-dozen employees stopped whatever they were doing and stared at Ramsay. Dressed in his boonie hat, Roy sunglasses, and little girlie vest, he was either the coolest terrorist this side of the Khyber Pass, or the strangest looking canoeist ever to come down the river.

Ramsay immediately put them at ease by announcing we were the two coots going Source to Sound. One of the workers had heard of us. He introduced himself as Jud, a hydro engineer. Jud might have been hired as a hydro engineer, but he was a natural PR man. He showed us around the office, explained what all the dials did, and told us to disregard the warning, that they weren't releasing all that much water and we'd be fine. Then he asked, "So, how's the trip going?"

Somewhere between *Beg, Borrow, and Deal* and meeting Krazy Kate, I happened to mention how I couldn't find a girlie calendar for Luke Eaton. "Ridgid Tools," Jud said. "They still make one."

He sat down at his computer and opened the website for Ridgid Tools. When he clicked on "Calendar," the screen instantly filled with twelve bikini-clad maidens. It was a great promotion. Ridgid's girls were no more pornographic than *Sports Illustrated*'s swimsuit maidens, but any one of these busty beauties was sure to make a young man's tool ridgid. "Perfect," I said, examining each month in great detail. "Modest enough to get by Lorna, risqué enough to pole vault Luke into puberty. Jud, can you print me out a copy of the order form?"

"I suppose so," Jud said, looking around. "Just don't tell anybody where you got it."

Back on the river, we were looking for two boulders known as Hen and Chicken Rocks. Riverview Farm, the home of Paul and Nancy Franklin, our strangers for the evening, was located just above the rocks. The problem was the river was loaded with rocks, and like clouds, they could be made to look like whatever fit your imagination. "Ramsay," I said, as we passed the confluence of White River, the location of White

River Junction, "how'd you let Nancy talk you into having two rocks in the river be our takeout? You're the guy who keeps saying, 'For all we know, we could be in Montana.'"

"Bugsy, they look like a hen and a chicken. How difficult can that be? Nancy said we can't miss them."

"Did you happen to mention to Nancy that we're the same guys who missed a whole bridge?"

Ramsay did not respond. He was running out of steam. Hen and Chicken Rocks were a good sixteen river miles from the Ompompanoosuc landing. That was four miles beyond our comfort zone, plus we had the portage. We paddled in silence letting the release from Wilder Dam carry us along. Four miles below the dam, we passed under Interstate 89, by far the biggest bridge we'd seen so far. After another thee miles, we came upon two huge rocks on the New Hampshire side. "Bugsy, what do you think? Is that a hen and a chicken?"

"They could be a cow and a pig for all I know, but they're in the right place at the right time and that house on the bluff has a good view of the river, so pull over."

Nancy and Paul Franklin were sitting on the front porch of their traditional New England farmhouse waiting for us. Like the Eatons, the Franklins had hung out an American flag. Ramsay's notes on Nancy Franklin read "nice lady, two grown daughters, a son starting college, likes to laugh." With her pert blond hair, girlish good looks, and all-American smile, Nancy looked too young to have two grown daughters and a son who was about to graduate from high school. The same could be said for Paul. Except for a hint of gray in his neatly trimmed mustache, he too looked too young to be facing an empty nest.

Riverview was not like the rich bottomland farms we'd seen upriver. It was set high on a bluff at the base of a hill, and unlike the Eatons, the Franklins were not full-time farmers. Paul's real job was with the Board of Tax Appeals for the state of New Hampshire. Nancy was a full-time mother. For the Franklins, farming was a hobby that had grown into a part-time business. From late summer through early fall, Riverview was a "pick your own" farm. "At first, it was just apples," Nancy said, "but over time, we kept added things, like flowers and vegetables."

Before dinner, I asked Paul if he'd give us a tour. At the end of the tour, Paul took us through the farm stand, a rustic wooden shed with a long counter. In one corner, I noticed a big farm scale. "Is that scale accurate?" I said.

"To the ounce," Paul said.

I was feeling a little heavy and wanted to check my weight. I jumped on the scale and began moving the weight along the top of the bar. When it finally balanced at 221, I couldn't believe it. That was the heaviest I'd ever been, by ten pounds. So much for Ruth's snack bag.

After a delicious lamb dinner, where I could have had seconds, but didn't, we retired to the porch to watch the sunset. Once we were settled, Paul brought out a bottle of his special apple juice. The label was a drawing of a head in the shape of an apple. The mustache left no question the head was Paul's. Around the head were the words PAUL'S SPECIAL APPLE JUICE. NOT YOUR AVERAGE BREAKFAST DRINK—BREWED AND CONSUMED BY PAUL AND HIS FRIENDS. At the top of the label was the disclaimer NOT FOR SALE—JUST FOR TRADE; at the bottom, ALCOHOL CONTENT: YOU DON'T WANT TO KNOW.

"Paul, is this stuff legal?" I said, studying the label.

"Sure," he said. "You're allowed to make two hundred gallons per family member. You just can't sell it. Here, try some."

"Where'd you get the label?"

"One of our friends made it for us," Nancy said. "Would you like one?"

"Definitely. It would look great on the canoe."

While Ramsay went out on the bluff to have a smoke, Nancy, Paul, and I sat on the porch enjoying our Paul's Special Apple Juice. "Dave," Nancy said, "you guys seem to know a lot about business. Paul and I have a question we'd like to ask you. For the past couple of years, people have been pushing us to take credit cards. They say we'd get a lot more business if we accepted them. What do you think?"

"I really don't know how credit cards affect a business, but I bet Ramsay does. Let's ask him."

When Ramsay came in, I said, "Ramsay, Paul and Nancy have a question maybe you can answer. People are bugging them to take credit cards. They say it would help their business. What do you think?"

"I think it'd be a waste of money. Who's going to pick more apples just because they can pay for them with a credit card? What's your average sale now, around twenty bucks?"

"Twenty-two sixty-three," Paul said without hesitation. Obviously, the Franklins had been thinking about this for awhile.

"How do most people pay?"

"Cash and checks, but mostly cash."

"How many bad checks do you get a year?"

"Very few," Nancy said. "Since we're not on the main road, most of our customers are people we know, or friends of friends. I bet we've had less than half a dozen bad checks the whole time we've been in business."

"Look," Ramsay said, "if you took credit cards, people would use them because they want the frequent-flier miles or whatever the credit card companies are offering. That's going to cost you at least two percent right off your gross, and that's not including additional fees. Plus, you'd have to rent a terminal. That's another three hundred a year even though you're only going to use it a couple of months. In short, if you start accepting credit cards you can figure you're going to give away at least three percent of your gross, and I can tell you right now, there's no way you're going to make that up from additional sales."

A look of relief swept over Paul and Nancy. In two minutes Ramsay had answered a question they'd been wrestling with for two years. "Let's open another bottle of this stuff," Paul said.

Why not? Ramsay had earned it.

11

JUNE 7
PLAINFIELD, NEW HAMPSHIRE

Wrong Shoes

After a big blueberry pancake breakfast with homemade maple syrup, Nancy took us on a tour of Plainfield. At the library, Nancy told us she was chairing the million-dollar campaign for a major renovation. That seemed like a lot of money for a little town like Plainfield. When I mentioned this to Nancy, she said, "We need a good library, we have J.D. Salinger."

"J.D. Salinger?" Ramsay said. "I thought he was dead."

"No," Nancy said, "he lives in Cornish, and we're his library."

"Have you ever seen him?" I said.

"Sure, when he comes in."

It was nice to know J.D. was still alive, but time sure does fly. It was tough to picture Holden Caulfield as another coot on Medicare.

There'd be no paddling this Saturday. We had a job that day. To thank Witty Sanford for all she'd done promoting our trip, we'd agreed to represent CRWC at the "Big Splash, A Celebration of the Life, The People & Communities, The Land & Rivers of the Connecticut River Watershed." The celebration was being held at a park we'd passed the day before just above Wilder Dam. In addition to the Green Mountain Highlander Bagpipers, the Hunger Mountain Boys string band, Marge Bruchac's Abenaki songs, and Carol Langstaff's

FLOCK dance troupe (traditional Irish dancing), Ramsay and I were featured as part of the entertainment. Our job was to sit in CRWC's booth and chat up people who came by and wanted to know more about the river. Only there were no people. A steady, heavy rain was keeping them away.

The Big Splash typically drew thousands, but when Nancy dropped us off just after noon, only a couple of hundred soggy souls had shown up, and most of them were volunteers working the event. Yesterday, the Big Splash would have been a grand success. Today, it was a total washout. The bagpipers weren't piping, the stringers weren't fiddling, Marge Bruchac in her Native American attire wasn't singing any Abenaki songs, and nobody was talking to Ramsay and me. Much to their credit, the little Irish dancers did try a jig or two, but they could hardly hold their footing on the rain-soaked stage. River gods are fickle. Who else would rain on their own parade?

Our strangers that night were Linda and John Hammond, owners of North Star Canoe Rentals in Cornish, Vermont. North Star was supplying the canoes for the Big Splash, so Ramsay had arranged for us to ride back to Cornish with Linda and John's son, Jabe. We arrived at the Hammond's farm at five thirty, which was good because the Belmont Stakes, the final leg of the Triple Crown, was being run at six, and I, like most Americans, wanted to see Funny Cide.

Funny Cide was a three-year-old gelding from Philadelphia who was trying to become the first horse in twenty-three years to capture the Triple Crown. In a society where bloodlines meant everything, both for horses and people, there was nothing fancy about Funny Cide and his owners, a group of high school buddies from Saratoga. Now, they were the odds-on favorites to capture Thoroughbred racing's greatest prize. The press loved it. It was the American Dream about to come true, and I was sure the Hammonds would be up for watching it.

John and Linda Hammond were direct opposites. John, dressed in a red T-shirt and well-worn jeans, was a big man with a full beard. When we came in, he was sitting in the living room reading the paper. He seemed plenty relaxed, much like a bear in hibernation. Linda, on the other hand, never sat down. She was moving around like a whirling dervish. Between getting us settled, making dinner, and conferring with Jabe on Sunday's canoe rentals, it was easy to see how she kept her trim figure.

John didn't come to life until I asked if there was any chance we could turn on the Belmont. "Sure," he said, but after pushing a bunch or buttons on two different remotes, it became apparent he had no idea how to work the cable TV. It wasn't until Jabe came in and took over the controls that we joined the 120,139 fans who'd made their way to Belmont Park in Elmont, New York, to watch the race. Unfortunately, on this day, their biggest in twenty-three years, the racing gods appeared as fickle as the river gods. The stands were a sea of umbrellas, the track a bowl of mud.

At post time, the three Hammonds, Ramsay, and I were joined by Eric, a ski instructor at Mt. Ascutney who helped Jabe and Linda run North Star Canoes in the off-season. "Since there are six horses and six of us," I said, "let's get a pool going. Everyone throw in a buck, winner take all."

As the host, John picked first. He took Empire Maker, a horse Funny Cide had beaten soundly in the Kentucky Derby.

When I made note of this, John said, "Not today. Funny Cide's going to have trouble in this slop. He's not shoed right."

It was then we learned that renting canoes was not the Hammonds' principal business. In real life, John was a professional blacksmith. Still, with all the mud on the track, you couldn't even see the horses' hooves, let alone their shoes. John had to be blowing smoke.

At six on the dot, the starting gate sprang open and the 134th running of the Belmont Stakes was under way. As the horses rounded the first turn, Funny Cide had the lead. He kept it all the way down the backstretch and was still in front as the horses rounded the far turn into the homestretch. Not shoed right, my ass.

It's the homestretch at Belmont that makes or breaks a Triple Crown hopeful. When horses turn into it, they literally have to run all the way to the next county. At the three-sixteenths pole, Empire Maker, with his impeccable pedigree, claimed the lead from Funny Cide. He never looked back. Then Ten Most Wanted, another blueblood, stormed by to place. By the time Funny Cide staggered in for the show, the American Dream was long over. "Damn," I said, "you can't beat breeding."

"Wrong shoes," John said, pocketing his six bucks. "Let's eat."

After a homegrown turkey dinner with mashed potatoes, acorn squash, and a johnnycake smothered in Hammond's own maple syrup, John invited us to come along on a ride he was taking up into the hills to check on his horses. In addition to blacksmithing, John raised Suffolk draft horses, a rare breed he'd imported from England.

The entrance to Windsor, Vermont, from Cornish, New Hampshire, passes over the Connecticut River through the longest covered bridge in America, 460 feet. Rumbling through the dark over the wooden boards, we expected the light at the end of the bridge to expose one of the prettiest little towns in all of New England. It didn't. Windsor was kind of a dump. As if sensing our disappointment, John said, "Goodyear Tire & Rubber destroyed this town. They had a plant here that made rubber insoles for shoes. It employed over twelve hundred people. In 1986, they had a big party celebrating the plant's fiftieth anniversary. The whole town showed up. It was a great day. Then two weeks later, Goodyear shut the plant down and shipped all the jobs overseas. People here have never gotten over it."

Once we got up into the hills, things were different. Gentleman farms with clean white fences, lush manicured pastures, and well-tended fieldstone walls graced the landscape. At one particularly beautiful home high on a hill overlooking emerald green fields separated by interlocking stone walls, John pulled over. "Wow," I said, "even for this neighborhood, this is some spread."

"This is where I keep most of my horses. It belongs to Andy Stewart, Martha's old husband. Andy likes to look out and see horses, but he doesn't want to own them so he lets me use his fields."

"Hot damn," Ramsay said, "talk about Martha'd out."

"Andy's just a regular guy," John said, implying Andy was nothing like Martha. He could have fooled us. Andy's place had Martha written all over it.

The Suffolk is a very pretty horse: smaller than the standard draft horse and palomino in color. Two dozen of them were grazing in a field just below the house. Watching them in the twilight, it was easy to see why Andy liked having John's horses around. Sitting on his porch, having a cocktail, soaking up all the pastoral splendor around him would be any city slicker's dream.

Seeing John, the Suffolks stopped grazing and began moseying over. It was then I noticed none of the horses had shoes. "John," I said, "they look like the cobbler's son. How come none of your horses have shoes?"

"Don't need them," John said. "They're not going anywhere."

When we got back to the farm, Linda asked John if he would drive into Cornish and pick up Matilda, their youngest daughter. Matilda was a sophomore at Windsor High and like all the Hammonds had a job. Tonight she was just finishing her shift at the local pizza parlor. Having never seen Cornish, and on the off chance we might be treated to a rare J.D. Salinger sighting, Ramsay and I went along. There was no sign of J.D., but on the ride home I asked Matilda, a pretty, clean cut teenager, how she like Windsor High. "Not much," she said, and left it at that.

Later, when we were sampling some of John's super hard cider, which was much more potent than "Paul's Special Apple Juice," I mentioned Matilda's comment to Linda. She told us she was not surprised, that Windsor High was a real blackboard jungle: kids swearing at teachers, gangs, no discipline, and no control. "Since the Goodyear plant shutdown," she said, "things have gotten real bad."

"You know, I bet Hanover doesn't have those problems with its high school," Ramsay said, and then launched into his diatribe of how Dartmouth's wealth was out of sync with the rest of the region.

"Hanover's always had more money than the rest of us," John said. "When I was a kid, they sent me to Hanover High. The first day I showed up in my work boots. That's what kids from around here wore, but all the faculty brats from Dartmouth had on Weejuns. They looked at me like I was some kind of hillbilly."

Ramsay got a big kick out of that. "Hot damn, John," he said, "you were like Funny Cide. There was no way you could win. Wrong shoes."

12

JUNE 8
CORNISH, NEW HAMPSHIRE

Coming to Cincinnati

The next morning, Linda dropped us off at the Hen and Chicken Rocks. We pulled the Mad River out from the high grass where we'd stashed it and pushed off into the river. As the current caught us, we were treated to one last look at the Franklin's Riverview Farm. "Ramsay," I said, "I've been meaning to tell you how great it was the way you were able to analyze Paul and Nancy's question about credit cards. They'd been worrying about that for two years, and you gave them the answer in about two minutes. You know, instead of fooling around with your golfing buddies, you ought to get back into business. Any day you're not running something is a waste of your time."

"It's too late. I tried to buy a mail-order swimsuit business a couple of years ago, but I couldn't make the deal work. That was my last shot. When the market went south, it wiped out forty percent of my net worth. Now, I can't afford to buy anything until it comes back, and by that time, I'll be too old."

Sumner Falls was a pleasant two miles from Riverview Farm and marked the halfway point between the Fourth

Connecticut Lake, the river's source, and Long Island Sound, its terminus. We'd made it in eleven days, not too bad for two coots mooching their way down the river. Of course, we'd taken a few senior citizen discounts, like having Earl Bunnell ferry us around Lyman Falls and Scot Williamson drive us around the Fifteen Miles Falls Development. On the other hand, we'd taken time from our trip to spend a whole day with Carl Demrow and another at the Big Splash.

The portage around Sumner Falls was easier than either McIndo Falls or Wilder Dam. We only had to go a couple of hundred yards, and the whole while we were entertained by two eagles circling high overhead. They, along with a dozen or so human anglers, were working the pools at the base of the falls. The human fishermen were the first we'd seen the entire trip. After talking with one of them, we found out why. Once a year, the New Hampshire Department of Game and Fish declares a free weekend for fishing. On those two days, anyone can fish anywhere in the state without a license. Since New Hampshire owns the river, both sides of the Connecticut were open to fishing. This year, the free weekend was Saturday and Sunday, June 7 and 8. "Hell," Ramsay said, as we watched a kid land a good-size trout, "if I'd known that, I'd have packed a rod."

Because Sumner Falls had not been dammed, the next six miles offered the best canoeing on the entire Connecticut. The river ran straight, the water flowed fast, and the banks on both sides were wooded and wild. Mt. Ascutney, looming high in the distance, gave us a constant benchmark of our progress, and we were flying along enjoying the run until we came to Windsor. There, the good feeling abruptly ended. Starting about a quarter-mile above town, the bank on the Vermont side was littered with old washing machines, sofas, stoves, tires, and other junk people were either too lazy or too cheap to lug to the dump. Crossing America's longest covered bridge you couldn't see it, but from the river it was a problem Windsor couldn't hide.

With Windsor's easy access off Interstate 91, location just south of Dartmouth, the best canoeing on the river, great skiing at Mt. Ascutney, and all that New York and Connecticut money sitting up in the hills, it had everything going for it, but instead of reinventing itself like Littleton, Windsor seemed content to wallow in its misfortune. After seventeen years, the town's collective mentality was still, "Yeah, we might look like a dump, but it's all Goodyear Tire & Rubber's fault. They're the ones that screwed us."

Hey, it wasn't Goodyear that threw all that crap into the river.

We were spending the night with Mark and Sandra Blanchard, who, according to Ramsay's notes, "sound like fun and have a cozy camp right on the river." The key to finding this cozy camp was spotting a sign on a tree that read BLANCHARD'S BEND. "You can't miss it," Mark had told Ramsay. "It's on the big bend two miles below Ashley Ferry boat ramp."

Once again, I was surprised Ramsay had agreed to such an arrangement. Finding Hen and Chicken Rocks must have buoyed his confidence. On top of that, he'd decided to make up for our day at the Big Splash by going twenty miles. After Windsor, the weather had changed and turned hot and sunny. At twelve miles, we began to fade. There had been no convenience store between the Hammonds and Riverview Farm, so for the first time Ramsay had been unable to buy a six-pack.

At fifteen miles, he was dying and actually asked a fisherman if he'd give us a tow. At eighteen miles, we came to Ashley Ferry, an old river crossing between Claremont, New Hampshire, and Springfield, Vermont. "Bugsy, we're stopping here," he announced. "I've had it."

"Fine with me," I said, happily stowing my paddle.

The ramp at Ashley Ferry was packed with boaters. After eight cold months, the good citizens of Vermont and New Hampshire were coming out of hibernation and eagerly exposing their creamy white skin to the bright June sun. Ramsay borrowed a phone from one of the boaters waiting to launch and called Mark Blanchard. Mark said he'd be there in half an hour.

We were watching an obnoxious Jet Skier buzz back and forth, back and forth when a shiny red pickup pulled into the parking lot. A stocky, friendly-looking guy smoking a cigarette got out. "You Ramsay and Dave?" he said.

"I'm Ramsay. He's Bugsy, and I got to tell you, Mark, we sure do appreciate your coming to get us. We'd about run out of steam."

"I figured as much," Mark said, flipping open a large cooler sitting in the bed of the truck. "You sounded like you might need a beer so I put a few on ice. I wasn't sure what you drank, but there should be something in there you like."

We looked in the cooler. It was full of Coronas, Sam Adams, Buds, and Bud Lights, all packed in ice, all frosty and cold. "Hot damn, Mark," Ramsay said, "we like 'em all."

As it turned out, we could see Blanchard's Bend from the landing. If Mark had just told us to keep paddling, we could have been there in twenty minutes. Instead, he'd driven eight miles south to the bridge connecting Springfield with Claremont, crossed the river, then gone ten miles north to the ferry landing, but Mark didn't seem to mind. On the way back to Blanchard's Bend, he showed us the sights of Claremont and Springfield.

Mark was head of maintenance at the Claremont-Springfield Hospital. His wife, Sandra, was a nurse at the hospital. He and Sandra had just bought the camp on the river and were in the process of fixing it up. When we got there, we could see Mark had been hard at work. He'd finished building a new deck, put on a new roof, new siding, and replaced all the windows. Now, he was starting on the inside, which was all torn up. As Mark spread out his plans on the kitchen table, he lit up a Camel. Ramsay, realizing he could smoke indoors for the first time the whole trip, pulled out a Carlton. After walking us through the plans, Mark said, "Maybe you guys can give me some advice. Sandra wants these six-thousand-dollar cherry cabinets for the kitchen. I think that's too much for a cabin. What do you think?"

"Of course it's too much," Ramsay said, "but you don't have a choice. It's her kitchen. If she wants them, you get them. That's the way it works."

That was not what Mark wanted to hear, so he took a long drag on his Camel and turned to me. "So Bugsy, what do you think?"

"Sorry, Mark, Ramsay's right. Sandra will be looking at those cabinets for the rest of your life. When she does, you want her to be happy."

Mark rolled up the plans. He had enough of our advice.

We were going to have dinner out on the new deck. After Ramsay and I got cleaned up, we went outside and parked ourselves in comfortable chairs overlooking the river. While we drank beer, nibbled cheese puffs, and watched the sun set,

Mark and Sandra prepared dinner. On one side of the deck, Mark had cranked up his new, superdeluxe grill. It was big enough to cook a whole steer, which was good since the piece of meat Mark unwrapped looked like the better half of a cow. "I hope you guys are hungry," he said, slapping the slab onto the grill.

"Hot damn, Mark, bring it on," Ramsay said.

Next, Mark unwrapped a pound of bacon. "What's the bacon for?" I said.

"That's for Mark's special salad," Sandra said. "Bacon and fried onions."

That was dinner, a big grilled steak smothered in fried onions and bacon. There were no greens, no tomatoes, not even a potato. Ramsay couldn't have been happier. "Mark," he said, inhaling deeply on a Carlton, "you ever get to Cincinnati, you be sure to give me a call." Ramsay liked inviting people to call him whenever they got to Cincinnati. He knew they'd never call. Who'd go to Cincinnati?

"You know, Ramsay," Mark said, "we might just do that. If the Pats are playing the Bengals this year, we could make it a long weekend. Leave on Friday, come back on Monday. What do you think, Sandra?"

"Sounds good to me," Sandra said. Ramsay didn't say a thing, but that was the last time he ever invited anybody to Cincinnati.

13

Awaking Dreams

The smell of cigarette smoke woke me up. When I opened my eyes I saw Ramsay sitting up in his bed puffing on a Carlton. Behind him a hard rain was beating against Mark's new windows. Mark and Sandra hadn't spent the night with us. The inside construction wasn't far enough along for that, but we didn't mind. After staying with strangers every night, having the place to ourselves had been a nice break. Mark showed up with coffee and donuts at eight. "You guys sleep all right?" he said, shaking the water from his hat.

"Hell, Mark," Ramsay said, taking another satisfying drag, "if it had been any better, I'd have bottled and sold it."

"This storm's supposed to blow out by noon," Mark said. "so if you guys want, you can stay here, and I'll drive you up to the boat ramp later on."

"We'd better go now," Ramsay said. "We don't want to mess up your day."

Mark assured us it would be no problem, but Ramsay was anxious to get back to the canoe. He'd made his calls the night before and didn't want to deviate from his plan. Then Mark made a good suggestion: "Why don't you leave your bags here and pick them up when you come by. That way, at least they'll be dry, and if the weather's still bad, you can decide if you want to wait it out here or keep going."

As he shoved us off into the cold, wet Connecticut, Mark showed no sign of wanting to come with us, and with good reason. The two miles from Ashley Landing to Blanchard's Bend were the toughest we'd faced the entire trip. The storm was blowing directly into our face. We'd paddle forward, the wind would push us back. We'd paddle forward, the wind would push us back. All the while the rain kept beating against our glasses. By the time we reached Blanchard's Bend, we'd had it.

Once inside, a smoke along with a couple of Bud Lights seemed to revive Ramsay. The rest of the donuts and a short nap did the same for me. By noon we felt well enough to give the river another try. It wasn't easy. Even though the rain had stopped, the wind was still a problem. We were plowing along, lost in our own thoughts, when Ramsay stopped paddling, lit up a cigarette, and said "Bugsy, you ever have any trouble with the IRS?"

"Not really," I said. "I got audited once, but it was a nonevent. My rule is to declare all earnings and take every deduction, whether it's clear or not. If the IRS disagrees, make them prove it. The tax code's so screwed up, half the time your guess is as good as theirs."

"And it worked?"

"The agent I met with tried to screw me, but when we got into the details, it turned out she couldn't figure out what was allowed any more than I could. She won some, I won some, but I've never been audited again. My income's not big enough for them to care."

"Damn, they're on me like fleas. I can't get rid of them. It's always something, and the hell of it is those bastards don't care how long it takes. They get paid the same, win or lose."

"You gotta be like the fox. The next time they audit you, put a stick in your mouth and go for a swim. That'll get rid of them."

"Yeah, right." Ramsay threw his Carlton into the river and started paddling, hard. When Major Rogers and his Rangers paddled this stretch of river in the fall of 1759, they'd been trying to outrun the French and Indians. Now Ramsay was paddling like he was trying to outrun the IRS. It's amazing the inner strength you can muster when you think somebody's coming after your scalp.

We were sitting on a log taking a break when we saw two kayaks coming downstream. "Bugsy, what do you make of this?"

"I don't know but whoever they are, they're really moving. Maybe it's the power kayakers Whitty told you about."

Ramsay would check in with the Watershed Council every few days so they could update our whereabouts on their website. On one of his check-ins, Whitty Sanford mentioned she'd heard there were two other Source to Sounders on the river. She thought one of them was a group of nurses raising money for medical research, the other a couple of kayakers doing a power run from Fourth Lake to the Sound.

"Too bad it's not nurses," Ramsay said, "but signal them in. We'll give 'em a beer and chat 'em up."

I stood up and waved. The kayakers stopped paddling and started drifting toward us. They were two guys, probably in their late thirties, decked out in expensive rain suits. As they got closer, we could see their kayaks were loaded with gear and they hadn't shaved in awhile. "You the guys running the whole river?" I said.

"Yeah. You the gray-haired paddlers?"

"That's us," Ramsay said, pleased with the recognition. "I'm Ramsay, he's Bugsy. How about a beer?"

"I'm Chuck and that's Tom," Chuck said, feathering his kayak about fifteen feet offshore, "but no thanks. We're going to stop for lunch at the park just ahead."

"What are you having?" Ramsay said. He didn't like the fact Chuck and Tom were somewhat standoffish. Ramsay expected everybody we met on the river to be our instant buddies, like Krazy Kate.

"We've got some granola," Tom said.

"Oh, that's too bad," Ramsay said. "If we'd known you were coming we'd have called one of our guys and had him make you a couple of turkey sandwiches."

"How about a snack," I said, holding up Ruth's snack bag. Tom and Chuck hesitated, reluctant to accept candy from a stranger.

"Have a See's chocolate," I said, throwing them each a bar. "It'll give you energy."

"Thanks," they said, taking the chocolates, but still not coming any closer.

"Those are sure good looking kayaks," I said. That broke the ice. Tom and Chuck immediately paddled closer so we could get a better look at their kayaks.

By not camping, Ramsay and I had missed a big part of the adventure. Spending days, even months, researching sleeping bags, tents, mattresses, packs, rain gear, footwear, stoves, food, and all the other crap that goes into camping is at least half the fun of an outdoor trip. Serious hikers and paddlers delight in debating the pros and cons of each piece of equipment, trying to prove why their stuff is better than yours.

Tom and Chuck were very serious paddlers. Now that I'd noticed their kayaks, they started playing the my-equipment's-better-than-yours game; opening compartments, pulling things out, and telling us how much they weighed, what they were made of, what they cost, and why they were the best. "So how much you figure you've got into this stuff?" Ramsay said, popping another Bud Light.

Chuck looked around, taking inventory. "Well, each of the kayaks costs over a grand, so I guess we're in for close to three thousand. What about you guys?"

Ramsay inventoried our stuff every bit as seriously as Chuck and Tom had theirs, then said, "With the two duffels and Bugsy's life vest, I guess we're in for close to a hundred."

"Don't forget my cushion," I said.

"Oh, yeah," Ramsay said, "Bugsy's cushion. That would make it about a hundred and seven."

Sitting there in his Roy sunglasses, boonie hat, and little girlie vest, wearing a deadpan expression, Ramsay looked like such a screwball Chuck and Tom couldn't tell if he was serious or not. Either way, they were ready to go. Playing the equipment game was no fun with us. I threw them each another See's, wished them luck, and off they went. Ramsay couldn't stop laughing. He kept replaying the conversation as we watched them and their three thousand dollars' worth of equipment disappear downriver. There was no question in his mind we'd won the game.

A mile downstream, we rounded a bend and saw the Union Jack flying over a wooden stockade in a field just above the river. It was the Fort at No. 4, the same fort Major Robert Rogers and three of his Rangers were trying to reach after they'd been stiffed at the Fort at No. 5. Having lost two rafts, nearly starving, and almost freezing, Rogers and his Rangers must have been overjoyed at the sight of the Union Jack. Ramsay could have cared less. He was focused on his schedule. "Bugsy, what time is it?" he said, guiding the Mad River up to a modest wood dock. "And how far do you figure it is to the New England Power landing in South Charlestown?"

I looked at the sun, which was now shining through a bright blue sky dotted with puffy white clouds. "I'd say it's close to two-thirty." Then I took out my maps and found the landing in South Charlestown. "The landing's about four miles. Why?"

"That's where the Doc suggested we meet. We should be able to make it by four, right?"

Dr. Charles Cunningham and his wife, Marija, were our strangers for the evening. Ramsay's summary of the Cunninghams was "pleasant older couple, canoeists with car-top capability."

"Why keep going?" I said, looking up at the Union Jack flapping in the bright blue sky. "The river's nothing but a lake from here to the dam at Bellows Falls. Let Chuck and Tom paddle it. I'd rather take a tour of the fort."

"What'll I tell the Doc?"

"Tell him to meet us here. What does he care? According to your notes, he's got car-top capability. We can put the canoe on the car and drop it off below the dam tomorrow. That'll save us a portage, and who knows, we might even pass Chuck and Tom."

Ramsay frowned and popped a Bud Light. It took him a whole beer, but finally, he agreed to ask the Doc to pick us up at the fort. The thought of passing Chuck and Tom had tipped the scales. Ramsay was sure if Chuck and Tom came down the river in their $3,000 worth of equipment and saw us ahead of them, it'd blow their minds. Having missed the Fort at No. 5, I was looking forward to taking a tour of No. 4.

Walking into the fort was like walking back into the mid-1700s. All the personnel were dressed like loyal subjects of George II. A genial colonist about our age dressed in black shoes with silver buckles, white linen knee socks, dark breeches, a white ruffled shirt, and a black tricorn hat introduced himself as our guide. He led us through the gardens, by the blacksmith shop, around the saw pit, past the cow barn, and into the stockade. "The stockade is made of seven hundred and twenty-four posts," he explained. "As you can see, the posts were set four to five inches apart. That way, they were close enough to keep the French and Indians from crawling through, but far enough apart so they could not be set on fire."

And so it went. After we'd toured the Great Chamber, a two-story wooden structure that contained the south gate and the watchtower, Ramsay wandered off for a smoke leaving me to listen to the guide's detailed explanation of the cooking utensils in Captain Spafford's lean-to, which were the same as the ones we'd seen in Lieutenant Willard's house. Finally, I said to him, "Is this a full-time job?"

"Oh, no," he said. "I'm retired. I just do this for fun. Most everyone here's a volunteer."

"So this is how you spend your retirement, showing people around the fort?"

"Just in the summer. In the winter, I go to Florida, but

you should understand being a volunteer at the fort is a lot more than just showing people around. During the six months it's open, we put on two dozen different programs. In fact, the Thanksgiving dinner has gotten so popular, we've had to divide it into two sittings. You know how it is when you're retired, some people enjoy playing golf, I like working here."

When the tour was over, I collected Ramsay and we went into the reception area where he called the Doc. The Doc said it would be no problem picking us up at the fort and he'd be there in about an hour.

"So, Bugsy," Ramsay said, as we walked back to the canoe, "I'm sure you must have gotten that guy's story? How bored do you have to be to dress up like a colonist and walk around a fort all day?"

"It's a social thing. Most of the people are volunteers. In addition to showing people around, they put on programs, dinners, dances, all that stuff. For them, it's a great way to spend their retirement."

"One of my golfing buddies refuses to use the word *retired*. Whenever he sees me he says, 'So Ramsay, how long have you been useless?' He claims that's a more accurate description."

"Jeez, Ramsay, you got to get some new friends. Your golfing buddies sound like they're just sitting around waiting to die."

"No, they're good guys, and you know something, he might be right."

"About what?"

"*Retirement* is just another word for *useless*."

What could I say? If Ramsay honestly believed he was useless, was it any wonder he was bored?

Now that the sun was out, Ramsay found a comfortable log under a big, shady oak and settled back for a smoke and a beer. He'd had some skin cancer removed a few years back and was careful to keep covered up. I, on the other hand, stripped down to my shorts and lay on the dock. I was tired of the cold and rain, and I wanted to bask in the warm sun. My last thought before falling asleep was of Major Robert Rogers. He was never useless. He'd no sooner gotten to the Fort at No. 4 than he turned around and headed ninety-one hard miles back upriver to rescue the men he'd left at No. 5.

"Bugsy, wake up." It was Ramsay shaking me. "There's somebody coming." I thought he meant the Doc, but when I sat up, I could see he was looking upstream. A kayak and canoe were making their way toward us, their paddles flashing in the bright afternoon sun. The kayak was in the lead. It contained a very attractive young woman. Another attractive woman, who looked a little older, was in the bow of the canoe. A man about the same age was in the stern.

"Who do you think they are?" Ramsay said.

"I don't know, but they're not packing any gear. Maybe they're just coming down from the park where Chuck and Tom had lunch. Then again, they could be the nurses."

"Hot damn, signal them in. We'll give 'em a beer and chat 'em up."

I waved, and they stopped paddling. The kayak fell back, giving the lead to the canoe. Like Chuck and Tom, they seemed hesitant to come too close. The canoe gingerly made its way forward, the kayak hovering in its wake. "Welcome to Fort at No. 4," I said. "You wouldn't happen to be Rogers's Rangers would you?"

The woman in the bow of the canoe gave us an appraising look: me almost naked in my shorts, Ramsay fully covered in his hat, sunglasses, and little girlie vest. "No, we're Awaking Dreams," she said.

"We thought you might be some nurses who are paddling the river to raise money for medical research," I said.

"We are paddling the river to help medical research, but we're not nurses."

"Whatever." Ramsay reached into the stern of the Mad River and fished out two cans of Bud Light. "How about a beer?"

While the couple in the canoe were wary, the girl in the kayak was very relaxed, even whimsical. Instead of piles of gear strapped to the bow like Chuck and Tom, her kayak was sporting a pink plastic flamingo. When she saw the beer, she immediately paddled around the canoe and up to the dock. Ramsay almost fell in handing it to her. God, was she good looking.

The canoe, a sparkling new Old Town Discovery 169, came in and tied up next to the Mad River. Seeing the CON-NECTICUT RIVER WATERSHED COUNCIL sticker on its side, the woman in the 169 said, "Are you the two old guys mooching your way downriver?"

"That's us," Ramsay said, handing her the other Bud Light. "I'm Ramsay. He's Bugsy. So, who are you again?"

The woman took a sip of the Bud Light and passed the can back to the guy in the stern. "We're Awaking Dreams. I'm Jamie Malone, this is my husband, Chris, and that's my sister, Brooke Derrick. In 1996, our brother was in an automobile accident. He's been in a coma ever since, so we're doing this trip to raise money for the National Brain Injury Association."

For the next twenty minutes, we sat on the dock and listened as Jamie, Chris, and beautiful Brooke told us about themselves and Awaking Dreams. They came from Southern California where their brother, Kyle, was in a rehabilitation center. Apparently, there are only a few centers in America that will accept patients who are in long-term comas. The Derrick family had created Awaking Dreams to help raise public awareness of this problem. One way they did it was by undertaking challenges most people only dreamed about. In 1999, Jamie hiked the entire length of the Appalachian Trail. That trip had raised close to $10,000 for the National Brain Injury Association. Now, she, Chris, and Brooke were taking on a similar challenge by paddling the entire length of the Connecticut River. Casey, a third sister, was providing support for them from a van, which explained why they had no gear.

As they left for a tour of the fort, Jamie gave Ramsay and me a copy of the press release they'd put together for the trip. Basically, it was a recap of what they'd just told us, but at the bottom in italicized print I saw, "*Sponsored by Old Town Canoe, Immersion Research & Stohlquist WaterWare.*"

"Dammit, Ramsay, will you look at this. We ought to sue Old Town."

"What for?"

"Age and sex discrimination, that's what for. When I asked Old Town if they'd sponsor our trip, they told me they'd had a lousy spring and weren't making any charitable contributions. What they should have said was, 'If you're old and male, no canoe, but if you're young and female, here, have a nice new one.' That's discrimination."

"No, Bugsy, that's just good marketing. If you were Old Town, who would you rather see in one of your canoes, you and me, or Brooke and Jamie?"

Of course, he was right, but I was still pissed.

The Doc, a robust octogenarian in a Dartmouth baseball cap, met us in the parking lot outside the fort. The Flamingo Kids, which is what we'd labeled Brooke, Jamie, and Chris, came out while we were loading the Mad River onto the car. We wished them well, and said we might see them downstream. They laughed and said they'd be looking for us, thinking for sure we'd never catch up with them.

On the way to the Cunninghams', we briefly described Awaking Dreams to the Doc. "So, what do you think," I said, "is there any chance of that kid coming out of a coma after seven years?"

"There's always hope, but I wouldn't count on it. After seven years, I doubt he's going to wake up."

Charles and Marija Cunningham lived about eight miles northwest of Bellows Falls in a beautiful brick and stone farmhouse originally built in 1791. The house was a good three miles back from the river, but sat on the crest of a hill that commanded a spectacular view of the valley. The Cunninghams had bought the house and a hundred acres back in the mid-fifties, right after he'd finished his residency at Mary Hitchcock Hospital, now Dartmouth-Hitchcock Medical Center. "Back then," the Doc told us, "Mary Hitchcock liked to seed its residents in local hospitals around the area. I accepted a position at Springfield, and we've been here ever since."

After drinks and a wonderful meal, we went for a walk through the fields behind the Cunninghams' house. A cart path led past a pond just beyond the barn. The Cunninghams told us that was where their four kids had learned to swim. Since he was a pathologist, I asked the Doc what he thought about swimming in the Connecticut, especially as we got farther downriver.

"Do you like swimming in treated or untreated crap?" he said. "The storm drains and sewer plants in towns like West Lebanon and Springfield use the same lines for water runoff and sewerage. When it rains, they divert everything directly into the river. When the weather's dry, the sewerage is treated. When it's wet, it's untreated. They're working to straighten it out, but treated or untreated, crap's still crap."

I was glad I asked. With the water getting warmer, I was thinking I might start swimming every day. Now, I wasn't so sure.

Back at the house, we settled into the Cunninghams' comfortable den, and the Doc said, "Boys, would you care for some dessert?"

We said that would be nice, but Marija dissented. "Charles, I don't believe we have any dessert." Then turning to us, she added, "We watch our diets pretty carefully."

I bet she did. Before they were married, Marija had been a head nurse at Mary Hitchcock, and judging from the orderly way she ran her house, Marija went by the book. If dessert wasn't on the diet, there wouldn't be any dessert.

"Oh, don't worry," the Doc said, bounding out of his chair.

"I picked up a little something when I was out doing my errands."

We could hear him happily humming in the kitchen and soon he came out carrying a tray with four big bowls of vanilla ice cream smothered in chocolate sauce. Marija nearly fell out of her chair. "Charles, what are you doing? You know you're not allowed to have ice cream."

"It's for the boys, dear," he said, handing us each a bowl. "I figured they'd enjoy a treat after a long, hard day on the river."

We did enjoy it, but not as much as the Doc. He savored every precious bite.

14

A Good Daughter

The next morning, the Cunninghams drove us to a put-in just below the dam at Bellows Falls, a nice little town with small winding streets and graceful brick buildings, more European than American. It wasn't until we saw the dam that things got ugly. The dam had destroyed the very thing that made the town of Bellows Falls unique—the falls.

Waterfalls are the most interesting parts of any river. That's where rivers get to flex their muscles and show the world what makes them great. With a drop of fifty feet, Bellows Falls had plenty to flex. Two hundred years ago, we would have seen hundreds of thousands, maybe millions, of Atlantic salmon packed in the pools below the falls, each summoning strength to attempt the climb. Along the banks eagles, bears, catamounts, and, of course, man would have been waiting to feast on the losers. And there would have been plenty of losers. In its heyday, Bellows Falls was a firm enforcer of Darwin's survival of the fittest, but on this day, we saw nothing. Thanks to the dam, the Connecticut had no muscle to flex. Above the dam, the river was a placid lake; below it, an empty gorge. The falls were gone.

The top of the dam formed a bridge that ran from Bellows Falls to Walpole, New Hampshire. The Doc stopped the car on the bridge to show us the gorge. "There are some Indian petroglyphs on those rocks down there. If you want, we can park and climb down to see them," he said.

The gorge was dark, dreary, and devoid of life. Neither Ramsay nor I had any desire to climb down there. "We've got a long day," Ramsay said. "I think we'd better keep moving."

I looked down into the gorge and wondered how John Ledyard in his big fifty-foot canoe had ever made it over the falls. "Doc," I said, "did you ever make the annual Ledyard Canoe Club run to the sea when you were at Dartmouth?"

"No, I never tried it."

"Do you ever come down and watch the kids from the club when they come by?" Ramsay said.

"Ha, those rowdies. They're a disgrace to the college. Drinking and mooning the town. I'm too embarrassed to watch them."

We said goodbye to the Cunninghams and pushed off into the tamed waters of the Connecticut. I was paddling along enjoying another perfect spring day imagining Julie and Allison mooning the good citizens of Bellows Falls when Ramsay said, "Bugsy, do you have a living will?"

"Yeah, I've got one." While I'd been daydreaming about Julie and Allison, Ramsay must've been thinking about the Flamingo Kids and their brother Kyle.

"What does it say?"

"You know, the usual: do not resuscitate, nothing heroic, when it's time to go, sayonara."

"Who makes the decision?"

"Ruth, I guess, along with the doctors."

"Do you trust her?"

"Yeah, Ruth knows the drill. It's her sister I worry about. I want to be cremated, but when Ruth's sister heard that, she told me she doesn't believe in cremation and Ruth should bury me. When Ruth's sister gets a bee in her bonnet, she can be tough. I'm worried if I'm not around, she might talk Ruth out of it. God, if I end up in a box someplace in New Jersey, that will be hell."

"So what are you going to do?"

"I'm going to have my lawyer redraft my will to say if I'm not cremated, my whole estate goes to charity. I've got the sister's kids in for a good chunk so I figure when they see that, they'll have me cooking before I'm cold. What about you? You got a will?"

"Yeah, it sounds about the same as yours. Theresa makes the call, and she's good. Theresa keeps my ass covered front and back."

"What about organ donations? You done any of that?"

"As far as I'm concerned, they can have whatever they want, but I can't imagine anybody wanting any of my organs."

"Maybe the lungs," I said. "That way, whoever gets them won't have to give up smoking."

Ramsay and I liked to joke how most of the CRWC members who offered to put us up were young, single women. In truth, Mary Lynch was the only young, single woman who actually offered. We met her at the Putney town landing, and liked her immediately. In his notes, Ramsay had described Mary as "great laugh, loves to cook." Mary did have a great laugh, but what really won us over was she was wonderfully whacky, like Krazy Kate. Plus, like Kate, Mary had frizzy hair.

As we buzzed back to Bellows Falls in Mary's economical little sedan, we quizzed her about her business. Mary was a freelance graphic artist who worked out of her house. When Ramsay asked her if she were busy, Mary said, "I have a couple of monthly newsletters that keep me going, but when you called, I was redesigning the jacket for Natalie Merchant's new CD."

"Who's Natalie Merchant?" I said.

"Natalie's a very popular folk singer." That didn't help. The only folk singer we knew was Joan Baez, and Ramsay thought she, like J.D. Salinger, was dead.

"Don't worry," Mary said, "I'm having a party for you guys tonight, and Gary Smith will be there. Gary owns Myth America Records and is Natalie's agent. Gary can tell you anything you want to know about the music business."

Ramsay was delighted to learn that Mary was throwing us a party. "Will Natalie be there?" he said.

"No, Natalie lives in Hawaii. She won't be able to make it."

Rather than take the interstate back to Bellows Falls, Mary was driving us along a scenic dirt road that ran next to the river. I was sitting in front with Mary, Ramsay was in back with the bags. I was about to ask Mary why what sounded like a major record company with a big-time client like Natalie Merchant would be located in a little out-of-the-way town like Bellows Falls when Ramsay yelled, "Stop! Stop! Stop the car!"

He sounded like Natalie Wood in the movie *Miracle on 34th Street* when she sees the house she asked Santa for.

"Look, Bugsy" he said, pointing to the river, "it's the Flamingo Kids."

Sure enough, there they were, Jamie and Chris in the Discovery 169, and Brooke, looking as lovely as ever, in the kayak. Mary stopped the car, and we all hopped out. Ramsay was so excited he ran to the river's edge and yelled, "Hey, where you been? We've been waiting for you all afternoon."

The Flamingo kids looked up, totally surprised. "How did you guys get ahead of us?"

"Hell, we must have passed you on the portage around Bellows Falls. We made it in one trip, and Bugsy didn't carry a thing."

"Somebody has to take care of the women," I said, putting my arm around Mary. "By the way, this is Mary. She's our hostess for the evening. You guys need anything?"

"No, our sister's meeting us at the Putney landing. That's where we're spending the night."

"That's where we left the canoe," Ramsay said. "We'll see you there tomorrow. In the meantime, watch out for bugs."

"Bring some beer," Brooke said. With that, she pointed the pink flamingo downriver and Awaking Dreams was gone.

Given our party that night and the prospect of seeing the Flamingo Kids tomorrow, we headed for Bellows Falls in high spirits.

Before we got to Mary's house, we stopped at a little market in Bellows Falls. Mary said she had to pick up a few things for our party. As we rolled up and down the aisles, loading the cart with hamburger, hot dogs, rolls, condiments, corn, beer, and wine, we realized Mary hadn't bought anything for our party, but we didn't mind. At the checkout, Ramsay insisted on paying for everything, which was only right. Mary was about the same age as Kim, Ramsay's daughter, and that's how we started to feel about Mary, like she could have been our daughter.

The first guests to arrive were Mike and Wendy Harty, Mary's next-door neighbors. Wendy was carrying a big bowl of salad and Mike was rolling a grill. When I asked Mike if he always brought his own grill to parties, he told me, "Mary likes to cook out, but she doesn't own a grill, so we have to bring ours over whenever she has a party."

The next guest to show up was Bob, Mary's boyfriend. The seriousness of their relationship immediately came into question when I asked Bob what he did. He told me he'd worked for an electronics company, but had just quit. "I'm going to spend the summer and fall traveling around the country fishing and hunting with my dogs. If I find some place I like out west, I might not come back." There was no mention of Mary.

The final guest was Gary Smith, Natalie Merchant's agent and the owner of Myth America Records. Like any high-powered agent, Gary arrived with an entourage, Gabe and Brian. The three of them seemed more Hollywood than Bellows Falls. When I asked Gary about Myth America Records, he told me they had offices in London, Paris, Hong Kong, and Bellows Falls, but before I had a chance to ask why a major record company like Myth America would be located in Bellows Falls, Gary moved outside. Like Ramsay, he, Gabe, and Brian were serious smokers.

Mike and Wendy not only brought the grill and the salad, they did all the cooking. Mary, as hostess, fluttered around injecting her great laugh. That left me talking to Bob. Fortunately, there were two shots left in the Myers's Rum bottle Scot Williamson had hung under the Lancaster Bridge. I went through both of them while Bob prattled on about his trip and described in great detail some of his dogs' greatest points. By the time we sat down to dinner, the conversation had been well lubricated. With lively discussions about topics ranging from dams to farming, to the record business, to politics, our party was a grand success. As we sat on the porch watching Mike and Wendy roll their grill back home, we thanked Mary for going all out for us. She had done us proud. She would have made a good daughter.

15

JUNE 11
BELLOWS FALLS, VERMONT

A Hole in the Hedge

When Mary dropped us off at the Putney landing, we found a note taped to the Mad River. It read:

Hey Old Kindness Guys,
We've been waiting for you ALL morning & now the River is callin'. We were hoping for a cold beer & another chat but we're sure we'll see y'all on the River. Our plan is Brattleboro for lunch & a quick jaunt then to another island to camp. Have a wonderful day paddling & keep those high spirits.
Paddling onward,
The Flamingo Kids ☺

Finding the note got Ramsay all excited. He'd bought a six-pack and was looking forward to sharing it with Brooke. "Bugsy, let's get going. We've got to catch up with the Flamingo Kids."

That wasn't going to happen. It was almost eleven and we were seven river miles from Brattleboro. We weren't going to see the Flamingo Kids today. My guess was we'd never see them again. I was leaving for a wedding in Texas the next day and Ramsay was going to Boston to spend the weekend with his daughter and her family. We wouldn't be back on the river until Monday, and by that time, the Flamingo Kids would be in Connecticut.

As she pushed us off, Mary really had that I-wish-I-was-coming-with-you look. She was still standing on the bank waving goodbye as we rounded the bend. The seven miles to Brattleboro were tough. It was raining, the wind was blowing into our faces, and we were worn out from our party. We were quickly running out of steam. The thought of having a beer with Brooke kept Ramsay going for a while, but the closer we got to Brattleboro, the more he began to realize there was no way we were going to catch the Flamingo Kids.

"Bugsy," he said, "let's pull in at the next takeout. I've had it."

The next takeout was the West River Marina, just north of Brattleboro. We'd planned to take out at Vernon Dam, about four miles below Brattleboro, but once again, thanks to the dam, the river had turned into a lake so what was the point? We turned off at West River, paddled under the railroad bridge, then under Route 5, and went another quarter-mile until we came to the West River Marina. As we pulled into the docks, a kid came out and asked if he could help us.

"Did a girl in a kayak with a pink flamingo on the front come in here earlier?" Ramsay said.

"Not that I remember," the kid said, "but I was working the lunch shift up in the restaurant. I could have missed her."

"Not her," Ramsay said.

We lugged the Mad River up onto the shore, chained it to a tree, and went into the restaurant. It was only two o'clock, too early to call Mary Hepburn, our stranger for the evening, so we decided to have lunch. After we'd ordered, I picked up the local paper to see what was happening around Brattleboro.

The list of entries at Hinsdale Racetrack caught my eye. I knew about Hinsdale from my days at Amherst. It used to run trotters, now it was dogs. On a rainy Wednesday afternoon, the only people at Hinsdale would be hard-core losers, but sitting at the track playing the dogs would beat sitting around the marina doing nothing. "Ramsay, here's something we can do," I said, holding up the race card. "What do you say we go out to the track, have a few beers, and bet on the dogs?"

"You go if you want, I'm having a beer right here."

I wasn't surprised. Catching the Flamingo Kids was the only thing that would have tempted Ramsay to deviate from his plan. I wasn't going to the track by myself, so I told him to call Mary Hepburn and see if she could come get us early. Mary said she'd be there in an hour.

We were sitting outside the marina waiting when I said, "This time tomorrow, I'll be on my way to Texas and you'll be heading to Boston. It'll be good to take a break."

"Maybe for you, but I'm not looking forward to calling Theresa. She's going to tell me my aunt in Baltimore's is either dead or dying, and she's either put both our dogs down or is about to."

"God, Ramsay, you sound like Somerset Maugham's *Appointment in Samarra*. You can't hide from death. You'll have to deal with it sooner or later."

"Not if I don't call home."

Ramsay's notes had Mary Hepburn as "very agreeable." That was an understatement. Mary's mailing address was Bellows Falls, but she lived in Saxton's River, a little town back in the hills. Saxton's River was at least an hour's drive from

Brattleboro. Mary had to be "extremely agreeable" if she were willing to come all that way to pick us up.

As we headed up into the hills, Mary told us she was the head of the art department at Vermont Academy in Saxton's River. Her husband, Ryan Ostebo, was a financial advisor catering mostly to clients in southern Vermont. It was a second marriage for both. Mary had two daughters by her first marriage, which is why she kept the Hepburn name, but they both were grown and out of the house so she and Ryan were empty nesters. It sounded like we were in for a quiet evening, which after our big party the night before was just fine.

Saxton's River was a classic New England prep school town: small, quiet, quaint, and prosperous. Mary's house was on Pleasant Street, just a few doors down from the entrance to Vermont Academy. Pleasant Street could not have been more aptly named. Everything about it was pleasant: big trees, nice homes, well-landscaped yards, shaded sidewalks. Since we had some time before dinner, I decided to go for a run through the academy, which is a very pretty little school.

When I got back, Ryan was sitting at the kitchen table with Ramsay. They were discussing why silos were no longer financially feasible for farmers. I introduced myself, and went to get cleaned up. I'd just gotten out of the shower and was drying off when a little boy opened the bathroom door. Seeing me standing there naked, he turned and ran out. Once dressed, I went into the kitchen, Mary was cooking pork chops for dinner. Ryan and Ramsay were outside touring Ryan's flower beds while Ramsay had a smoke. The little boy was sitting at the kitchen table giving me the stink eye. I went over and whispered to Mary, "That little boy came into the bathroom while I was drying off after my shower. When he saw me, he was pretty surprised. I hope I didn't scare him."

"That's Hayden. He lives in the house behind us. I should have warned him you were in there. He thinks that's his bathroom."

Ramsay and Ryan came in, and we all sat down to dinner. Hayden never said a word, but he kept giving us the stink eye. Obviously, he wasn't happy having Ramsay and me moving in on his sweet deal. However, having us there didn't dampen his appetite. Hayden had his pork chop down to the bone before any of the rest of us were even close to finished. "Hot damn, Hayden" Ramsay said, "for a little kid, you sure can eat."

Hayden snagged another pork chop and attacked it with the same gusto. When he was through, he got up and walked out. "Interesting little kid," I said, as we watched him disappear through a hole in the hedge that ran across the backyard. "Do his parents work at the academy?"

"No, we don't really know his parents," Mary said. "Hayden just showed up one day. I think he's adopted us."

"Kids are like cats," Ramsay said. "Feed 'em, and they keep coming back."

After dinner, Ryan opened another bottle of wine and we retired to the den. When I complimented him on his house, he said, "It was a wreck when we got it, but we're about through here. We're looking at a house up the street. The lady who owned it just died. It needs a lot of work, but we're thinking of making the kids an offer."

"She just passed away last week," Mary said. "We probably should wait a while. They might be offended if we asked them now."

"If I had a house and was planning to sell it," Ramsay said, "I'd sure as hell want to know if somebody was interested."

"Is it that old cape up the street?" I asked Ryan. "I saw some people walking around there when I was out running.

They were taking notes on a yellow pad, like they were making an inventory of things to do. I bet it was the kids. Come on, let's take a walk up there. You can pretend you're showing me around town and maybe we can find out what's going on."

When Ryan and I got to the house, the car was gone and everything was dark. "They must have gone out to get something to eat," Ryan said. "Here, let me show you the barn." We walked around to the back. "Look at those lines. Beautiful, don't you think?"

It was hard to tell. Most of the barn had fallen down, and the house, while still standing, wasn't in much better shape. If Ryan wanted to tackle another fixer-upper, this was the place.

Back in the den, I noticed a framed photograph hanging over the fireplace. It showed a quarterback standing over the center getting ready to take the snap. The team with the ball was Middlebury, the one on defense was Amherst. "When was this photo taken?" I said, standing up to get a better look.

"The fall of eighty-eight," Ryan said. "That's my son, Tim, playing quarterback."

"So what's he doing now?"

"Tim's gone. He died ten years ago when his car spun off a road in Colorado."

Once again I was left speechless, and, of course, Ramsay was outside having a smoke. I was fumbling for something to say when a car drove by. "That's the kids coming back," Ryan said, getting up. "I'm going to go see them."

"You know," I said to Mary as we watched Ryan go, "this is the third time we've stayed with someone who's lost a child."

"You don't know the half of it," Mary said. "Ryan had two

sons. The other one, Tim's younger brother, drowned in the river here when he was a senior at the academy."

I had to sit down. When Ramsay came in, I told him about Ryan's sons, and he too sat down. Then Mary told us more about Ryan. He was from Minnesota and had gone to Dartmouth where he was an All-American hockey player. During his senior year, he'd played every minute of every game, which led Rusty Ingersall, the author of *Skates, Sticks, and Men: The History of College Hockey,* to dub Ryan "the last sixty-minute man." From Dartmouth, Ryan had tried out for the 1960 Olympic team, the one that won the gold medal at Squaw Valley, and had been the last player cut. Ryan still played hockey for some old-timer teams, but Mary thought getting this house would be good for him. "Ryan always needs a project."

Ryan was in high spirits when he came back. He'd found the kids and had a nice talk with them. They told him they were planning to sell the house, and as Ramsay had predicted, were very pleased to learn Ryan and Mary were interested. They said they'd give Ryan a call just as soon as they were able to get their mother's affairs in order. Once again, Ramsay's advice had been right on the money.

As I lay in bed listening to Ramsay floss his teeth, I couldn't stop thinking about Ryan losing his two sons and how Hayden had just showed up. This strange little boy must have sensed a void on the other side of the hedge and crawled through to fill it. Now, if Ryan and Mary moved, would he follow them? Having to walk up the street wouldn't be the same as just crawling through the hedge. Then I remembered how Hayden had polished off those pork chops and fell asleep betting he would.

16

The Shrinking Canoe

Tom Miner, Whitty Sanford's husband and the executive director of CRWC, was waiting for us at the West River Marina. Tom was going to drive us to CRWC's offices in Greenfield. Ruth was going to meet us there at noon. Then Ramsay would ride with us to Hartford where Ruth and I would catch a plane for the wedding in Texas while Ramsay took the car to visit his daughter in Boston. Before Ruth arrived, I had some work to do with Whitty. She had a bunch of projects that local land trusts on the river had submitted for our review. After looking them over I wanted to check in with the foundation to make sure I was still its one-month, unpaid project manager for the Connecticut River.

Ramsay's original plan was to leave the Mad River chained to a tree at the recreation area just below Vernon Dam, but when Ramsay called Tom to let him know where to pick us up, Tom had told him, "I've been thinking about where to leave the canoe, and since you're going to be gone for the weekend, it would be safer if you leave it inside the fence at the power plant. We have a good relationship with New England Power. I'm sure they wouldn't mind if you just call and let them know what time we'll be coming."

Ramsay had tried the number Tom had given him for the

power plant several times, but no one ever answered. Ramsay mentioned the fact as we were lifting the Mad River onto the top of Tom's car. Tom took out his cell phone. "I'll try again," he said, dialing the number. "We won't be able to get in unless there's somebody at the gate to meet us. With the country operating under Code Orange, that plant will be locked up tighter than a frog's behind."

Tom, like Ramsay, failed to get an answer. "Don't worry," Ramsay said, "we'll get in. Bugsy and I can talk our way in anywhere."

With the canoe now resting on top of Tom's car, I stood back to see what would happen. When we'd picked the Mad River up at CRWC's offices on our way north, Ramsay and Tom had a little tête-à-tête over how a canoe should be tied onto a car. Although they both claimed never to have met before, it turned out Ramsay and Tom had been in the same class at Princeton. For some reason I could never figure out, they went at each other like old rivals. Ramsay maintained the stress of falling off was on the front and back of the canoe. Ever the planner, he'd gone into his duffel and fished out two ropes with loops previously prepared for tying down a canoe. With these, he'd proceeded to secure the bow and stern to the front and back bumpers. Tom, on the other hand, had said the stress of falling off was on the sides so he'd taken out two straps and lashed them over the hull. I hadn't said a word. Only a fool would have gotten between these two Tigers, but one thing was for sure: Once they were through, the Mad River wasn't going anywhere.

This time, there was no Princetonian debate. Ramsay and Tom each did their thing. Ramsay tied the bow and stern front and back. Tom lashed the hull side to side. Once again,

when they were through, the Mad River wasn't going anywhere. For all practical purposes, it might as well have been
welded to the roof.

Because we'd quit paddling before we reached Brattleboro, Tom decided to give us a quick tour of the town. At first,
Brattleboro looked like Littleton, an old mill town trying
somewhat successfully to reinvent itself. Then Tom drove us
across the Route 119 bridge so we could see Brattleboro from
the other side of the river. It was not a pretty sight. The riv-
erbank above the railroad tracks was covered with old ten-
ements. Their black-stained brick; dull, dirty windows; and
lines of laundry hanging between unpainted wooden porches
looked bleak. "God," Ramsay said, "it's like something out of
a Dickens novel."

"Brattleboro's turned its back on the river," Tom said.

Clearly, that was a mistake. Towns that had embraced
the river like Bradford and Bellows Falls seemed to be pros-
pering. Towns that ignored it like Woodsville and Windsor
seemed to be going nowhere. Making parks and green space
along the river part of a downtown area capitalizes on a tremendous resource. Any city or town that doesn't understand
that deserves to fail.

Completed in 1909, the Vernon power station was one
of the early hydro- and fossil-fuel-fired plants still operated
by New England Power. The dam was six miles south of the
Route 119 bridge and had turned this stretch of river into
another lake. Having Tom drive us around it was just fine.
When we pulled up to the entrance of the plant, the gate was
wide open. Tom stopped the car, honked the horn, and waited
for somebody to come out. Nobody did.

"With Code Orange," he said, "you think we can just
drive in?"

"Damn straight," Ramsay said. "The gate's wide open, and nobody's coming out. What are they going to do, shoot us?" Having spent the last two weeks on the river, Ramsay and I had forgotten about terrorism. Except for the cop who'd driven Ramsay around Colebrook, nobody we'd met in the last two weeks seemed too concerned about security. Everybody had greeted us with open arms, and none of our strangers even bothered to lock their doors.

When we pulled up in front of the plant's office, Tom said, "Dave, go in and tell them we're from the Watershed Council. Ask them where they want us to leave the canoe." Tom must have figured if somebody was going to get shot, better me than him.

I got out and went into the office. Nobody was there. "Hello," I shouted. Nobody answered. I walked out onto the main floor of the plant. It easily could have accommodated two football fields. Turbines the size of dump trucks were whirring away unattended. It was useless trying to shout above the noise so I started wandering around looking for somebody. At the far end of the floor, I came across a set of metal stairs leading to the bowels of the plant. Down I went, still nobody. Now I was getting nervous. Maybe terrorists had threatened to blow the place up and all the workers had gotten out. I ran back up the stairs, sprinted through the turbines, and out the big bay doors into the parking lot. With this type of security, who'd ever be so arrogant and ignorant as to publicly challenge Al Qaeda to "Bring it on"?

Tom and Ramsay were waiting by the car. Tom was pacing up and down nervously, Ramsay was having a smoke. "This is weird," I said. "I've been all through this place and there's not a soul here."

At that moment, a guy in a yellow safety hat with the NEW ENGLAND POWER logo on the front came walking around the corner of the building. He didn't seem surprised to see us. "Hi, I'm Tom Miner from the Watershed Council," Tom said, stepping forward. "We called about leaving a canoe here for the weekend?"

"Just put it over there by the fence," the guy said, not asking for any identification.

We lugged the Mad River over to the fence where Ramsay said, "Bugsy, give me the chain. This place is about as secure as a Mickey Rooney–Liz Taylor marriage. We're locking this sucker to the fence."

In May, on my recommendation, the foundation had made a $5,000 grant to CRWC. The check had come with a letter signed by Barry Tobias, Treasurer. Rather than bother Dan Lufkin, I dialed the number listed on the letterhead. "Peter Sharpe and Company," the woman who answered said. "This is Linda."

"Linda, this is Dave Morine. I'm trying to reach Barry Tobias."

"Hang on, I'll see if Barry's free." From Linda's tone, I got the impression Peter Sharpe and Company was a small, informal operation.

Barry Tobias could not have been nicer. He told me he'd sent a check for $10,000 to the Upper Valley Land Trust and was waiting for our next request. The more we talked, the more it became clear Barry's real job was running Peter Sharpe's real estate holdings and managing the foundation was something he and Linda did on the side. That was typical of Dan. Keep the overhead low, put the money into grants.

When I went to find Whitty, she and Peg McDonough, CRWC's outreach coordinator, were in the conference room with Ramsay. He was regaling them with stories of our trip. "Hey, Bugsy," he said, as I walked in, "tell Whitty and Peg how I had you looking for a Panamanian flag at the Eatons."

"I don't have time for stories," I said. "Whitty and I have to go over some projects. If we can get our next proposal to the foundation today, we might be able to present a check to one of the projects when we paddle by it next week. That would fire up the local conservationists and give the Watershed Council some good PR."

"That *would* be good PR," Whitty said, "and speaking of local conservationists, Nathan Tufts called. He said he'd be happy to put you guys up."

Nathan Tufts was one of the founders of CRWC. I'd never met Nathan, but friends in conservation told me he was a real character, and we should try to spend a night with him. "Great," I said, "we'll give him a call. We can stay with him Monday night. In fact, Ramsay, while Whitty and I are going over the projects, why don't you call Nathan. And Peg, while Ramsay's doing that, could you make a couple of copies of his index cards. That way, we'll all have a list of the people who offered to put us up."

By noon, when Ruth arrived, Whitty and I had reviewed all the projects and written a proposal to the foundation to help with the purchase of a tract right on the river in Hadley. I was feeling good as we turned onto Interstate 91 heading south to the Hartford airport. Ruth was just about to put on a Natalie Merchant CD Mary Lynch had given me when Ramsay said, "Hold on, Ruth. Bugsy and I have to clear the air on a few matters."

"Clear the air?" I said. "On what?"

"I didn't like the way you were acting back there, ordering me and Whitty and Peg around like we were your slaves."

"Slaves? Look, Ramsay, I apologize if I seemed rushed, but I had a bunch of things to do and only an hour or so to do them. Plus, most of the stuff I was doing was for the Watershed Council so I doubt Whitty and Peg minded."

"Well, I minded, and another thing, I didn't like the way you started changing where we're going to stay. I didn't call Nathan Tufts because he wasn't on my original list, and I have us staying in Greenfield Monday night."

"I thought we were staying in Greenfield on Tuesday night?"

"We are."

"Believe me, Ramsay, I've spent a lot of time in this area and we don't want to be staying in Greenfield for two nights, especially when we can spend a night in Northfield with Nathan Tufts."

"It's too late. I've already picked the people we're staying with and they're both in Greenfield."

"Ramsay, look, now that we're in Massachusetts things are different. It's not like up north where neither one of us knew anything. I know what's going on around here, and if we can stay a night in Northfield with Nathan and then a night in Greenfield, it's going to make the trip more interesting and fun."

"Okay, if you want to take over the planning, you've got it.

"Ramsay, I'm not taking over the planning. You've done an amazing job, but you've got to loosen up. All your planning's taking the adventure out of the trip. So what if we stay with a guy who wasn't on your list. Isn't it better than spending two nights in the same place? Hell, you're the one who said we can never go back."

"Then you call him on Sunday. You tell him when and where to meet us on Monday."

"Ramsay, please, don't do this to me. On Sunday, I'm going to be flying back from Texas; you're going to be sitting at Kim's house right next to a phone. If you don't want to call Nathan, that's fine. Make any arrangements you want. I don't care. It's your trip. I'm just trying to make it a little more interesting. Is there anything else?"

"Just one more thing. I don't like the way you always pick the tree where we chain the canoe."

"Ramsay, I'm not believing this. I have one lousy job, and now you're telling me you don't like the way I do it?"

"What I don't like is you ask me what tree I think would be good, then you pick some other one and tell me to move the canoe, like you're the Lone Ranger and I'm fuckin' Tonto."

"Okay, from now on, I promise I'll take your pick of trees more seriously. Is that it?"

"That's it."

Before Ramsay could change his mind, Ruth quickly hit the Play button and Natalie Merchant's folksy voice filled the car. Natalie's first song was "Sally Ann," and it was pretty good, in a down-home sort of way. None of us said another word until we reached the Hartford airport.

As I squeezed into my seat on the plane, I was prepared to feel cramped and tight. Instead, I felt free and relaxed. Ramsay and I needed this break. If Ramsay's theory that "every day you spend on a boat with somebody, the boat shrinks a foot" was correct, after sixteen days on the river, our canoe was gone. Now the question was how many feet, if any, would grow back over the weekend?

PART III

MASSACHUSETTS AND CONNECTICUT

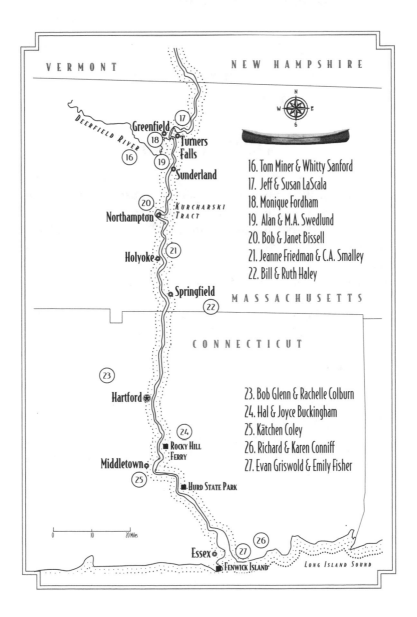

VERMONT NEW HAMPSHIRE

Deerfield River

Greenfield
17
18
Turners
Falls
16
19
Sunderland

20
Kurcharski Tract
Northampton

21
Holyoke

Springfield
22 MASSACHUSETTS

CONNECTICUT

23

Hartford

24
■ Rocky Hill
Ferry
Middletown
25
■ Hurd State Park

0 10 20 Miles

26
Essex 27
■ Fenwick Island *Long Island Sound*

16. Tom Miner & Whitty Sanford
17. Jeff & Susan LaScala
18. Monique Fordham
19. Alan & M.A. Swedlund
20. Bob & Janet Bissell
21. Jeanne Friedman & C.A. Smalley
22. Bill & Ruth Haley

23. Bob Glenn & Rachelle Colburn
24. Hal & Joyce Buckingham
25. Kätchen Coley
26. Richard & Karen Conniff
27. Evan Griswold & Emily Fisher

17

JUNE 16
CONWAY, MASSACHUSETTS

A Long Way Down

Ramsay was in high spirits when he picked us up at the Hartford airport late Sunday evening. Spending time with Kim, his sports-betting son-in-law, and his three grandchildren seemed to have revived him. He'd been able to do his laundry, and mine, and when he'd called home, Theresa told him death had not made an appointment with either his aunt or his dogs. Moreover, he happily reported he'd called Nathan Tufts, and we'd be staying with him in Northfield on Monday night. He even granted that Nathan sounded like a neat guy, which was a lot from Ramsay.

Ramsay, Ruth, and I spent Sunday night with Whitty Sanford and Tom Miner at their home in Conway, Massachusetts. When we came down to breakfast on Monday morning, Whitty was standing by the front door dressed in a business suit stuffing papers into a leather briefcase. "Hot damn, Whitty," Ramsay said, "you look like you're about to board the train to Wall Street."

"I have to go to a meeting of all the conservation groups working on the river," Whitty said. "We're trying to coordinate our efforts regarding the Conte Wildlife Refuge, but it's not easy. Dealing with these national organizations is like wrestling with an eight-hundred-pound gorilla."

Silvio O. Conte had been a long-term and much-beloved congressman from western Massachusetts. During his thirty-two years in office, conservation had been one of Conte's top issues, and when death caught up with him on February 8, 1991, he'd been working on ways to clean up the Connecticut River.

Shortly after his passing, President George Herbert Walker Bush honored the congressman by signing into law the Silvio O. Conte National Fish and Wildlife Refuge Act. This act authorized the U.S. Fish and Wildlife Service to undertake a study of the entire 7.2 million acres of the Connecticut River watershed, an area half the size of Vermont, New Hampshire, Massachusetts, and Connecticut combined. Then, based on this study, the Fish and Wildlife Service was mandated to create a new refuge like none it had ever established before.

Prior to Conte, national wildlife refuges typically were owned by the U.S. government and managed by the U.S. Fish and Wildlife Service. Conte was different. The bulk of the land designated for conservation would be protected by private groups under a cost-sharing program where the feds would provide up to 50 percent of the project costs with the rest coming from nonfederal contributions of land, labor, equipment or materials, and, of course, actual money. The program would be administered by the Fish and Wildlife Service and funding would be awarded through a competitive process. After a decade of surveys, site evaluations, reports, and meetings, many of which were done in conjunction with local conservation groups like CRWC, the study was done. Now, the land rush was on. With up to fifty percent of the total funding guaranteed, nonprofit conservation groups were lining up to stake out their claims. That meant developing proposals that would identify lands to be protected; explain why they were significant; describe how they would be managed; show where they fit into the overall protection scheme; and list potential sources of funding.

The problem Whitty and the other local nonprofits were facing was that the national organizations had a distinct competitive advantage. Even though most of the work on the study had been done by local groups, with their size and resources the national organizations could cherry-pick the biggest and best projects and muscle their way to the front of the line for funding. Already they'd begun announcing grand plans for saving the river and lobbying hard for the appropriations.

But the locals had one advantage. Since much of the 7.2 million acres that made up the Connecticut River watershed were inhabited by two million humans, the study mandated that the refuge had to be both scientifically sound and socially acceptable. That was like mixing oil and water. "Scientifically sound" means letting nature take its course while "socially acceptable" means making it comfortable for man, and these two uses are seldom compatible. Convincing farmers, timber companies, towns, and other landowners to embrace the refuge was going to be a tough sell.

"Whitty," I said, "don't let the national organizations push you around. The projects have to be socially acceptable and you're the ones that have the local credibility. The national groups need you more than you need them, so if they start pushing you around, tell them to pound sand."

"You might be right, but telling an eight-hundred-pound gorilla to pound sand might not be the smartest thing to do. If you get them upset, they can really rough you up." As

Whitty got into her car she added, "Keep checking in, and oh, by the way, Tom's got something to show you in the morning paper. It doesn't look like you'll be staying with Nathan Tufts tonight. He's had an accident."

Back inside, Tom handed us a copy of *The Recorder*, Greenfield's daily paper. The headline read ULTRALIGHT PLANE CRASH SENDS PILOT TO HOSPITAL. The plane, an Arnet Pereyra Adventura UL, was pictured lying crashed in a field. The caption read, "The pilot of this plane, Nathan Tufts, 73, of Northfield, remains in fair condition at Bay State Medical Center."

"Can you believe it?" I said. "A seventy-three-year-old guy flying around in an ultralight. I'm sorry we're going to miss Nathan."

"Hell," Ramsay said, "at least Nathan's got a bed for the night. Where are we going to stay?"

"Don't worry," Tom said. "I talked with the Mount Grace Land Trust this morning. They're having a party for you tonight, and they'll put you up." Tom handed Ramsay a piece of paper with a name and number on it. "When you stop for the day, call Chuck Levin at that number. Chuck works for the land trust, and he'll come pick you up."

After breakfast, Ruth drove us to Vernon Dam. Once again, the gate to the plant was wide open and once again, there wasn't a soul in sight. All that was missing was a sign that said, WELCOME OSAMA BIN LADEN. We collected the Mad River, but before we pushed off, Ruth suggested we look at the fish ladder New England Power had built next to the dam. Like the recreation area below, the fish ladder was part of New England Power's public outreach program. A set of steps ran next to the ladder so people could walk along and watch the fish as they fought their way around the dam. Only there weren't any fish. Even though it was the peak of the annual salmon and shad runs, all the pools along the ladder were empty.

Halfway up the dam there was a visitors center. In addition to glorious pictures of Atlantic salmon leaping high in the air, there was a blackboard that kept track of the fish using the ladder. So far, just a half-dozen Atlantic salmon had made it as far as Vernon Dam, which is only a third of the way up the river. Shad had done somewhat better. Between two and three thousand of them scaled the ladder, but that was a far cry from the millions upon millions that literally clogged the river in colonial times. As long as the dams are there, it's safe to say no one will ever see those great runs again.

Ruth gave us a shove and Ramsay pointed the Mad River south toward Long Island Sound, now just 138.5 miles away. It was good to be back on the river, but this part of the trip was going to be different. Between Deerfield, Amherst, and my work in conservation, I'd spent a lot of time in western Massachusetts and Connecticut. For me, the excitement of being someplace new wasn't going to be there, at least not totally, and our strangers probably wouldn't be complete strangers. In most cases, I'd know people they knew. Plus, word had gotten out that we were donors, and that meant our strangers would no longer be treating us as two old happy-go-lucky moochers. Now, they'd be putting on the Ritz. Instead of good cheer and friendly advice, giving as good as we got would be measured in terms of money.

After about six miles, we crossed into Massachusetts and entered a section of the river known as the Pond. It was called the Pond because Northeast Utilities had turned this section of the river into a public playground for boating, hiking, picnicking, even a riverboat ride. The reason for Northeast's largesse was simple. In 1958, it figured out how to apply the old Wall Street adage "buy low, sell high" to the production of power. It did this by building a three-hundred-acre reservoir on top of Northfield Mountain and installing four huge combination pump/generators down by the river. During periods of *low* demand, Northeast would move water from the river up into the reservoir by using cheap electricity in its system to power the four pumps. Then during periods of *high* demand, Northeast would release that water back down the mountain where the four generators would turn it into expensive electricity that Northeast would sell to its customers.

Unfortunately, unlike buying stocks and bonds, this trade required more than just shuffling paper. Once a day every day, five and a half billion gallons of water was sucked from the river then flushed back into it. That might explain why only five Atlantic salmon were able to make it as far as Vernon Dam, the rest being sucked up into electricity, and it definitely was the reason why the banks of the Pond looked like a giant mud hole. As compensation for this obvious plundering of the river, Northeast Utilities rewarded the public by dressing up the Pond with recreational trinkets like boat ramps, hiking trails, picnic tables, and the riverboat ride. The public seemed happy to accept this trade. Northeast had made the Pond socially acceptable.

We called it a day when we came to the Route 10 bridge. We'd only gone about ten miles, but we'd started late and Ramsay was anxious to find out where we were spending the night.

A house stood next to the bridge; its lawn ran right down to the river. On the lawn leaning up against a tree was a canoe. "Bugsy," Ramsay said, spying the canoe, "whoever lives in that house must be a canoeist. Lets pull in and I'll ask them if we can leave the Mad River here for the night."

The woman who answered the door not only told Ramsay we could leave the Mad River on her lawn, she said he could come in and use her phone to call Chuck Levin at the Mount Grace Land Trust, and then she and her little daughter Jessica brought us a pitcher of cold lemonade and a plate of chocolate chip cookies. People sure were nice to us.

Chuck showed up in a shiny little sedan. The car looked too small for Chuck, who was tall and lanky, but once inside, we had plenty of room. More to the point, we were embraced by one of the most pleasant aromas known to man, the scent of a new car. As was so often the case, I was up front with Chuck while Ramsay was in back with the bags. To break the ice, I said, "New car?"

Everyone likes talking about their new car, and Chuck was no exception. "It's a Toyota Prius," he said, "one of the new hybrids. When you're going slow, it runs on electricity. Then when you speed up, it switches over to gas. It's all automatic, and unlike pure electric cars, it's self-charging. You never have to plug it in."

"How many miles to the gallon?" I said.

"I'm still figuring that out, but it's over fifty."

"How much does one of these things cost?" Ramsay said.

"Around twenty thousand, but I didn't buy it. I won it in a raffle."

"A raffle?" I said. I'd never met anybody who'd won anything big in a raffle.

"Yeah. There's a nonprofit organization in Greenfield

called Greenfield Energy Park. It's trying to promote sustainable energy, so they raffled off a Prius. Five bucks a ticket. I bought three, one of them won."

"The IRS treats raffle winnings as ordinary income," Ramsay said, "so what did they hit you for in taxes?"

"Actually, next to nothing," Chuck said. "The government offers a two-thousand-dollar tax credit to anyone who buys one of these cars. Because winnings are treated as income, I was eligible for the credit. It just about covered the taxes."

Amazing. Some guys have all the luck.

Chuck was driving us to the little town of Gill where we'd meet up with Dick French. Dick was a board member of the Mount Grace Land Trust. He and Chuck wanted to show us a project they were hoping we'd support. Dick ran a two-man woodworking business from a barn next to an old farmhouse where he lived with his wife and two boys. He was just closing shop when we arrived. After welcoming us to Gill, he wasted no time suggesting we go see the project.

Seeing Carl Demrow's project and meeting the Dawg had given Ramsay more than his fill of conservation. He wasn't going. "Bugsy's the project guy," he told Dick and Chuck. "If it's just the same with you, I'm going to stay and get cleaned up."

The land the Mount Grace Land Trust was trying to protect was a 248-acre hollow that had over a mile of the Fall River, a tributary of the Connecticut, running right through it. The Commonwealth of Massachusetts had appropriated the money to buy an Agricultural Preservation Restriction (APR) over the land, but there was a catch-22. Before the APR Committee could approve funding the project, it had to have an appraisal establishing the Fair Market Value (FMV) of the APR, but when the legislature passed the funding for the APR program, it hadn't included any money for appraisals.

"If we can get the money for an appraisal," Dick said, "we can make this happen, but without it, we might lose the whole thing."

"How much for an appraisal?" I said.

"Somewhere between six and ten thousand," Chuck said. "There's three different properties involved."

"That sounds high to me," I said. "You're a nonprofit. You should find an appraiser who's interested in conservation and have him cut you a break. In any event, here's what we'll do. We'll recommend to the foundation that it give Mount Grace five thousand dollars for appraisals. If you can do it for that, fine. If not, you'll have to make up the difference. Then when the appraisals are done, have the landowners give Mount Grace an option to buy the APRs. Then when the state's ready to buy, you sell them the option for the cost of the appraisals. Buying the option would be part of the acquisition costs and that way you get your money back and can keep revolving it into new projects."

Back at the house, Ramsay had showered, shaved, and taken a nap. While I got cleaned up, he was going to review with Dick and Chuck the stretch of river we were going to paddle the next day. We'd heard parts of it could be tricky, especially going through French King Gorge. When I came out, the three of them were huddled over a map. Seeing me, Dick said, "Let's go for a ride. Chuck and I want to show you the best way around a couple of spots you'll hit tomorrow."

After talking to Ramsay, Dick and Chuck must have surmised we weren't the world's best canoeists and now with their grant, they didn't want anything to happen to us. We piled into Chuck's new Prius and drove to French King Bridge, the point where Route 2 crosses French King Gorge. I'd crossed that bridge many times and going through the gorge was one of the main reasons I'd agreed to come on this trip. Chuck parked the Prius in the lot on the east end of the bridge, just above where Millers River joins the Connecticut. From the parking lot, we had a clear view of the confluence. "Once you're under the bridge," Dick said, pointing to the swirling waters below, "stay well to the west side of the river. With Millers flowing in, it can get pretty choppy out in the middle."

From there we walked to the center of the bridge where we stopped and looked down at the river far below. "See that rock?" Dick said, directing our attention to a boulder sitting in the middle of the river at the head of the gorge. "That's French King Rock. The river's very deep here. All you're seeing is the tip of the rock. While it might look calm, there's a hell of a current caused by the water swirling around the rock so stay away from it."

"Anybody ever jump from here?" Ramsay asked, looking down at the water.

"At least a couple of dozen," Chuck said. "I think Walter Jones, the insurance guy, was the last. The day Walter found out he had terminal cancer, he drove up here, parked his big Cadillac in the lot, took off his Rolex, laid it on the front seat next to his medical report, walked out to the middle of the bridge, and jumped. That was the end of him."

"How far down is it?" Ramsay said.

"Around a hundred and seventy-five feet."

"Anybody ever jump and live?"

"A few years back, a couple of kids from Connecticut made it," Dick said. "They were too drunk to be scared, which probably saved their lives, but they were pretty well beat up."

"Sounds like ol' Walter was taking a chance," Ramsay said.

"How's that?" I said.

"Hell, Bugsy, there's no guarantee you won't make it. If you're going to kill yourself, you ought to do it right." He paused and looked down at the river. "The first time my brother tried, he screwed it up. I mean, how feeble is that? How hard can it be to kill yourself? He finally got it right the second time."

That was a conversation stopper. Ramsay had mentioned he had an older brother who died, but I didn't know he'd committed suicide. Ramsay had made it clear he never really liked him, but like him or not, saying he'd screwed it up on his first try seemed a little tough. Now that his brother was gone, you'd think he would cut him some slack, but apparently not. On the bright side, at least Ramsay and Katharine Hepburn would have something to talk about. Katharine also had a brother who'd committed suicide.

As we were leaving the bridge, we heard a bulldozer working in the woods along the east side of the river. Heavy machinery working along a river is always suspicious. When we got back to the Prius, I asked Chuck if we could drive by and see what was going on. What we saw was a crew working on a road they'd hacked through a stand of old hemlock next to the river. "What do you make of that?" I said.

"Probably putting in a new picnic area," Dick said.

That made sense. The gorge is arguably the most scenic part of the river, and given the ugly banks of the Pond, Northeast Utilities probably figured a picnic area overlooking the gorge would be a public relations plus. Too bad it was cutting down so many trees, but what are a few trees to a power company?

When Chuck had picked us up, he told us we'd be staying with Jeff and Susan LaScala, members of the land trust who had a beautiful home overlooking Barton Cove, an area of the river just above Turner's Falls. Chuck had assured us we'd be very comfortable with the LaScalas, and we believed him. Now that we were donors, the land trust wanted us in the spiffiest place it could find. But first, they were throwing us a party at the Frenches. The party was a potluck supper, the preferred fare of most grassroots conservation groups. Each of the half-dozen couples who'd been invited brought a different dish. The guests were relatively young and all looked decidedly liberal, not exactly Ramsay's crowd. Being surrounded by so many conservationists made Ramsay uneasy so after we'd been introduced, he stepped outside for a smoke.

I felt fine so I stepped up for a beer, which is how I got to know Alden Booth. Alden and his wife, Lissa, both of whom graduated from Amherst in the class of '83, had contributed a keg of beer to the potluck dinner, but it wasn't just any keg. Alden owned The People's Pint, a combination microbrewery/pub in downtown Greenfield. As Alden explained, this keg was cask-conditioned, which meant the beer had to be hand-pumped from the keg. "It's like the real ale you get in an English pub," he said, pumping me a glass.

"So how's that differ from other beer?"

"Remember back at Amherst when you used to tap a keg, you'd pump CO_2 in to force the beer out."

I did, quite fondly. "Yeah, getting the pressure just right was a big deal."

"With cask-conditioned beer, you don't use any outside CO_2. CO_2 is produced naturally during the fermentation process so if you cap the keg during fermentation, you trap the

CO_2 inside. That way, when you hand-pump the beer out, the carbonation is all natural. That's what makes this beer so malty and smooth."

Alden was serving a dark, creamy, brown ale. As he pumped, he kept holding the glass up to the light to see how much was ale and how much was foam. When it had settled to his satisfaction, he handed me the glass. I took a long sip, the foam forming a mustache on my upper lip. The beer was nutty and delicious.

Thanks to Alden's keg, everyone soon was in good spirits. The food was tasty and during dessert, Emily treated us to a short flute recital. Even Ramsay ended up having a good time. In addition to spending some quality time with Alden's keg, when he brought up Chuck's car, he discovered that conservationists were not above petty jealousies. Everyone he spoke to felt that they should have won the car, especially since all of them had bought more than three tickets. "Hell, Bugsy," Ramsay said, as the party was ending, "those people are okay. They get pissed off just like anyone else."

18

A Great Abenaki Warrior

When I first woke up, I had no idea where I was. It wasn't until I looked out the window and saw a white cloud hanging over the river that I remembered we were at the LaScalas. Watching the wisps of morning mist rise off the water into the sun like ghost soldiers made it easy to see why the land trust wanted us to stay with the LaScalas. Their home, standing alone high on a bluff overlooking the cove, was a perfect spot for entertaining donors.

Downstairs, Ramsay was out on the deck with Susan LaScala. He was looking through a telescope. "Bugsy," he said, calling me over. "Come see this. It's really neat."

I went over, put my eye to the lens, and was face to face with a bald eagle. It was sitting atop a dead tree in a huge nest made of sticks. The eagle had a fish in its talons and was ripping it apart with its beak, then feeding the pieces into the nest. "This is neat, how many chicks are in there?"

"Two," Sue said. "If you want a better look, we can go up to my bedroom."

Up to her bedroom? That sounded strange. Susan was a very attractive woman, and Jeff, her husband, an emergency medical doctor, had already left for the hospital. "Susan," I said, "I've heard 'come up to my bedroom and see my etchings,' but never 'come up and see my eagles.' Is that your line for seducing old conservationists?"

"No, that's where we keep the TV that's set to Eagle Cam."

Eagle Cam was another one of the power company's outreach programs. In an effort to show the public it was eagle-friendly, the power company had installed a TV camera just above the nest and was broadcasting the eagles live, twenty-four hours a day, on a local cable station. The eagles' daily trials and tribulations was a popular soap opera. People couldn't get enough of them.

"I'm surprised the Fish and Wildlife Service let them put a camera up there," I said, as we watched momma eagle feeding her chicks. "The feds are pretty strict when it comes to eagles. They don't like people doing anything that might upset them, especially when they're nesting."

"It's not the eagles that are upset," Susan said. "It's the cat owners. When they installed the camera, they discovered the nest was full of cat collars. Cat owners went nuts. They couldn't believe the eagles were eating their pets."

It serves them right. Cats are killing machines. Studies compiled by the American Bird Conservancy show that the fifty million domestic cats that are allowed to roam free and the seventy to one hundred million feral cats that run wild kill well over a billion birds a year. While the feral cat population keeps increasing, bird populations worldwide are in a steep decline. Loss of habitat is the number-one cause, and with birds being forced into smaller areas, they've become very easy prey. When told that cats and humans are the only two species that kill purely for fun and that they should keep their cats indoors, most cat owners go into complete denial. "Oh, my little Tabby, Tigger, or Socks would never kill a bird." Having the eagles snatch a few Tabbys, Tiggers, and Socks isn't going to solve this problem, but it might scare some cat owners into being more responsible.

We were still watching the eagles when Dick French arrived. On our way back to the canoe, he gave us a tour of Gill. Hidden between the river and Interstate 91, this little community of just over 1,200 people was rural in the best sense of the word: clean, neat, prosperous, but not yet yupped up or Martha'd out. And Dick was doing everything he could to keep it that way. Not only had he and Emily placed an ADR over their six hundred–plus acres, it became obvious Dick had a plan for protecting every large undeveloped parcel of land left in Gill. That made me feel good. Grants are really made to people, not organizations, and in Dick French we couldn't have picked a better Dumbo.

We'd paddled a couple of easy miles when we came to a stretch of shoreline that had been completely leveed. It was easily the length of a football field and looked like hell. The lower part of the bank was riprapped in stone, while the upper part was covered with grass and sumac. At the far end, we could see where some farmland had eroded. "That erosion must be caused by all that water the power company's sucking up and letting go every day," Ramsay said. "They probably had to put this levee in because the farmers were bitching about losing their land."

"God, it's ugly," I said. "It would have been better if they'd used old cars, like the ones we saw up around Lancaster. They would have been a lot cheaper and a lot more interesting than this crap."

Then we noticed a half-dozen people wandering over the levee. They had their heads down like they were searching for something. "Bugsy, what the hell are they doing?"

"Beats me. Pull over and we'll ask."

A young, fuzzy-faced guy wearing Timberland boots and a big straw sunhat was bent over edging his way along the bank. Every now and then, he'd stop, pick something up, examine it, and make a note on a clipboard. "Pardon me," I said, as we pulled up next to where he was standing, "could you tell us what you're doing?"

The guy jumped. He'd been so intent on his search, he hadn't seen us coming. "Oh," he said, regaining his composure, "we're looking for dragonfly skins."

"Dragonfly skins?"

"We're doing a study on what effects the levee has on the dragonfly population."

Due to the levee there were no eddies where we could pull in, and with the rocks, no place we could land so before we could ask him why, we'd been swept downriver. Once we were out of earshot, Ramsay said, "And I thought paddling with you was boring. Can you imagine spending the day looking for dragonfly skins? Those people have to be nuts."

"What's really nuts is trying to control flooding with levees. You build a levee here, it's going to push the water over there, which means you have to build a levee over there, and so it goes. Before you know it, all that's left is a ditch that's devoid of life and always overflowing. You want to control flooding, preserve wetlands. That's the best way."

"That's it, Bugsy, get pissed," Ramsay said. "Somebody's got to save those dragonflies."

We rounded a bend and there, towering over the river, was French King Bridge. The moment I'd been waiting for had arrived, we were about to run French King Gorge. Better yet, it was a perfect day: The sun was shining, the sky was blue, a gentle breeze drifted up from the south. The river gods who'd treated us so shabbily at the Big Splash were now smiling on us. Like Athena, protector of virgins, French King Rock was the only thing between us and our entry into the Gorge. The water around the rock looked calm, but thanks to Dick French's warning, we knew not to get lulled into its grasp. "Ramsay, take it wide. That rock's just waiting to grab us."

As Ramsay steered toward the east bank, we got our first good look at the place where we thought the power company was building a new picnic area. What we saw was a swath of frontage that had been totally stripped of all trees and vegetation. A big, yellow backhoe was gouging huge chunks of earth from the bank where they were scooped up by two massive front-end loaders and dumped into a line of waiting trucks. The backup beeps from the backhoe, front-end loaders, and trucks kept echoing around the Gorge. The little road through the hemlocks we'd seen the day before had been a ruse. The power company wasn't building a picnic area, it was constructing a new levee on the east side of the Gorge. "Dammit," I said, "those assholes are turning the most scenic part of the river into a mess. Who the hell wants to look at this crap? They're wrecking the gorge."

"Don't worry, Bugsy, just start paddling. I'm going to make you feel like a great Abenaki warrior."

Ramsay put the Mad River into a U-turn and headed for the west bank. From there, the construction wouldn't be staring us in the face. Unfortunately, he'd made the turn too late. The current, which thanks to the levee upriver felt like it was on steroids, was pushing us right into French King Rock. I put my head down and dug deep. My seat immediately started squeaking, not from frustration, but fear. From the stern, I could hear Ramsay shouting, "Harder, Bugsy, harder! Give me everything you've got."

I did. My head was down, I was pulling hard, but just waiting for the crunch. There was no way we were going to get around the rock. Ramsay was still yelling when we kissed the face of French King Rock, only I could hardly hear him. His shouts were muffled by Athena's angry roar. For one scary moment, I could smell the moss, touch the granite, and feel the Mad River's bottom buckle on the rock. Water gurgled up to the gunnels. We were going over, but Ramsay was still yelling so I dug deeper and somehow the Mad River slipped free. When I looked up, we were in the gorge zipping for the bridge. Ramsay had done it. He'd risked everything to make my day, and he had. As we swept past the wooded shore, damn if I didn't feel like a great Abenaki warrior.

When we rounded the bend at the end of the gorge, the current slowed to a crawl. Thanks to Turners Falls Dam, the river had turned into another long, boring lake. As we plowed along, two things caught my eye. First, an eagle soaring high above Barton Cove. Second, a mat of milfoil covering the cove. Thanks to the mist, I hadn't seen the milfoil that morning. Now, I couldn't miss it. It was a green carpet running wall to wall.

Most everybody's seen milfoil. It's the aquatic weed pet stores throw into fish tanks to make them look more natural. A native of the Far East, milfoil went wild sometime during the sixties when a fish tank owner dumped it into a lake. Since then, milfoil's been running wild, infesting lakes and rivers all over the country.

Milfoil's aptly been called the AIDS of lakes. Like AIDS, it's easily spread and almost impossible to control. Once a lake becomes infested, the only way to treat the spread of milfoil is by hiring divers to pull it out by hand. That's an expensive proposition, and there's no way divers can get every piece. As with AIDS, without constant and expensive treatment, a lake infested with milfoil will slowly die. Barton Cove, which had looked so good hidden in the morning mist, now looked dead, which explained why the eagle was flying so high. It was looking for another place to fish.

We straggled up the boat ramp and dropped the Mad River under a tree. After a smoke and a Bud Light, Ramsay walked over to the public phone and called Monique Fordham. Monique was our hostess for the evening, and the only stranger I'd rejected, but Ramsay had overruled me. He thought Monique was neat. When he'd called, she'd laughed at all his lines and told him she was a five-star cook. That was enough for Ramsay. He'd rated her just below John Harrigan, editor emeritus of the *News and Sentinel*, and Bill Webster, Katharine Hepburn's next-door neighbor.

Ramsay might have thought Monique was neat, but all the conservationists I knew avoided her like the plague. That's because Monique Fordham was a fanatic, an ideologue who was willing to sacrifice everything for the cause. I'd met my share of true believers when I was with The Nature Conservancy and they scared the bejesus out of me. I was always afraid they were going to ask me to do something crazy, like lie down in front of a bulldozer or chain myself to a tree. Mainline conservationists like me don't do things like that. We say it's more productive to work within the system, but in truth, we're too established and too comfortable to risk everything for the cause.

Not Monique, she was neither established nor comfortable, and didn't seem to care. This fact had become clear during her five-year fight to protect Wissatinnewag, a sacred site of her ancestral tribe, the Abenaki Indians. Wissatinnewag (Abenaki for "Shining Hill") was a sixty-four acre tract located in Greenfield, just above the Turners Falls Dam. Before the dam, Wissatinnewag overlooked a waterfall that was even more spectacular than Bellows Falls. Every spring for thousands of years the Abenaki, Narragansett, Wanpanoag, Nipmuc, and other New England tribes had put aside their tribal differences and congregated at Wissatinnewag to feast upon the annual shad and salmon runs. From their communal camp above the falls, they'd fish, hunt, trade, hold powwows, and generally celebrate having made it through another long, cold winter.

On May 19, 1676, that life ended forever. Under the cover of darkness, a colonial militia led by Captain William Turner attacked the camp at Wissatinnewag and massacred over three hundred Indians. Turner launched his attack while the warriors were off hunting so most of those killed were women and children and old men, some of whom fell to their death trying to escape over the falls.

Since renaming the site Turners Falls in honor of Captain Turner, the white man had not been kind to Wissatinnewag. The actual falls were obliterated by the dam in 1886, and during the construction of Route 2, symbolically known as the Mohawk Trail, much of Wissatinnewag was turned into a sand and gravel pit. The final ignominy came in 1993 when Wal-Mart announced it was buying the land for a big-box store. That was when Monique decided to defend her Abenaki heritage and joined a broad-based coalition that had come together to oppose Wal-Mart's plans to build a store in Greenfield.

After a long, hard battle, Wal-Mart decided to build its store in neighboring Orange. That should have been the end of it, and for the coalition it was. Unlike Monique, most members had no attachment to the sand and gravel pit. They just wanted Wal-Mart out of Greenfield. Once Wal-Mart was gone, the otherwise pro-growth Greenfield town council decided to rezone Wissatinnewag for an industrial park, leaving Monique and a few friends to face a new and publicly supported threat to develop what they knew to be a sacred site.

In her efforts to save Wissatinnewag, Monique wrote to everybody from Bill Gates to Camille Cosby asking for money. She also besieged numerous conservation organizations—national, regional, and local—with persistent calls for help. She was the Abenaki's David going against Greenfield's pro-growth Goliath. Despite her dismal odds, Monique would accept no compromise. Nothing was going to stop her from saving Wissatinnewag, and nothing did, not even personal bankruptcy. In 2001, Friends of Wissatinnewag (FOW), a nonprofit organization founded by Monique and her friends, took title to the entire site.

When it came time to close, they'd clumped together all but $17,000 of the $780,000 purchase price. At the last moment, Monique was forced to take a loan from a local land trust. I didn't know the details of the loan, but I knew Monique was still looking for money, and as the head of FOW, she would have seen Whitty's e-mail alerting conservation groups along the river that Ramsay and I had money in our canoe for land conservation. Monique certainly wasn't going to let that opportunity go floating by. That's why she'd volunteered to put us up.

"Did you get Monique?" I said when Ramsay came back from making his call.

"She's on her way."

"You know, it's not going to be a fun evening. All Monique wants from us is money."

"Bugsy, that's your problem. All I want from Monique is a five-star meal."

Monique and her boyfriend, Rick, showed up driving an old, faded Pontiac LeMans. After all the stories I'd heard about Monique, I expected her to be dressed like an Indian, like Marge Bruchac, the Abenaki songster we'd seen at the Big Splash, but she wasn't. In her T-shirt, faded jeans, and sandals, Monique looked like any other college student. Rick, on the other hand, with his slender build, pasty white skin, dark framed glasses, and white short-sleeve shirt, looked like a computer geek, which he was.

After we'd introduced ourselves, Ramsay asked Monique if we could take the Mad River with us. The portage around Turners Falls was about three miles, and there was no way we were going to walk that. Monique said taking the canoe would be no problem, so Ramsay went into his duffel and dug out his ropes and some special Styrofoam pads he'd brought for putting canoes on the top of a car. As he worked, neither Monique nor Rick offered any advice on how a canoe should be tied onto a car, which further confirmed Ramsay's high regard for Monique.

"Is there anything special you guys want to see?" Monique said, as we piled into the LeMans.

"I'd like to see The People's Pint," I said.

The People's Pint was the pub in Greenfield owned by Alden Booth, the publican we'd met the night before. It was hot, my throat was dry, and one of Alden's cask-conditioned beers would taste good, but that wasn't the only reason I wanted to see The People's Pint. I had a hidden agenda. Every place we stopped, people would ask, "You guys want a beer?" and we'd reply, "Sure," and they'd say, "Any particular brand?" and Ramsay would say, "We don't care, just so long as it's cold."

With that low expectation, we were always handed a Busch, or a Miller Lite, or a Bud Light, but unlike Ramsay, I did care. I wanted a beer I could taste, like a Sam Adams, or a Bass Ale, or one of Alden's cask-conditioned beers. That's why I was eager to visit The People's Pint. I was hoping a tour of the brewery might expand Ramsay's taste.

We pulled open the heavy wood-and-glass door and entered Greenfield's version of an old English pub: a long mahogany bar running along the wall to the right, cozy wooden booths along the wall to the left, and overhead fans suspended from the pressed tin ceiling recycling the sluggish afternoon air. On this lazy Tuesday, The People's Pint was almost empty. We claimed four stools at the bar and began studying the big blackboard on the wall behind it where Alden chalked in his beers of the day: Farmer Brown Ale ("like any good farmer, outstanding in the field"), Pied PIPA ("a colorable India Pale Ale"), Impeachment Porter ("it speaks for itself"), and I.R.A. ("the Irish Red Ale"). I ordered a dark, creamy, brown ale, like the ones I'd had the night before. Rick, Monique, and Ramsay settled on a pale ale, which was much lighter.

While the bartender was pumping, I asked her if Alden was around. She said he was downstairs in the brewery. Once we'd been served, she went down and got him. Alden seemed glad to see us, and asked if we'd like a tour of the brewery. I said that would be great, but much to my surprise, and embarrassment, Ramsay said we didn't have time, we had to go shopping for dinner.

I couldn't believe it. Forget the fact we might actually learn something about beer, Ramsay's refusal was just plain rude. We'd walked into a guy's bar, asked him to leave what he's doing to come up and say hello, he offers to show us how he makes his beer. I say yes, and Ramsay says no, we have to go shopping for dinner. What was the matter with him? What would it take, fifteen minutes? We weren't on any schedule, we could shop for dinner anytime. It was like the Fort at No. 5. Was it any wonder Ramsay found life so boring? What did he expect if he had no interest in trying anything new? I was steaming as we left The People's Pint.

After we'd finished shopping, Monique drove us to a two-family home on the backside of Greenfield. Monique lived near Rutland where she was just completing her second year at the University of Vermont Law School. To host us, she'd borrowed the two-family house from some friends connected with Wissatinnewag. Fortunately, they weren't home. Judging from the candles, beads, and feathered dream catchers scattered around the house, it was a sure bet they danced to a different tom-tom.

While Ramsay, Rick, and Monique went into the kitchen to start working on our five-star meal, I poured myself a big glass of wine and went out onto the front porch to blow off some more steam. I still couldn't get over the way Ramsay had snubbed Alden. I was sitting there drinking my wine watching a steady stream of smokers, beer drinkers, and lottery-ticket buyers going in and out of the bodega directly across the street when Ramsay came out. "Hell," he said, lighting up a Carlton, "I got these great steaks, but there's no grill and the broiler in the oven doesn't work. It turns out Monique can't cook for shit so Rick's in there frying the steaks on the stove. They'll probably end up tasting like shoe leather."

"I warned you not to mess with Monique. Why don't you *ambulante* over to the bodega and buy a lottery ticket. Maybe your luck will change."

"My luck's fine. Except for the steaks, things couldn't be better." There was no way Ramsay would ever admit he'd been wrong.

As it turned out, the steaks were a little tough, but much to my surprise, Monique was not your typical ideologue. Unlike most fanatics, she was able to laugh at herself, and during dinner she entertained us with stories about her battles with Wal-Mart and the pro-development forces on the Greenfield Town Council. After dinner, Monique gave each of us a brochure on Wissatinnewag and said she'd like to tell us about FOW and what it was doing with the site. "That's Bugsy's area," Ramsay said. "You can tell him while Rick and I do the dishes."

Monique sat me down on the couch and proceeded to walk me through the brochure. She had done her homework. Knowing I'd been with The Nature Conservancy and its goal was the preservation of biotic diversity, Monique focused on the gardens FOW had planted at Wissatinnewag that contained indigenous varieties of corn, beans, and squash: the 'three sisters' of the Native American diet. "One of the things we want to do at Wissatinnewag," she said, "is educate people on the importance of protecting biodiversity in food seed."

"Education's good," I said, "but tell me more about this note you're trying to pay off."

"Well, you know, Wal-Mart had agreed to pay four million for this property. When they pulled out, that's how much the owner still wanted. After years of negotiation, Terry Blunt, head of the state's program for protecting the Connecticut River, and I finally got him to agree to take seven hundred and eighty thousand. Of that, the state would put up three hundred and fifty thousand, the U.S. Fish and Wildlife Service would add another two hundred and fifty thousand, and

FOW committed to raise the balance of one hundred and eighty thousand. When it came time to close, we were seventeen thousand short so I borrowed it from the Valley Land Fund, a local land trust. Since that time, paying back the loan has been FOW's top priority."

That was going to be a problem. It's tough to raise money for land that's already been saved. Once the threat of development's gone, there's no sense of urgency, plus in this case, the loan had come from a local land trust that was supposed to be saving the valley, so why hadn't the land trust just given FOW the money? My guess was they did, but never told Monique in the hopes that she still might be able to raise it.

"Monique, it says here Wissatinnewag is listed on both the State and Federal Registers of Historic Places. Wouldn't that make you eligible for federal or state funds? Hell, what happened at Wissatinnewag sounds as bad as Wounded Knee. You'd think the feds would be throwing money at the Abenaki."

Here Monique made an interesting point. Unlike the western tribes that had their treaties broken and were forced onto reservations by the United States government, the Abenaki never dealt with the United States. Turner's attack on Wissatinnewag had taken place exactly one hundred years before the start of the Revolutionary War. It wasn't the U.S. government that had massacred the Abenaki and driven them off their land. It was the colonists. As such, the United States government had no legal obligation to honor any Abenaki claims. If the Abenaki wanted restitution, Monique would have to petition Queen Elizabeth.

"What about the Pequots?" I said. "They're making millions off their casino in Connecticut. Can't they help?"

"We've sent them several proposals, but all we got back was a form letter rejecting our requests. They even spelled Wissatinnewag wrong." Monique paused, took a deep breath, "So, what about you?"

A fair question. In my letter to Dan Lufkin, I stated we wanted to help little land trusts get into new projects. To do that, we were looking for people like Carl Demrow and Dick French who just needed a push to start them flying. Monique had been flying for years. Now, she was looking for a place to land. "Monique," I said, "the foundation we represent wants to help local land trusts get into new projects along the river, not pay off old ones. Look, you've done your job, you've saved Wissatinnewag. It's time for you to get on with the rest of your life."

"Not until I've paid back the loan. That's what I promised to do."

Over dinner Monique had told us her life plan was to finish law school and find a job where she could represent Indian tribes, but obviously she felt obligated to put all that on hold until she paid off the loan. Ramsay was right. Even if she couldn't cook, Monique was neat. How many kids today respect nature, would go bankrupt protecting their heritage, and would put their lives on hold to repay a debt they're not legally responsible for?

And to think, Captain William Turner wiped out a whole tribe of people who held these values. For what it's worth, the captain got his comeuppance. When the warriors hunting down river heard the gunshots, the rushed back to Wissatinnewag and seeing the carnage, went after the colonial militia. Before that long, sad day was over, they had tracked down Turner and killed him and thirty-four of his men.

19

JUNE 18
GREENFIELD, MASSACHUSETTS

A Good Grave

We woke up to a hard, cold rain that steadily got worse as the morning wore on. Ramsay wandered over to the bodega and along with his daily beer and cigarettes, came back with coffee and donuts. We were in no hurry to get on the river, but Monique had to get back to Rutland for a class so we couldn't hang around forever. Still, when we got to the put-in on the south side of Turners Falls, Monique and Rick were reluctant to let us go. "We can drive you down to Sunderland," Monique said.

"Thanks, but we've got nothing better to do," Ramsay said. "Besides, the cold and the rain beats the heat and the wind we had yesterday."

I wasn't sure of that, but it let Monique and Rick off the hook.

The confluence of the Deerfield River, a major tributary to the Connecticut, was just across the river from the put-in. That meant the current would be both fast and tricky, but dealing with the current was not our immediate problem. We were having trouble just getting down to the river. There was no regular put-in, like a beach or a boat ramp. The best entry we could find was a steep path that dropped straight to the water. With the rain, the path was wet and slippery. At the bottom, there was no room on the bank for the canoe or the duffels. We'd have to slide the Mad River directly into the water, then load it.

"Hell, Bugsy, we've got a problem," Ramsay said, looking at the path. "Trying to load the canoe in that current's going to be like dancing on a log. One wrong move and we're all in the river."

"What option do we have? You go down the bank, brace yourself on that tree, and I'll lower the canoe to you. Once you've got it in the water and tied to the tree, I'll come down and we'll have Monique and Rick throw us our bags."

Somehow we got packed and seated without tipping over. We said goodbye to Monique and Rick, who were standing at the top of the bank looking very pleased they weren't coming with us, untied the Mad River, and immediately were swept away. With the rain beating against my glasses, everything was a blur, but before we'd gone too far, I heard the grinding of steel on steel. Cleaning my glasses, I looked up and saw a diesel engine slowly pushing a row of freight cars across a trestle bridge spanning high over the river. The engineer, warm and snug in his cabin, was leaning out the window watching us. He must have been surprised to see anyone on the river in this weather. I raised my arm and gave him the sign for a toot. He waved back and gave us a blast that made our goose bumps shiver.

The river ran straight and fast and around noon the rain let up so we could start seeing the land around us. The shoreline was mostly wooded with a mixture of silver maple, cottonwoods, a few shagbark hickory, and some tall white pine. In one of the pines, a bald eagle was sitting watching us, hoping we might scare up a fish. When we got close, it took off. An eagle really is big and monarchal. Whoever talked Ben Franklin out of making the more democratic turkey our national bird did the country a grand service. More to the point, seeing the eagle was proof that at least along this part of the river, conservation efforts by CRWC and other groups were starting to show results.

Alan and Mary Alice Swedlund were our strangers for the evening. The Swedlunds lived on the river somewhere north of Sunderland, but there were no Hen and Chicken Rocks or other landmarks in front of their house, so Ramsay had asked them to pick us up at the Route 116 bridge in Sunderland. Since banks along this stretch were all mud, we had no desire to pull over and were making very good time. We'd only been paddling a couple of hours when we saw the Route 116 bridge. Before we reached it, we had to go by three islands. The middle one was a good quarter of a mile long. As we approached it, we saw something splashing in the shallows. My first thought was a weasel or a mink hunting for frogs or crayfish, but as we got closer, we could see the splashing was being caused by fish. Ramsay was ready for a smoke so I said, "Pull over. Let's see what's going on."

Unlike the banks of the river, the shore of the island was mostly gravel, so we were able to get out and walk around. The splashing, we discovered, was being caused by carp, big carp, rolling in the shallows. As we stood watching them, Ramsay lit up a Carlton and said, "Bugsy, what the hell are they doing?"

"They must be spawning. I guess all that splashing is them rolling on the rocks trying to get the eggs out. Whatever it is, it's definitely sexual."

Ramsay took a long drag on his Carlton. "You know, we must be really bored if the highlight of our day is standing around watching fish fuck."

"Hell, it beats listening to your golf stories."

We pulled into the landing just above the 116 bridge, locked the Mad River to a tree, grabbed our duffels, and walked into the little town of Sunderland. Since we'd made such good time, we had an hour to kill before Ramsay could call the Swedlunds, so we decided to treat ourselves to a late lunch. Harvest Gold, a nice restaurant, at least by our standards, was right in the middle of town. Being wet and grubby, I wasn't sure they'd seat us, but the hostess cheerfully took Ramsay's boonie hat and little girlie vest, hung them up, and showed us to a table. No one seemed to mind that our river rat attire might stain the spotless white tablecloth and starched linen napkins. Our waitress was pleasant and we had a nice meal.

When Mary Swedlund, or M.A., as she liked to be called, picked us up, the rain had stopped and the sun was shining. At the house, we met Alan, M.A.'s husband, and almost tripped over an old black lab lying just inside the front door. "That's Sadie," Alan said. "Don't mind her. She's too old to move."

At the mention of her name, Sadie's wagged her tail and tried to get up to greet us, but she couldn't quite make it until Alan reached down and gave her a boost. Watching her, I noticed M.A. looked very sad. "I should tell you," she said. "We're going to need a little time to ourselves tomorrow morning. The vet is coming to put Sadie down."

"We've got two old dogs at home," Ramsay said, "and my wife and I are wrestling with the same decision. God, it's awful. There's just no right time to do it."

"We don't have a choice," Alan said. "We're leaving for Wyoming Thursday morning, and the girl who house-sits isn't here during the day so she can't deal with Sadie's incontinence. We tried the kennel, but they won't take her because she's too old. There's nothing else can we do."

There was something we could do. Back in 1990, Percy, our fourteen-year-old golden retriever, was steadily failing, and Ruth and I were dreading the thought of having to put him down. Like the great dog he was, Percy made it easy for us. Before we could screw up enough courage to call the vet, he died peacefully in his sleep.

Ruth and I had just started to dig Percy's grave when some friends of friends who'd just moved to Washington dropped by to meet us. Seeing what had to be done, and realizing we were having a tough time doing it, these wonderful strangers told us to go sit with Percy while they did the digging. It was one of the nicest things anybody had ever done for me. Now, here was my chance to pass that kindness on. "Well," I said, patting Sadie, "let's go find a spot overlooking the river and dig Sadie a grave."

Alan and M.A. hadn't thought about that. They insisted they'd do it while we were getting cleaned up, but we convinced them to let us do it while we were still dirty. We all walked down to the river and found a wooded bluff that not only looked nice but smelled wonderful. "What's that aroma?" I said, breathing it in.

"Mountain laurel, wild rose, Russian olive," M.A. said. "It grows all along this part of the river."

"Then this is the spot."

I laid out a grave and began digging. The soil was sediment from the bottom of Lake Hitchcock, the 170-mile-long lake that had covered the Connecticut River Valley 17,000 years ago, and that made the digging easy. When Ramsay spelled me, I began rummaging around an old fieldstone wall until I came across a flat slab of arkose, a reddish sandstone that's common to this part of the Connecticut. I pried the rock loose, lugged it over to the hole, and set it on end facing the river. Once Sadie was resting in peace, Alan and M.A. could carve her name into the sandstone. It was a good grave for a good dog. Percy would have been proud.

Alan and M.A. had put together a small dinner party in our honor. In addition to Ramsay and me, there was Tom Miner and Whitty Sanford; Mark Zenick, the executive director of the Franklin Land Trust; and Terry Blunt, head of the Department of Environmental Management's program to protect the Connecticut. I knew Mark because for the past ten years I'd been doing volunteer work for the Franklin Land Trust. I knew Terry because back in the early seventies he'd worked for The Nature Conservancy, and after leaving the Conservancy, he'd spent the next thirty years protecting the Connecticut.

I made a point of sitting with Terry during dinner. He was on the board of the Valley Land Fund, the group that had lent the $17,000 to Monique, and it was Terry who'd put together all of the public funding for Wissatinnewag. I told him we'd spent the night before with Monique and that she was very upset that she hadn't been able to pay off FOW's debt to the Valley Land Fund.

"That land never would have been saved without Monique," Terry said, "and to be honest with you, nobody ever thought she'd raise as much money as she did."

"She told me you were the one who finally put the deal together."

"Monique and I were the good cop, bad cop. After Wal-Mart dropped out, we'd go see the owner and Monique would keep telling him how important the property was, and I'd keep telling him there was no way we could match the four million Wal-Mart had offered. Finally, he said he'd take $1.2 million. I knew I could get $350,000 from the State and $250,000 from the Fish and Wildlife Service. Monique said she thought she could raise $180,000, so I called the owner and said, 'Seven Eighty, that's it.' He called me back the next morning and said he'd take it. I thought Monique was going to jump through the roof. I'd never seen anybody so happy."

"Well, she's not very happy now. Trying to raise this seventeen thousand is wearing her down. She feels she can't go on to anything new until she pays off the loan, but to be honest with you, it's time for Monique to get on with her life."

"First off, seventeen thousand's not right. The last time I looked, the outstanding balance was only twelve, and as I said, everyone was surprised Monique was able to raise as much as she did. Despite what she says, she's the one that saved Wissatinnewag. I'll call her tomorrow and see what we can work out."

I couldn't have asked for anything more. If nothing else, Monique's loan had gone from seventeen thousand down to twelve, and if I heard Terry right, he was going to try to figure out a way to get her completely off the hook. I was about to go find Ramsay, who, as usual, was outside having a smoke, and give him the good news, when Sadie struggled over and flopped down by my feet. Obviously, she was looking for an easy handout and, like any lab worth her salt, had correctly surmised I was a soft touch. As I slipped her a juicy chunk of my hamburger, it occurred to me this probably would be Sadie's last treat. What the hell, life's too short. I gave her the whole damn thing.

20

Another Lousy No

When I came downstairs just after 7 a.m., M.A. was heading out the door. Judging from her outfit, she was going jogging. "Going for a run?" I said.

"No, I'm going to Sugarloaf Mountain. A group of us walk up there every morning."

"Every morning?"

"Well, not all of us make it every morning, but there's eight women in the group so there's always somebody. It's a wonderful way to start the day. We've been doing it for sixteen years. Would you care to come along?"

"I would, if you're sure the other women wouldn't mind." Ruth's in a few women's groups, and I've learned that while they claim men are welcome, they usually don't mean it.

"Just keep up, and you'll be fine."

M.A. was right. Climbing Sugarloaf was a wonderful way to start the day. Rising just 652 feet, Sugarloaf is hardly a mountain, but it does offer spectacular views of the farms, villages, and river spreading out across the valley below. Like M.A., the four other women who showed up that morning were all in terrific shape, both mentally and physically. They moved right along with constant and interesting conversation, and I was able to keep up on both counts. When we'd finished, not only had I worked up a sweat, I felt like we'd settled many of the world's problems.

Back at the house, Alan and Ramsay were sitting in the kitchen having a cup of coffee with Bob Schmitt, the vet who'd come to put Sadie down. Bob was a big, unpretentious man with a quiet, comforting manner. He'd do his job, and do it with dignity. Seeing the time had come, Ramsay suggested we go upstairs and pack. After zipping up my duffel, I looked out the bedroom window and I saw Alan and M.A. pushing a garden cart across the field. Sadie was lying in the cart. Her pain was gone, she was at peace. When Alan and M.A. reached the grave, they wrapped Sadie in her blanket and gently lowered her into the hole. Even from a distance their grief was palpable. God, it's hard losing a good friend.

Downstairs, Ramsay was back at the kitchen table drinking coffee with Bob. I figured he might be asking Bob what he should do with his two old dogs, but he wasn't. Instead, they were discussing the demise of family farms. Bob, who was about our age, had gone to Cornell's school of veterinary medicine. After getting his DVM, he'd come back to the Pioneer Valley to be a large animal vet. Bob said he'd had a pretty good run, but now it was tough to find any large animals. "In twenty years, I doubt there'll be a commercial dairy farm left in all of New England."

"Not one?" I said.

"Well, maybe one or two will figure out a way to survive, but that'll be it. Family dairy farms are a thing of the past. The kids don't want to do it. It's too much work for too little return."

"We'll put our money on Auburn Star Farm," Ramsay said, and proceeded to describe our night with the Eatons.

"Sounds like they might have a chance," Bob said, "but along this part of the river, we're at the end of the line."

M.A., who was eager to get home and start packing for Wyoming, pushed us out from the shade of the Route 116 bridge into a hot sun. We'd gone about five miles when we came to a long lazy bend in the river. As we rounded it, we saw a big, sandy beach. After miles of mud, the beach came as a complete surprise. "Hey, Ramsay, pull in. I bet that's where we're going to have the ceremony tomorrow."

The proposal Whitty and I had sent to the foundation just before I left for Texas was for $10,000 to help buy fifty-seven acres in North Hadley known as the Kucharski tract. After ten years of trying, Terry Blunt finally had been able to sign a purchase and sale agreement with the Kucharski family for $235,850. The property contained three quarters of a mile of frontage and the finest beach on the entire river, but there was a catch. To get to the fifty-seven acres you had to go through the rest of the Kucharski's farm, and they didn't want that. Therefore, the purchase was dependent on the commonwealth being able to secure an alternative right-of-way, and much like the situation we faced with the appraisals in Gill, the department had the funds to close on the purchase, but no money for the right-of-way.

The Valley Land Fund, the same group that had made the loan to Monique for Wissatinnewag, had been able to secure an option on a right-of-way, but needed $10,000 immediately to buy it. That was the proposal we'd sent to the foundation, and seeing the chance for some good PR, Whitty had quickly arranged a ceremony on the river for Friday, June 20, the next morning.

All that beautiful sand looked like one big ashtray to Ramsay. He steered the Mad River to shore. While he lit up a Carlton and popped a Bud Light, I got out and walked the beach. I could see why Terry Blunt had worked so hard to buy it. There was nothing else like it on the entire river. "Bugsy," Ramsay said, pointing to a rope swing tied to a limb hanging out over the water, "why don't you give that swing a try."

Not a bad idea. It was hot and there was no one around. I stripped down, grabbed the rope, and walked up to the top of the bank. I was about to launch myself out over the Connecticut when it hit me. I was fifty-nine, not nineteen, and this was a major league swing. At the rope's apex, I'd be twenty feet above the river, and dropping ass backward from that height would be a good way to break my neck. I let go of the rope, put on my clothes, and walked back to the Mad River.

"Bugsy, I'm proud of you," Ramsay said. "It's not like you to show that much common sense."

"To hell with common sense. You know what they say, 'common sense comes from experience, but experience comes from a lack of common sense.' I like experience, only I didn't have the guts for this one. If I'd tried and made it, I'd have felt like a million bucks. Now, I just feel like an old fart."

We came out of the bend, went a couple of miles, and entered a curve that pushed the Connecticut around the town of Hadley. Here, things got ugly. The whole south side of the river was held in place by a massive levee. It looked like something you'd see on the Mississippi: long, high, and unnatural. I hated the sight of it, but nobody in Hadley was complaining. One look at the map showed the Connecticut clearly was itching to cut through this bend and head down Hadley's main street. Without this levee, Hadley was a goner.

I thought back to the riprapping along the Pond and the new diking being built in French King Gorge. For every action there's an equal and opposite reaction. The more they keep channeling the river above Hadley, the faster the water was going to be moving when it reaches this bend. If I lived in Hadley, I'd be fighting any diking upriver. One of these days, even with the levee, the Connecticut might have enough power to scratch that itch.

As we paddled to the landing in Northampton, Ramsay was in an unusually good mood. We were going to meet Bonnie Obremski, a reporter with the *Daily Hampshire Gazette*. Meetings with the press were Ramsay's favorite parts of the trip. After chaining the Mad River to a tree of Ramsay's choosing, I found a phone and called Bonnie.

We were lying in the sun, Ramsay puffing on a Carlton and sipping a Bud Light, I looking up at the big, white, puffy clouds, when a girl wearing a helmet, sneakers, shorts, and knapsack came zipping toward us on a bicycle. She braked to a stop and said, "Are you Ramsay and Dave?"

"That's us," Ramsay said. "Who are you?"

"I'm Bonnie Obremski."

"The reporter?" Ramsay said. "You've got to be kidding. You're too young to be a reporter."

Bonnie wasn't kidding. She parked her bike, took off her knapsack, pulled out her notebook, and said, "So, tell me about your trip."

"Hot damn, Bonnie," Ramsay said, "hang on here a minute. While you've been lounging around in an air-conditioned office all day, we've been out in the hot sun paddling our butts off. Let's find some place where we can sit down and have a cold beer."

Captain Cook's fish shack was just across the road so that's where we went. "Bonnie, can we buy you a beer?" Ramsay said, sliding into a booth.

"Thank you, Mr. Peard," she said, "but I'm not old enough to drink."

"Hell, Bonnie," Ramsay said, "even Jimmy Olson, cub reporter for the *Daily Planet,* was old enough to drink."

It wasn't clear whether Bonnie knew who Jimmy Olson was, but at Ramsay's insistence, she had a Coke. As we drank our beers and Bonnie sipped her Coke, she told us she was a student at Hampshire College working as a summer intern for the *Daily Hampshire Gazette.* As it turned out, for a cub reporter, Bonnie was pretty good. She politely endured Ramsay's rendition of *Beg, Borrow, and Deal,* and when I explained my "Dumbo's feather" theory, she immediately grasped the merits of making seed grants to local conservation groups. Bonnie got a kick out of Ramsay's claim that I sat in the bow taking notes while he did most of the paddling, but what really interested her was the fact that we were staying with strangers every night. "That sounds like a wonderful way to experience the river," she said. "More people should try it."

"Whoa, Bonnie," I said. "Let me tell you something. Staying with strangers is no game for small boys. You can't just knock on somebody's door and think they're going to take you in. Mooching at our level requires skills honed by years of experience: places we've been, people we've met, things we've done."

After we'd finished telling her about the trip, Bonnie posed us on the dock holding our paddles, took our picture, and peddled off to make her deadline. Watching her go, we felt very old.

Bob and Janet Bissell were our strangers for the evening. Ramsay's notes on Bob read, "Guy's an outdoorsman. Wants to paddle his own canoe with us for a while. Going to Boundary Waters Canoe Area in August. Grown children." As a fellow canoeist, Bob undoubtedly would make sure we were well wined and dined, and we liked staying with people who had grown children. People with grown children typically keep their kids' rooms in tip-top shape in the hope that someday they'll be filled with visiting grandchildren. In the meantime, those rooms were open to us.

Bob picked us up at the dock. On the way back to his house, he gave us a quick tour of downtown Northampton. Northampton was a lot different than the town I remembered from the mid-sixties. Back then, except for the streets abutting Smith College, Northampton was a played-out mill town with a bar on almost every corner. Now, the town was Martha'd out with most of the bars having been replaced by coffee shops, flower shops, bagel shops, and a plethora of yupped-up restaurants serving sushi, grilled zucchini pizza, and vegetable mousse terrines.

With the downtown Martha'd out and the food yupped up, one expected to see the sidewalks filled with swells dressed in pinks and lime greens, but that wasn't the case. Main Street Northampton was dominated by women in black, many sporting lavish tattoos, numerous body piercings, and butch hair dyed blond, purple, and green. Some were strolling hand in hand. It was these women who'd made Northampton prosperous and vibrant. They'd turned this dying mill town into the lesbian capital of the Northeast.

Bob and Janet lived in a well-established neighborhood on the north side of the Smith College campus. Its stately trees, shaded streets, and fine homes set well back on landscaped lots had a fifties feel, like the set for the TV show *Leave It to Beaver*. Bob pulled into the driveway of a comfortable colonial and led us in through the kitchen door. On the refrigerator was a photo of a black bear rummaging through a garbage can. The way the bear's big rump was sticking out of the can made the photo look like a joke, like something Janet and Bob had stuck on the refrigerator door to discourage snacking, but the more I studied the picture, the more the setting became familiar. "Bob, where was this picture taken?" I said.

"Right here." He pointed out the kitchen window to a garbage can sitting next to the garage.

"You've got to be kidding."

"No, one day we looked out and there she was, a big sow with three cubs. When food gets scarce, they wander up from the wetlands down below. The sow and her cubs were here three or four times last spring. Once, we even had a moose."

That was not good. In recent years, many species like raccoons, fox, coyote, white-tailed deer, even an occasional moose have become suburbanized. While they eat shrubbery and upset garbage cans, they are, for the most part, viewed as something of a novelty. Not so with black bears. They're too big, too powerful, and too carnivorous to be a novelty. In the wild, black bears pose very little danger to humans. In suburbia, it's a different story. I could just picture Bob dressed in a chef's hat and apron standing over his backyard grill cooking a big, juicy steak while on the other side of the hedge a huge black bear was on his hind legs sniffing the air. Gary Larson has a cartoon like that. The caption reads, TROUBLE BREWING.

Ramsay was fascinated with Bob and Janet Bissell, not because they lived in Northampton but because they were undergoing a change of life. Bob, who was at least ten years younger than us, had been a very successful pediatrician, but after twenty-two years had just given up his practice. When Ramsay asked why, Bob said he had two projects he wanted to undertake before he got too old. The first was to write a novel about a young woman growing up in western Massachusetts as America drifted into World War I. The second was the restoration of an old wood and canvas canoe he'd always loved.

Janet had her own list of projects. With a master's degree in microbiology, she was going to keep working part-time in the lab at Cooley Dickinson, the local hospital, but her main interest was horticulture. In addition to leading tours around the Smith greenhouse, Janet spent endless hours tramping through the woods of western Massachusetts checking out invasive and endangered plant species for the New England Wildflower Society. Unlike Ramsay, Bob and Janet seemed to welcome change and were never in the least bit bored.

After all our partying, we would have been content spending a quiet evening at home with Bob and Janet, but that wasn't going to happen. Bob recently had gone on the board of a little land trust dedicated to protecting Broad Brook, the stream that ran into the Smith campus, and Janet volunteered for Arcadia, a very popular seven hundred–acre preserve that abutted the Great Oxbow of the Connecticut. Bob and Janet had planned a dinner in our honor with some of the people connected with these groups. When they gave us the news, I could see Ramsay's eyes glaze over. He was tired of meeting conservationists, and who could blame him. Since we'd entered Massachusetts, conservation had taken over our trip.

Being somewhat new to the conservation community, Bob had opted for a cookout rather than a traditional potluck supper. While veggie burgers were the food of choice, Bob snuck on a couple of real hamburgers for Ramsay and me. Better yet, he'd set out a big washtub full of ice and cold beer from a local microbrewery. Still, the beer wasn't enough for Ramsay. When the dozen or so guests started telling us about different projects they were working on, Ramsay headed to the street for another smoke.

As the sun set, it started to get buggy so Janet suggested we move inside for dessert. I was just about to take my first bite of a tasty-looking strawberry shortcake when Mary Shanley-Koeber handed me a packet. Mary was the director of Arcadia Wildlife Sanctuary. The packet was a proposal for a donation to the Mass Audubon Society, the organization that owned and managed Arcadia. "We have an opportunity to add a sixty-acre inholding to the sanctuary," Mary said. "Initial estimates indicate it'll cost approximately one hundred and ninety thousand dollars, but this piece is the hole in the donut, and we're hoping you can help us fill it."

I gulped. There was no way we were making a donation to Mass Audubon. Mass Audubon was the largest and oldest conservation organization in New England. Arcadia was just one of thirty-six preserves it owned and managed. With its impressive nature center, four miles of well-maintained trails, 250 active volunteers, and full-time professional staff, Arcadia itself was larger than any of the groups we'd supported. A grant to Mass Audubon was impossible. It was no Dumbo.

At first mention of the proposal, Ramsay stepped out for yet another smoke. Once again, I was left on my own. I'd always thought giving money away would be fun, but it wasn't. It was work, hard work, and what I was beginning to understand was more often than not you had to say no, and you weren't saying it to just anybody. These were really good people trying to do really good things.

I'd felt terrible not being able to give something to Monique. Now, I was going to have to say no to Mary and everyone else at the party. This no was going to be especially tough because Mary wasn't some naive volunteer. She was a seasoned pro who wouldn't sit back and meekly accept no. She'd immediately give me ten good reasons why I should say yes and have a well-thought-out case for every one of them. As I watched the whip cream curdle on my strawberry short-cake, I had an idea. Sometimes the best decision is no decision, so that's what I'd do. "Mary," I said, putting down the proposal and picking up my strawberry shortcake, "I appreciate this information. It sounds like an exciting opportunity for Arcadia and Mass Audubon. I'll be sure to take a look at it tomorrow."

Tomorrow was another day, and tomorrow we'd be gone.

21

Unasked, Untold

The next morning. I was in high spirits. Bob was driving us to the Kucharski Tract where we were handing over a check for $10,000 to the Valley Land Trust. After saying no to Monique and on the verge of saying no to Mary, it would be nice to see all the faces light up and hear the big crowd's enthusiastic applause when we made our own "Big Splash." Only there was no big crowd. Once again the river gods chose to rain on their own parade. When Bob, Ramsay, and I arrived at the tract, all we found was a soggy handful of hard-core conservationists who couldn't wait to grab the check and run. After my very short, but very complimentary remarks about Terry Blunt and all he'd done for the river, Tom Miner handed the $10,000 check to Judith Eiseman, president of the Valley Land Trust. Then, everybody headed for their warm, dry cars.

Between the rain and the hard-core conservationists, I expected Ramsay might fall into one of his funks, but on the ride back to Northampton he was quite animated. "Did you see how Tom Miner tried to steal our show?" he asked Bob and me.

"Steal our show?" I said. "What are you talking about?"

"Didn't you notice? In all the pictures, Tom made sure he was the guy presenting the check, like it was his money."

"Ramsay, it was raining, everybody wanted to get the hell out of there. So what if he presented it? He's the one trying to save the river. Better for CRWC to get the credit than us. We'll never see any of these people again."

"It wasn't right. I was standing next to the reporter from the *Hartford Courant* and he didn't even know it was us who were making the gift."

"I'm sure you corrected that oversight."

"You're damn straight I did."

The rain was still coming down in buckets when Bob pushed us out into the river. Originally, Bob was going to canoe along with us for a while but decided at the last moment that this would be a good day to work on his book. As we paddled south under the Calvin Coolidge Bridge, I remembered driving over it in the spring of 1966 on the way to my army physical, which thank God I flunked. "Ramsay," I said, "how did you manage to stay out of Vietnam?"

"By the skin of my teeth. When I got out of Princeton I got lucky and found an opening in the Coast Guard reserves as a corpsman. Most guys didn't even know the Coast Guard had corpsmen. I never had to leave the States."

"You ever treat anybody who'd been shot?"

"Once. I was down at Camp Lejeune doing my two weeks' active duty, and they were having war games. War games weren't restricted to the base, so we had guys running all over these little towns in southeast North Carolina pretending to shoot at each other. Somehow, one of the patrols was issued live ammunition, and a guy ended up getting shot in the gut. I was the medical officer on duty that night, so the medics threw me in the ambulance and rushed me out there."

"How bad was it?"

"Bugsy, let me tell you something. A bullet's a messy

thing. You don't want to be fooling with anyone who's been shot. I took one look at this kid and said we've got to get him to a hospital. Luckily, there was a local hospital just a few miles down the road, so I had the medics stabilize him as best they could and told the ambulance to hotfoot it down to the hospital. At that point, a colonel shows up and says, 'No, we're taking the kid back to the base. If we take him to the hospital, they'll have to report the shooting to the local police and all hell'll break loose. The fact that some Marines were issued live ammunition would lead to an inquiry, which would mean the end of somebody's career.'"

"What did you do?"

"I said, 'Fuck you, sir.' I was the medical officer on duty and even though he outranked me, he couldn't rescind my order. I wasn't about to risk this kid's life to save some chicken colonel's ass. We went to the hospital, but when I got back to the base, they put me on the first bus back to Baltimore. They didn't want anybody asking me any questions. They just wanted me the hell out of there."

"Bugsy," Ramsay said, as we approached the dock in South Hadley, "I should warn you. I think Jeanne Friedman might be gay." Jeanne Friedman was the head coach of Mount Holyoke crew and our stranger for the evening.

"What makes you think that?"

"When I called her, she mentioned something about living with a friend."

"So, maybe the friend's some guy like Monique's Rick?"

"No, the way she said it, I think she was giving me a heads-up."

"Gay rights is a hot issue. If you're right, we could be in for an interesting evening."

Ramsay probably didn't think so. From past discussions, I knew his conservatism extended to gay rights, but in Ramsay's defense, he brought some personal baggage to the issue. Earlier in the trip, he'd told me he had a cousin who was a lesbian. Nobody in the family knew about it until she showed up pictured in *Time* magazine as one-half of the first civil union in Vermont. That had come as quite a shock to the very Republican Peard clan.

My own feeling on gays could best be described as indifferent. I've had limited exposure to the gay community and, to the best of my knowledge, nobody in my immediate or extended family is gay. With issues like the war in Iraq, the Federal deficit, the failure of public schools, and the religious right's attack on science, gay rights wasn't something I'd spent much time thinking about. If Jeanne and her friend were in fact gay, staying with them could be my first chance to have a serious discussion with a lesbian couple.

When Jeanne Friedman stepped out of her small Subaru station wagon, my first impression was Scout from *To Kill a Mocking Bird*. Dressed in a sweatshirt and jeans with no makeup and close-cropped hair, Jeanne looked like a little tomboy. She walked with an easy, athletic gait, and her only concession to self-adornment was a gold band on her ring finger. "You must be the paddlers," she said amiably.

"That's us," I said.

"Well, throw your gear in the car, and I'll take you up to the house so you can meet my partner, Carol Ann, and our son, Jacob."

So much for guessing. Jeanne was openly gay, but did the gold band mean she and Carol Ann were married? If Jeanne and Carol Ann had a son, they must have had some type of legal relationship, but what was it, what rights were involved, and how did they differ from a traditional marriage? I had a bunch of these questions, and if Jeanne and Carol Ann were comfortable talking about their relationship, it *was* going to be an interesting evening. But right now, while we were at the dock, I wanted to ask Jeanne about the Mount Holyoke crew. "Jeanne," I said, "before we go, could you show us around the boathouse? We saw the one at Dartmouth and it was really something."

"Sure, but it's no Dartmouth. We're planning to build a new rowing center as soon as we can raise the money."

Jeanne was right: The Mount Holyoke boathouse wasn't much. It sat inconspicuously behind a restaurant and a marina in a surplus World War II Quonset hut. Except for some hand-painted banners displaying slogans like WE PULL TOGETHER and ALL POWER TO ALL WOMEN, the inside of the hut was dark, cramped, and dreary. The nine sleek shells resting on racks looked out of place, like debutantes stuck in a biker's bar. "Jeanne, how much does one of these boats cost?" Ramsay asked, running his hand over the *Joanne V. Creighton,* the queen of the shells.

"An eight like that goes for around twenty-three thousand."

I walked over to a stack of oars piled in the corner. "How much for an oar?" I said, hefting one, testing its weight.

"Each of those costs two hundred and thirty dollars."

"So," I said, doing the math, "it costs about twenty-five thousand to put an eight-man shell in the water?"

"You could spend a lot more," Jeanne said, apparently not offended by my eight-man faux pas, "but for us, twenty-five thousand would be about right."

There was at least a quarter of a million dollars' worth of equipment in Mount Holyoke's very modest boathouse. Launching a college team, even for a minor sport like rowing, wasn't cheap.

Jeanne was going to drop us off below the Holyoke Dam the next morning, so we were taking the Mad River with us. She pulled the Subaru down to the dock where Ramsay and I hoisted the canoe up onto the top. Ramsay got out his ropes and began to tie the Mad River down. "Front and back," Jeanne said, watching him work. "That's good."

Ramsay nodded approvingly. Jeanne might be gay, but knowing the Peard way of tying a canoe onto a car got her big points with Ramsay.

Jeanne's house was a modest brick ranch in a quiet, resi-dential neighborhood overlooking the backside of the Mount Holyoke campus. Her partner, Carol Ann, or C.A. for short, was waiting to meet us. C.A. was holding a very cute baby. "This is Jacob," C.A. said, patting the little boy's blond hair into place.

"And how old is Jacob?" I said, gently shaking his tiny hand.

"Eight months," C.A. said. Jacob smiled, happy to meet me. I was happy to meet him, but curious to know where he'd come from. Had he been adopted?

Back in the mid-seventies when it became obvious Ruth and I weren't going to conceive a child, we'd looked into adop-tion. What we'd discovered was it was almost impossible to adopt a healthy, white, American-born baby. Thanks to the pill, *Roe v. Wade*, and the fact that single, liberated women were keeping their babies, the supply had pretty much dried up. At the same time, more and more women were break-ing into professions like law, medicine, and business and were waiting longer to have children. Not surprisingly, the infertility rate among these older professional women had begun to soar, which made the demand for healthy, white, American-born babies even greater while the supply was getting smaller.

By the time Ruth and I started looking into adoption, I was thirty-four and Ruth was thirty. The adoption agencies we visited wouldn't even put us on their lists. They told us it would take at least three years for our name to come up, and by that time, we'd be too old to adopt. Jeanne might have looked like a little tomboy, but on the drive to her house, she told us she'd just turned fifty. C.A., as it turned out, was forty-three. So how had these two middle-aged lesbians gotten Jacob? I was hoping to find out.

We had a couple of hours before dinner, and I wanted to send Mary Shanley-Koeber a note telling her that I'd read her proposal and it was a great project, but the foundation wanted us to focus its grants on little land trusts, so we wouldn't be able to help. Jeanne had a meeting for a summer rowing camp she was running and offered to walk me through the campus to town. As we walked, we talked, and in the course of our conversation, she mentioned that C.A. was still on maternity leave after having Jacob. That answered the question about adoption, but raised a new one, what about conception? I sure hoped we were having a lot of wine with dinner.

Ramsay and I were sleeping in a playroom just off the kitchen. We had our own bathroom, but it didn't have a shower, or even a door. For our stay, Jeanne and C.A. had rigged a curtain over the doorway, which was fine, provided nobody was in the kitchen. When I got back from town, Jeanne and Ramsay were sitting outside on the patio while C.A. was inside putting Jacob to bed. I asked Jeanne where I could shower, and she told me to use their bathroom. "It's in the back," she said. "If Jacob's toys are in the way, just move them."

At that moment, as if on cue, we could hear Jacob crying. "Ha," Ramsay said, "it sounds like Jacob doesn't want Bugsy messing with his toys. I don't blame him. I wouldn't want Bugsy messing with my stuff either."

Once Jacob was down, Jeanne and C.A. became noticeably more relaxed. After eight months of parenting, they seemed to relish the prospect of having a meal with just adults. They'd set the dining-room table and prepared a lemon-baked chicken with boiled new potatoes smothered with butter and parsley and a fresh green salad.

The lubricant for the evening was a bottle of Yellow Tail merlot from Australia. As we ate, we learned Jeanne and C.A. were both serious rowers. That's how they'd met ten years earlier, and rowing was still a big part of their lives, at least it had been before Jacob arrived. Jeanne and C.A. had competed in meets all over the country. "In 1996," C.A. said, "we were favored to win the doubles at the Master Nationals, but it was too windy and our race got blown out."

"You must be big fans of Title Nine," I said.

Title IX of the Education Amendments of 1972 is the legislation that forces any educational institution receiving any federal aid, and almost every educational institution receives some form of federal aid, to provide equal athletic opportunities for men and women. Since the law was enacted, women's athletics has undergone a complete transformation. When Ramsay and I were in college, the most visible women in sports were perky cheerleaders bouncing up and down on the sidelines of men's games. Today, thanks to Title IX, women are playing their own games in their own venues at skill levels quickly approaching those of men.

"Title Nine is good for women," Jeanne said, "but it hasn't been all that good for Mount Holyoke crew."

"How's that?" asked Ramsay.

"It's helped because it's gotten more women into sports, but it's hurt us because it's forced the coed schools to add more women's teams. Rowing's a relatively cheap sport that's easy to learn, so where Mount Holyoke used to have its pick of rowers, now we're up against a number of new and better-funded programs. In the battle for top students, reputation's no longer enough. Having top facilities is all part of the academic arms race. That's why we need a new rowing center."

"So Jeanne," Ramsay said, "how do your teams do?"

Jeanne's teams did fine, and listening to her war stories led to a broader discussion of college sports. We got into recruiting, training, and conditioning. We were surprised to learn how prevalent anorexia was not only in women's sports, but also in men's. Jeanne said she wouldn't allow a scale in the boathouse. "Women athletes still feel the societal pressure to look thin. I work them into good shape, but the last thing I want is for them to be worrying about their weight."

When the first Yellow Tail kicked, Jeanne popped open a second. As she refilled my glass, the gold band on her ring finger caught my eye. I was about to ask her if the band meant she and C.A. were married when I froze. It was obvious Jeanne and C.A. were comfortable with who they were, and if I wanted to know more about their relationship, its legality, and even Jacob's conception, they probably wouldn't mind talking about it. But I hesitated. Was it any of my business? We were having a good time. Why jeopardize it by going someplace I didn't belong. Still, this might be my only opportunity to have a meaningful discussion with a same-sex couple on something I knew nothing about. Digging deep for some courage, I took a big slug of merlot, but before I could say anything, Ramsay, sensing where I was headed, blurted out, "So how 'bout those Red Sox?"

That was it. We had a nice, comfortable evening talking about nice, comfortable subjects, but I couldn't shake the feeling that I'd missed my chance, probably my only chance, to get to know two very interesting people.

22

The Longest Day

Jeanne launched us at the put-in just below the Holyoke Dam. Unlike most of our strangers, there was no I-wish-I-were-going-with-you look in her eyes. The coach was used to pushing people into the river. She was gone before we got the Mad River pointed south. "Bugsy, start paddling," Ramsay said, turning the Mad River back to shore.

"Why?"

"I've got to use that Port-a-John."

Like the other power companies along the river, Holyoke Water Power did a superb job maintaining their recreational area at the base of the dam. Their Port-a-John was clean and tidy, and Ramsay took to it like a bear to honey. He came out puffing a Carlton and looking like a new man. "Bugsy," he said, climbing back into the Mad River, "these Port-a-Johns are neat. At home, Theresa won't let me smoke inside, but you can sit in one of those things and nobody cares."

There are seventeen dams on the Connecticut River. All the dams are degrading, but the one at Holyoke is the worst by far: dirty and disgusting, like a ball of hair clogging up a drain. Most of the river above the Holyoke Dam is rated

Class B, "somewhat swimmable, but never drinkable." By the time it oozes its way over Holyoke Dam, the water is downgraded to Class C, as in Crap.

Below the dam, we paddled through clumps of chemical foam that lay on the surface. Fish, hundreds of them, mostly shad, were floating dead upside down, their white, swollen bellies rotting in the sun. The smell alone was enough to make any paddler want to take a shower. Holyoke Dam had taken away whatever shred of decency the once mighty Connecticut had left. The river was now repulsive. Canoeing it was like driving through the Bronx, we couldn't wait to get out of there.

"You know," I said, surveying the mess around us, "when it's time to check out, I've been toying with the idea of calling Earth First! and telling them to wire me up and drop me off just above the Glen Canyon Dam. I figure I could swim out, hit the button, and blow the dam up with me. That was Ed Abby's dream, blowing up the Glen Canyon Dam."

"Sounds like a plan," Ramsay said.

"Yeah, but now I'm thinking, why go all the way to Arizona? Why not blow up the Holyoke Dam? Getting rid of this piece of crap would be a great legacy."

"You could do worse."

Saturday, June 21, was the longest day of the year. The farther we went, the more miserable it got. The weather had turned hot and muggy. We could feel the stench of dead fish clinging to us. When Ramsay pulled over for a smoke, he slipped and fell face-first in the mud. For a guy who spent fifteen minutes every day flossing his teeth, was so fussy about his clothes that he wouldn't let anybody do his laundry, and for sanitary reasons had cut his own hair for thirty years, it was a terrible fall from grace. In addition to smelling like a dead fish, he now looked like one.

Someplace between Holyoke and Springfield we passed the Chicopee River, the Connecticut's largest tributary, only with all the highways, run-down factories, steel and concrete bridges, antiquated sewer pipes, and mishmash of power lines, we never saw it. We did see a few yellow warblers flitting through the shrubs along the banks, but the constant hum from traffic crossing the bridges on Interstates 391, 90, and 91 droned out any warbles. Our only pleasant vista was Memorial Bridge, one of the two bridges connecting Springfield to West Springfield. Its seven spires had a refreshing touch of old-world charm.

Once we'd passed under Memorial Bridge, we saw Springfield's aborted attempt to embrace the river. In the late 1990s, Springfield had initiated a major riverfront redevelopment by turning the land between the east bank of the river and Interstate 91 into a park. The centerpiece of the park was a concrete amphitheater nestled next to the river. The pilings sticking out of the water revealed that at one time a dock for boats was next to the amphitheater, but the dock was long gone. "Bugsy," Ramsay said, guiding the Mad River towards the pilings, "go see if there's a men's room up there. I've got to get cleaned up. This smell is killing me."

I got out and started walking up the steps of the amphitheater. Urban graffiti covered each tier. At the top a paved path wound along the river. No one was on it. The only person I saw was a guy trying to push a lawnmower through the overgrown grass. The mower, overwhelmed by the grass, conked out as I came up to him. "Pardon me," I said. "Is there a men's room around here?"

"Naw," the guy said, mopping his brow, "nothin's open anymore. The place's gone to hell."

"That's a pretty small mower to be cutting all this grass," I said, looking at the little twenty-one-incher. "The city should get you one of those big riding jobs."

"The city's broke. It doesn't have money to buy anything. That's why the park's gone to hell, and this is my mower, not the city's."

"You don't work for the city?"

"Hell, no. I just hate seeing what's happening to the park so I figured the least I could do was cut the grass."

When I reported to Ramsay there was no men's room, he announced that he couldn't go any farther without a shower and some clean clothes. "But Ramsay," I protested, "it's only noon. We've gone less than eight miles. We can't quit now."

"Wanna bet?"

Now what? Our stranger for the evening was Mark Noonan, but Mark was not a real stranger. He was the head of the Winding River Land Trust in Westfield, Massachusetts, and a friend of Mark Zenick's, the head of the Franklin Land Trust. Noonan was one of the hardy, waterlogged conservationists who'd attended the ceremony at the Kucharski tract, and Zenick had urged him to put us up for a night. Zenick considered Noonan a bright young star of conservation and felt it would be good for him to spend some time with us. Ramsay had expressed strong reservation about spending the night with another tree hugger, but after meeting Noonan, a fun-loving Irishman with no wife or kids, he'd relented. "Mark's neat," he said. "He could be another Carl Demrow."

We'd agreed to meet Mark at Enfield Dam, about ten miles south of Springfield, around four o'clock. That gave us four hours to get there. Once past Springfield, the river flowed through woods and fields more like its natural self. If we could find a shady spot and rest for a while, maybe

Ramsay would rally. "Look, Ramsay, there's the West Spring-field town landing directly across the river. There's plenty of shade and maybe it won't smell so bad. Let's paddle over and take a break. Then if you still feel like quitting, I'll find a phone and call Mark."

Crossing the river, we passed through a flotilla of canoes frantically paddling upstream. "Hey," I yelled to one of them, "where you from, and what's going on?"

"The Pioneer Valley Yacht Club in Longmeadow. We're racing to Memorial Bridge and back." At least somebody was enjoying the river on this sunny Saturday afternoon. Between the smell, all the development, the continual noise of traffic, and the heat, we sure as hell weren't. I parked Ramsay down at a picnic table under a big cottonwood tree, and I walked up to a little one-story brick building set back from the river under some high-tension lines. The porch was strung with Christmas lights and a sign over the door read VALLEY BOAT AND FISHING: A SOCIAL CLUB. There was a skinny guy in a T-shirt sitting on the porch drinking a beer and smoking a cigarette. The T-shirt had MASSACHUSETTS TOBACCO CONTROL PROGRAM printed on the front and FREE ROLE MODEL FOR LIFE on the back. I asked him if there was a phone I could use, and he said, "Sure, right inside, and if you need a beer, we got that too."

Mark was surprised to hear from me. He said he was someplace in Connecticut, but thought he could be there in an hour or two. I bought a beer and asked the guy in the T-shirt if it would be okay if I sat on the porch. I figured sitting there would beat sitting with Ramsay who smelled like a dead fish and seemed happy to be left alone. "No problem," the skinny guy said, dusting off the seat next to him, "sitting here drinking a beer's a good way to beat the heat. I'm Dale, president of the club."

Dale seemed happy for my company, especially when I bought us each another beer, and told me the club had been built fifty years ago on land under the high-tension lines leased from the power company. It was easy to see why the power company had given the club a lease. The club and the West Springfield town ramp were located right next to the Bondi's Island Incinerator, a huge dump and waste water treatment facility. While the area around the club was neat and tidy and covered with bright green grass, the town landing was unkempt and littered with all kinds of trash. "The power company's lucky to have you," I said. "If the club wasn't here, their land would end up looking like the landing."

"Yeah, if the dump's closed when people come they don't want to lug their junk back home so they just throw it down here. If we catch 'em, we're tough on 'em so most people know not to mess with us, but West Springfield can't afford to have anybody patrolling the landing, so that's where they dump it."

"How big's the club?"

"We've got about a hundred members."

"Most of them fishermen?"

"Used to be, but not anymore. Thanks to the Holyoke Dam, in the summer you can wade across the river, and with all the crap from the treatment plant 'bout the only fish you catch these days are 'Bondi Island Brown Trout.' Now, we're just a social club, mostly for bikers."

After an hour of so chatting with Dale, I bought a beer and brought it to Ramsay. As we sat looking across the river, I mentioned it was too bad Springfield couldn't maintain its park. Unlike Windsor and Brattleboro, Springfield hadn't turned its back on the river, it just didn't have the money to capitalize on what should have been its greatest asset.

"Hell, Bugsy, money shouldn't be a problem. Look over there. The answer's staring you right in the face." Ramsay pointed to the south end of the park where the sun was shining on the Basketball Hall of Fame. "Between the NCAA and NBA, there's the money. The city of Springfield should figure out a way to make the park part of the Hall of Fame. Having a park as part of what they offer would be good for both the city and the Hall."

It made sense. Great parks help make great cities, and both the NCAA and the NBA had to be wishing that the Hall of Fame was in a great city. Right now, Springfield wasn't even a good city. It was bankrupt and on the brink of collapse. If the NBA and NCAA were to get behind the project, they could help the Hall and the city create a first-class riverfront park. Ramsay was right. The answer was staring us in the face. As with his analysis of credit cards, he'd hit another three-pointer.

By the time Mark Noonan showed up, we were more than ready to go. Spending a couple of hours next to the Bondi Island incinerator in ninety-degree heat was not our idea of a good time. We'd planned to throw the Mad River into the back of Mark's little Toyota Tacoma pickup but saw right away it would never fit. To get it in, Ramsay decided we'd have to tie the bow to the top of the cab and let the stern hang off the tailgate. At the mention of tying the bow onto his roof, Mark's normal Irish joviality suddenly evaporated. "It won't scratch my truck, will it? I just had it painted."

"Hell no," Ramsay said, opening his duffel. He fished out his two Styrofoam pads and attached them to the gunnels just behind the bow. "There," he said, satisfied with the placement. "You guys lift the bow onto the cab while I hoist the stern into the bed, and Bugsy, try not to scratch Mark's new paint job."

Once the Mad River was on the truck, Ramsay got out his ropes and began tying it down. If Mark had any opinion on whether side-to-side or front-and-back was better, he kept it to himself. With the canoe securely in place, a much-relieved Mark said, "There's a clambake I want to take you to, but it doesn't start for another couple of hours. In the meantime, is there anything you want to do?"

"I want to find a place where I can get out of these clothes and take a shower," Ramsay said. "Hell, I'll rent a motel room if we have to."

Mark assured him that would not be necessary, and off we went over Memorial Bridge, through downtown Springfield, and out into the suburbs. On the way, I asked Mark about Winding River Land Conservancy, the land trust he'd set up in 1998 to help protect the town of Westfield. He gave us the following summary. "Westfield's population has grown eighty percent since 1950. In 1978, there were seventy farms. Today, there are thirty-five. During that time, the town's issued an average of a hundred new single-family permits each year. Those new homes have chewed up over two thousand acres of farmland. What we're trying to do is save as much as we can of what's left."

Mark took us to the house where he'd grown up on the east side of Springfield. His mother, now a widow, lived there alone. Mark, who was forty and still a bachelor, was the youngest of Mrs. Noonan's eight children. Mrs. Noonan seemed pleased, but somewhat surprised, to see us. Mark introduced Ramsay and me as a couple of conservationists who were paddling down the river and asked if we could use a bathroom to get cleaned up. He sounded like a little boy who'd brought home a couple of stray cats and was asking his mother if he could keep them, but that was okay with us. We were a couple of strays, and we wanted to be kept.

Mrs. Noonan guessed it would be okay, but said she needed a few minutes to get some clean towels out and straighten things up. "Mrs. Noonan, you take all the time you want," Ramsay said.

When Ramsay came out of the bathroom, it was like a butterfly had emerged from its cocoon. The muddy, fishy, dour canoeist had morphed into a clean, fragrant, cheerful guest. Mrs. Noonan was so impressed she insisted we stay for tea and cookies. The more we chatted, the more we realized Mark was angling to get us an invitation for the night, but Mrs. Noonan wasn't biting. After tea, she politely showed us to the door. "So, Mark," I said, as we waved goodbye, "just where are we staying tonight, with you?"

"Well, that's a possibility," he said, "but I'm in the middle of a major renovation so I'm trying to find a place where you'd be more comfortable. I thought you'd be good company for my mother, but she felt unprepared because she hadn't made up the beds. I guess I should have told her you were coming."

"That would have been nice," I said, starting to question the wisdom of conservation's rising star.

Mark was taking us to something called the Great Clambake of 2003. According to the flyer Mark showed us, the idea behind it was to replicate the Great Clambake of 1915. At that time, the town of Hampden, Massachusetts, was in a state of social and economic decline. In an effort to save the community, a local farmer named Richard Stacy announced he was holding a clambake at his house "to unite the town in a day of food, fun, and festivities for all ages." Stacy's clambake had been a huge success and the town was saved.

The Great Clambake of 2003 was not being held to save the town, which was fine. Instead, the Hampden Land Project, a local land trust, was replicating Stacy's communal as a fund-raiser to save Minnechaug Mountain, a 166-acre local landmark. We were going because Deana, a friend of Mark's, was running the clambake. When she'd read in the *Springfield Republican* that we were paddling down the river making grants to local land trusts, she insisted Mark bring us.

The clambake was being held on a farm in Hampden, about ten miles east of the river on the Massachusetts-Connecticut line. As we got back into Mark's truck, I was sure Ramsay would want another clearing of the air, like the one we had when Ruth was driving us to the airport. I was in charge of making our plans for this night, and now it appeared I'd screwed up on two counts: First, we had no place to stay, and second, we were going to yet another conservation gathering. Much to my surprise, once we were in the cab all he said was, "Hot damn, Mark, let's go. I'm ready to party."

The party was in full swing. Most of the crowd were sitting at tables under a big tent, but a whole horde of kids and a fair number of adults were out in the field playing volleyball, having sack races, and lining up for a huge game of tug-of-war.

Mark's friend, Deana, was standing by the gate taking tickets. A thunderstorm had blown through earlier and

Deana was drenched from head to toe, which made her tight black dress even tighter, but the dress wasn't the only thing that caught our eyes. What really stopped us in our tracks was the ring of dark blue flames tattooed around her right bicep. Deana was hot. "Once I get you guys settled," Mark said, as we approached the gate, "I might not stick around, but when you're ready to leave, just call my cell phone and I'll come get you."

"Why wouldn't you stick around?" I said.

"It's complicated."

"We're used to complications," Ramsay said. "Try us."

"I used to date Deana, but now she's going with the guy who owns the farm. If he sees me here, he might think we're still seeing each other."

"Are you?" Ramsay said.

"No, but you know how it is, nobody likes having the old boyfriend hanging around."

"Oh, great," I said. "First you've got no place for us to stay, now you've got us in the middle of a love triangle. How about giving me the keys to the truck? That way, when you get shot, we can drive to a motel."

"Bugsy, back off," Ramsay said, enjoying this complication. "Watching Mark sneak around will be a hell of a lot more fun than talking to all these conservationists."

Seeing us, Deana came running over and gave Mark a big hug. "Mark, I was afraid you weren't coming." Then, turning to us, she said, "You must be Dave and Ramsay. Let me get you some food and introduce you to the people who run the land trust."

Deana got us each a lobster, an ear of corn, and a dish of potato salad, and placed us at a table with a bunch of people who were drinking plenty of wine and having fun. I was sure they were going to try and hit us up for a donation, but none of them ever mentioned money, or even the 166 acres they were trying to save. All of the five hundred people who had shown up for the Great Clambake of 2003 seemed to be there for just one reason: to have a good time. Even Ramsay was enjoying himself. That's when I realized the Hampden Land Project didn't need our money. They'd make their goal easy. They'd figured out the secret of fund-raising: make it fun.

Deana had put us next to Bill and Ruth Haley, an attractive middle-aged couple. Ramsay kept insisting Bill was the star of the rock group Bill Haley and his Comets, and the Haleys had kept pouring us wine. As the dinner was breaking up, Deana came over to us and said, "Mark told me you guys needed a place to stay tonight, and Bill and Ruth said they'd be delighted to have you stay with them."

"Hot damn," Ramsay said, "that's the best offer we'd had all day. Count us in."

The Haleys lived in an old New England farmhouse facing the town common. Once we were settled, Bill said he had one job to do while it was still light and was dreading it. "What's that?" Ramsay said.

"We're leaving for a family vacation in New Hampshire tomorrow. The bags, the dog, and a bunch of the kids are coming, so I bought one of those clamshells you strap onto the top of the car for the luggage, but for the love of me, I can't figure out how to put it on."

"Bill," I said, "this is your lucky day. When it comes to strapping things onto cars, Ramsay's the world's self-proclaimed expert."

Mounting the clamshell onto Bill's car was a job worth dreading. As the three of us stood in the driveway trying to make sense out of how screw A could possibly fit into clamp

B, which, according to Figure 3, somehow attached to bracket C, I was reminded of our aborted effort to fix Jeff Wheeler's lawnmower. We had absolutely no idea what we were doing. Where was Luke Eaton when we needed him?

Eventually, thanks to Ramsay's dogged persistence, we got to the point where we were reasonably sure the clamshell wouldn't blow off. Seeing we were done, Ruth said, "You boys look like you could use a drink, and I make a pretty good margarita."

By getting the clamshell safely secured to the top of Bill's car, I was sure we'd given as good as we got, but maybe not, Ruth made an exceptionally tasty margarita. After a couple, maybe more, we fell into bed feeling no pain. Thanks to the Haleys' outstanding hospitality, the longest day had ended in a pleasant glow.

23

Biocube

Sunday, June 22, started with a hard and steady rain that showed no sign of letting up. We hadn't heard anything from Mark, but that was okay. We were in no hurry to get back on the river. We were sitting in the Haleys' warm, dry kitchen drinking coffee when we heard a tapping on the back door. It was Mark. Lord only knows where he'd spent the night, but he was still in one piece and apparently there was nobody gunning for him. We thanked the Haleys for their kindness, wished them nothing but blue skies during their vacation, threw our duffels into the back of Mark's pickup, and headed off for the landing. "So, Mark," Ramsay said, once we were on our way, "you were pretty invisible at the clambake. Did Deana's boyfriend ever catch you sneaking around?"

"No, everything worked out fine. Did you guys have a good time?" He wasn't about to say anything that might incriminate him.

"Hot damn," Ramsay said, "we had a swell time, but you're crazy to give up on Deana. Except for that damn tattoo, Deana's neat."

That got a laugh from Mark. "Ramsay, that was a henna."

"A henna? What's a henna?"

"A fake tattoo. Deana just put it on for the party. It'll wear off in a few days."

"Man, that's really neat. It fooled the hell out of me."

Bob Glenn, Rachelle Colburn, and their eight-year-old son, Jake, were waiting for us at the Enfield state ramp, the first put-in in Connecticut. Bob and Rachelle were our strangers for the evening, but like Mark, they weren't real strangers. Before moving to Simsbury, Connecticut, they'd lived on the same street as Ramsay in Cincinnati. When they saw our press release, Rachelle had sent Whitty Sanford an e-mail that said, "We joined the witness protection program hoping to get away from Ramsay Peard, but now that he's found us, we would be willing to put him and his friend up for an evening."

When Ramsay called Rachelle to confirm we'd be staying with them, he'd invited Jake to ride with us for a day. Knowing our canoeing skills, I didn't think that was such a great idea, but Ramsay assured me Jake was a neat kid who'd do just fine. "Jake's my buddy," he said.

He might have been a neat kid, but as we got ready to push off, I could see Jake was having second thoughts. Ramsay's original invitation assumed it was going to be a nice sunny day and Jake could fish and do some paddling. Now with the rain and cold, there wasn't going to be any fishing or paddling. Rachelle, who must have sensed Jake was getting cold feet, said, "So, Jake, do you still want to go with Ramsay and Bugsy?"

"I guess so," Jake said, obviously not wanting to look like a wimp in front of his big buddy Ramsay.

"Jake, you might consider taking a rain check," Mark said, trying to give Jake an easy out. "You won't see much of the river today."

"No, I'll go."

"I'll tell you what," I said, consulting the *Guide*, "the Windsor Locks town ramp is the next takeout. It's only four miles downriver. Bob and Rachelle, why don't you meet us there in about an hour, and we'll see how Jake's doing. If he likes it, he can keep going. If not, he can get out, and you can pick us up later."

The minute the current caught us I knew we'd made a huge mistake. It was faster and stronger than anything we'd experienced so far. Although we hadn't seen Enfield Dam, according to the *Guide* it was breached in several spots and the stretch below it ran unusually fast. Today, with all the rain, it was ripping.

Kings Island, just below the landing, split the river in two. The east side looked shallow and fast, so Ramsay decided to cross over to the channel on the west, but that meant we had to get across the river before we were swept into the island.

"Paddle, Bugsy, paddle!" he yelled as soon as the current had us. It was like trying to get by French King Rock. Paddling sideways to the current is always tricky, but now, with Jake scrunched in between the duffels, we were out of balance. If I paddled too hard, we might tip over; if we were swept into the island, we definitely were going over. Either way, if we flipped, I knew I only had one job: grab Jake and get him to shore.

We didn't go over. Once again, the river gods saw fit to spare us and we squeaked by the tip of the island. When we were clear, Ramsay immediately turned the Mad River downriver. Going with the current improved our balance, but just to be sure, Ramsay said, "Jake, be sure to keep your weight right in the middle."

"Yes, sir," Jake said, and for the next four miles, he never moved. He also never complained, which was amazing considering he must have been cold, wet, and bored out of his mind. If I'd been Jake, I would have been complaining a lot.

Windsor Locks's town ramp was on the west side of the river just below the Interstate 91 bridge. Our first view of the river had come from that bridge driving north from the Hartford airport almost a month earlier. Now, going under it, I never thought I'd be so happy to hear the hum of an interstate. Poor Jake was drenched and shaking. I was afraid he might be getting hypothermia.

"Jake was great," we told Bob and Rachelle as they ran down to meet us, "but get him home and into a hot shower, immediately."

"What about you two?" Rachelle said.

Ramsay dug out the *Guide*. "We gotta keep going. We need to get closer to Hartford. See this takeout just below the Route 291 bridge?" he said, showing Bob and Rachelle the map. "We'll meet you there in three hours."

The *Guide* said this section of the river offered great fishing and good birding. Except for two wet eagles sitting in a tree looking as miserable as we were, we didn't see a thing. The rain kept pelting us and we kept paddling. We'd just passed the confluence of the Farmington River when Ramsay said, "Bugsy, it's starting to rain harder. We'd better stop while we can."

The South Windsor town landing was just ahead, but it was on the east side of the river. Bob and Rachelle had planned to meet us on the west side. If we pulled in at South Windsor, they'd have a tough time finding us. It was only two miles to the Route 291 bridge. The smart thing to do would have been to keep going, but I was more than ready to quit. "Hell, Ramsay, I don't care what you do just so long as you get me someplace where it's warm and dry."

He pointed the Mad River toward the South Windsor town ramp, and none too soon. By the time we got to the ramp, the rain was coming down in sheets. The landing reminded me of Bedell Bridge State Park up in North Haverhill, New Hampshire. The parking lot was empty, there was no public phone, and the only way out was a long dirt road leading off through some fields. We looked down the road hoping to see a van full of happy, helpful Mennonites coming to save us, but no such luck. "Bugsy, you watch the bags while I go find a phone," Ramsay said, and started walking.

The park surrounded the landing had no welcome center, picnic tables, or even a Port-a-John to provide any cover. A little kiosk housed a hand-painted map of the area. Under the map was a plaque that said the park was a project of the South Windsor Land Trust. Studying the map, I could see the land trust had protected a sizable stretch of river frontage. That was good. That's what local land trusts should be doing, protecting land along rivers and streams. Unfortunately, some idiot had pumped seven shots from a .22 into the back of the map. Due to the thick plastic covering the front, the bullets never made it through. Instead, they were mashed behind the plastic like seven mushrooms sprouting from the map. My first reaction was to make a grant to the South Windsor Land Trust for a new map, but the more I looked at the bullets, the more I realized it was better leaving them where they were. Having the bullets framed as part of the map turned the kiosk into a piece of pop art that made a statement. For me, the message was, "We have to keep working to protect nature from the morons who are too stupid to respect it."

Water has a unique way of finding its way through any crack, crease, or crevice. The kiosk wasn't quite big enough for both me and the map, and no matter how I buttoned, zipped, or tied my poncho, the rain kept seeping down my neck, under my shirt, and into my pants. I was cold, wet, and very, very tired. Like a horse, I fell asleep standing up.

"Hey, Bugsy, wake up." It was Ramsay. He looked wet and tired and was a muddy mess.

"What the hell happened to you?" I said.

"Two guys in a pickup came down the road, but when I tried to flag them down they sped up and when they passed, they hit a puddle, and sprayed fuckin' mud all over me."

More likely, they saw Ramsay standing in the rain in the middle of nowhere and figured he was some nut like Drago, the mass murderer who'd killed Vicki Bunnell, but I didn't say that. "Did you get hold of Bob and Rachelle?"

"Yeah, they're on their way." Ramsay took off his boonie hat and wiped at the mud. "Damn it, look at this crap."

Bob, Rachelle, and Jake lived fifteen miles west of the river in a center-hall colonial set on a nicely wooded lot just outside Simsbury, Connecticut. Strangely, they had hardly any furniture, like they were still moving in. According to Ramsay, Bob and Rachelle were a couple of Texans who'd left home to pursue their careers. In Cincinnati, Rachelle was a registered architect, and Bob, who had a Ph.D. in mechanical engineering, had been a rapid automation consultant for a company called Robotica. When two of his colleagues left

Robotica to form their own company, Bob went with them. Their plan was to design and build robots for drug companies and since Pfizer, the world's largest drug company, was located in Connecticut that's where they decided to set up shop. As yet, it wasn't clear whether the new company was going to be successful.

When Ramsay and I came downstairs after taking long, hot showers and changing into dry clothes, Bob, who designed the software that ran the robots, said he had to go to the office and check on a program he was running. I'd never seen a robot at work so I asked him if I could come along. In yet another sudden shift in the weather, the day had miraculously turned sunny and warm. It had gotten so nice, Ramsay, Rachelle, and Jake decided to come with us. Bob's company, Protedyne, was located near the Hartford airport. As we entered a low, rambling, red brick office building typical of industrial parks built in the seventies and eighties, Ramsay noted that Protedyne was the first new manufacturing venture we'd seen on the entire river. Bob wasn't surprised. He told us Protedyne had looked at a number of similar buildings vacated by companies that had moved their manufacturing offshore.

Connected to the office building was a corrugated metal manufacturing facility the size of a commercial airplane hangar. Sitting all by itself in the middle of the concrete floor was Biocube, Protedyne's first robot. I'd expected Biocube to look like R2D2; instead it resembled a popcorn machine. While Bob and Jake went back into the control room to check on his program, Ramsay, Rachelle, and I walked across the empty floor to get a better look at Biocube. Up close, it was no popcorn machine. Behind its sealed glass sides, Biocube's mechanical arms were clicking away, moving stacks of trays filled with hundreds of test tubes through a series of different positions: up and down, side to side, over and over. Having a robot that could perform these functions obviously would be a great asset. If medical researchers had to do these same tasks by hand, it would take countless hours.

"Bob," Ramsay said, when Bob and Jake rejoined us, "what does one of these things go for?"

"We're thinking somewhere around $750,000."

"Have you sold any?"

"We're not quite ready to start marketing. We've been focused on raising more venture capital. We just got an additional twelve million. Hopefully, that'll buy us enough time to get our sales going."

Starting a new business, especially one that requires a lot of research and development, is a major gamble. Every time you have to go back to the market for more capital, you have to give up more equity. That was Protedyne's problem. With thirty to thirty-five employees, it could burn through $12 million in a matter of months, and if they hadn't started selling the robots by that time, Bob and his partners would have to go back to the market for another round of venture capital, which meant they'd have to give up even more equity. It was no wonder Bob was working on Sunday.

As if reading our minds, Bob told us that he and most everyone else at Protedyne had deferred taking a salary. That meant the Glenn-Colburns were living off their savings, which would explain why they had no furniture. These Texans had bet the ranch on Protedyne. To hell with chairs, they'd rather sit on their options.

Dinner was grilled steak and potatoes prepared especially for Ramsay. While we ate, Rachelle, Bob, and Jake pumped him for news of the old neighborhood. That got Ramsay going on about a fight he was having with his next-door neighbors, a young couple who were undertaking a major renovation of their house. Listening to Ramsay, it sounded to me like he'd been pretty tolerant. He'd never complained about the constant noise from the construction. He'd even given permission for the big crane needed to hoist the new joists into place to use his driveway. When the crane's stabilizers punched holes in his macadam, Ramsay told the neighbors not to worry about it, they could just patch the holes rather than redo he whole driveway. Then, as if to add insult to injury, the young couple installed a big bay window in their new dining room that looked right down onto Ramsay's deck, but even that didn't seem to upset Ramsay. What got him all pissed off was when the woman used his washing machine.

During one phase of the construction, the builders had to turn off the neighbor's water for a couple of days. The woman, having no water, came over and asked Ramsay if she could do laundry. Ramsay said that would be fine, but noted there was a small leak in his washing machine and she should keep an eye on it. After the women left, Ramsay went to do a load of wash and discovered water on the floor. "I still can't believe it," he grumped. "You borrow somebody's washer, you'd clean up when you're through."

"Maybe she didn't notice it," said Rachelle, who apparently kept in touch with this neighbor and might have heard the other side of the story.

Ramsay would hear none of it. To him, the woman had clearly stepped over the line. "You're supposed to notice. You don't leave water on someone's floor."

"Ramsay, I've got the perfect solution for you," I said. "You should put a Port-a-John on your deck. Then when the neighbors are having a dinner party, you can go out for a smoke. I can't think of anything more unappetizing than looking out the big bay window at you in your Port-a-John."

The only one who liked this suggestion was Jake. The more he thought about it, the harder he laughed. Ramsay was right. Jake was a neat kid.

24

JUNE 23
WEST SIMSBURY, CONNECTICUT

Thank You, Joe Marfuggi

Bob drove us to the South Windsor town ramp the next morning. At last, it looked like we were in for a totally sunny day. Ramsay had seen on the Weather Channel that we'd been paddling through the wettest June on record. Hartford already had received ten inches of rain, which beat the old record of 9.78 set in 1903, and June still had a week to go. One car was parked at the landing. As Bob pulled in next to it, a guy about our age hopped out and said, "You Ramsay and Dave?"

"That's us," I said, wondering who he could be.

"I'm Jim Woodworth, president of the Great Meadows Conservation Trust. I was hoping you might join me for lunch."

The Great Meadows Conservation Trust? That was one of the groups that had submitted a project for our consideration. I'd planned to meet with them once we got below Hartford, but how had this guy ever found us up here? "Jim," I said, totally confused, "how did you know we'd be here? We didn't even know we'd be here."

"I called Hal Buckingham. He told me you were staying with him tonight, so I figured you had to be someplace north of Hartford. I just kept checking each of the landings until I saw a canoe with a Connecticut River Watershed Council sticker on the side."

"Well, in that case we'd be happy to have lunch with you."

It seemed inconceivable anybody would go to all that trouble to track us down, but since Jim had, I couldn't say no.

"Good, I'll have one of our members waiting for you at the town landing in Wethersfield Cove, just below Hartford. Once you get there, he'll call me, and I'll make us up some bacon, lettuce, and tomato sandwiches. Would that be okay?"

"Don't forget the beer," Ramsay said.

"Any special kind?"

"Whatever you like, just so long as it's cold."

Having made it through the slime of Springfield and then a day of solid rain, we were feeling pretty good. Even the river was feeling more like its old self. The banks were wooded, the water was clear, and the two eagles we'd seen huddled in a tree the day before were circling high above us. The river looked a lot like the section from Sumner Falls to Windsor, Vermont, which was still our favorite.

The primary reason the river seemed rejuvenated was simple: no more dams. From Enfield to Long Island Sound, the Connecticut was its own master. Whatever power it could muster, it kept. This sense of entitlement had given it back some of its virility. The smell, the globs of chemical foam, and the dead fish all were gone. Rivers can't survive unless they're constantly moving. That's how they breathe. Flowing free had given the Connecticut a chance to take a deep breath and clean out its lungs.

We eased around a long, lazy bend and a railroad bridge came into view. Beyond it, framed in the trestles, was the city of Hartford. As with Springfield, Interstate 91 cuts the downtown off from the Connecticut, so I was expecting Hartford's waterfront to resemble Springfield's. The first hint that things might be different was a young woman rowing a scull upstream. Unlike Krazy Kate, who darted around the river like a waterbug, this girl's long, easy stroke was keeping the scull perfectly in line. The closer we got to the city, the more sculls and kayaks were coursing the river. Cruising among them were several sailboats, the first we'd seen. The hub of all this activity was a brand new boathouse nestled in the midst of a neatly wooded park right at the foot of downtown. "Ramsay," I said, "pull in here. I want to take a look at this place."

It was time for a smoke, so Ramsay headed the Mad River to the dock. While he lit up, I got out and walked up to the boathouse. It was an impressive structure. The lower level was in fact a boathouse, but above it the building blossomed into a beautiful community center with posh locker rooms, a well-appointed library, a state-of-the-art kitchen, offices, and a generous common area that opened up onto a spacious deck overlooking the river. A crew was in the process of breaking down tables and chairs in the common area. Wilting bouquets sat on some of the tables, the fading memories of a wedding reception. The father of the bride had gotten his money's worth. With all the rain, being in the comfy confines of the boathouse sure beat sitting under a soggy tent.

Bronze plaques on the walls acknowledged major donors. The community room had been made possible by a grant from Lincoln Financial Group; the entryway was courtesy of the Mass Mutual; the big barn doors leading into the boathouse itself were a gift of the Stanley & Elsie Roth Charitable Trust and the 2002 Jaycees of Greater Hartford. These plaques proved how much the financial and charitable leaders of Hartford were committed to making the river an important part of the city. Having them so deeply involved guaranteed the boathouse would be meticulously maintained and set the standard for the rest of the waterfront.

From the deck overlooking the river, I could see their investment was paying off. The grass in the park was freshly mowed, the pathways neatly raked, the trash cans emptied. Set into the bank of the river just down from the boathouse was an amphitheater much like Springfield's, but Hartford's was first-class. Each terrace was covered with a rust-colored stone rather than bare cement and the tiers were free of graffiti. To the east across the river, I saw another park, a boat launch, more walking and biking trails, and stylish new condominiums. Unlike poor Springfield, Hartford was looking at prosperity, not a huge incinerator and waste treatment plant.

The head of the cleaning crew came out onto the deck. "Excuse me," I said, "you wouldn't happen to know who's responsible for all these parks? Is it Hartford's Department of Parks and Recreation?"

"Naw, they're all projects of a nonprofit called Riverfront Recapture. A guy named Joe Marfuggi runs it. Joe's been at it for twenty years. He's got a plan for the whole waterfront. Now he's talking about turning the old Colt firearms complex into some kind of mixed-use development."

That came as no surprise. Behind every great project is some bulldog who just won't take no for an answer. While everyone else thinks they're crazy, these people keep pushing ahead, making calls, twisting arms, going to meetings until finally even the biggest naysayers become true believers. Joe Marfuggi had to be one of those people. His vision had taken hold; Hartford's waterfront was becoming an integral part of the community and was pulling the entire city up with it.

What Springfield needed was a Joe Marfuggi, someone who saw the benefits of putting the Basketball Hall of Fame and the city's park together and wouldn't take no for an answer.

Back in the canoe, I lifted my head to look up at the Charter Oak Bridge, the last of the four bridges crossing the river at Hartford. Beads of sweat dripped from my chin. The temperature had climbed well into the nineties. It was hard to imagine we'd been cold just twenty-four hours earlier. Mark Twain, who'd lived in Hartford for twenty years, had been right. If you don't like New England's weather, just wait a minute and it'll change.

About two miles below Charter Oak Bridge, we found the narrow channel leading to Wethersfield Cove, the place where we'd agreed to have lunch with Jim Woodworth. The channel ran for about a quarter-mile through dense bottomland forest. Just before reaching the cove, we passed under I-91. I stopped paddling and listened to the steady hum of traffic passing directly overhead. Due to the heavy undergrowth, none of those drivers would ever guess we were there. "Keep paddling," Ramsay said, "a cold beer and bacon, lettuce, and tomato sandwich will taste good, even if it means listening to more talk about conservation."

The cove itself was a hidden Eden: quiet, green, and serene. It was tough to believe we were just two miles south of the state's capital. A paved parking lot was to our left. On this quiet Monday we saw only two cars. "Jim's guy must be in one of those cars," I said. "He's probably got the AC on."

"Hell, Bugsy, we're not eating in some damn parking lot. Look at the heat coming off of that pavement. We're going over there." Ramsay pointed the Mad River across the cove toward a small clubhouse with shady trees and a dock.

The sign at the end of the dock said, WETHERSFIELD COVE YACHT CLUB: MEMBERS ONLY. A guy was working on a boat in one of the slips. Otherwise, the place seemed deserted. "Is it okay if we tie up here for a couple of minutes?" Ramsay said, pulling into the slip next to him. "We're meeting somebody here."

"Okay by me," he said, not bothering to look up.

"Is there a phone up there?" Ramsay said.

"Yeah, right under the porch."

We tied the Mad River to the dock and walked up to the clubhouse. I called Jim and told him where we were. "The Wethersfield Cove Yacht Club? How'd you get there? Phil Lohman's waiting for you at the landing. You must have gone right by him."

"Why don't you and Phil meet us here," I said. "There's nobody around, and it's too hot at the landing."

Jim didn't sound comfortable with the thought of sneaking into the yacht club, but he knew the first rule of fundraising: the donor is always right. He said not to move, he and Phil would be there just as soon as he finished cooking the bacon.

There was a picnic table next to the phone so we settled down in the shade under the porch. Before long, Jim and Phil showed up with a cooler full of Sam Adams beer, Gatorade, BLTs, and homemade cookies. While we drank and ate, Jim and Phil told us about the Great Meadows Conservation Trust (GMCT). For the last thirty years, this little all-volunteer organization had been pecking away trying to protect the Great Meadows, a 4,500-acre area of rich bottomlands that ran along the river through the towns of Wethersfield, Glastonbury, and Rocky Hill. To date, the trust had saved thirty-three separate tracts, totaling 130 acres, which wasn't much, but that was about to change. The study for the new Silvio Conte National Fish and Wildlife Refuge had listed the Great Meadows as an area of special concern, which meant land bought for conservation within this area would be eligible for federal funding.

Before we could get deep into a discussion on conservation, Ramsay got up and said we were meeting Hal Buckingham at the Rocky Hill landing, and if we were going to be on time, we had to leave now. "Here, you'd better take this with you." Jim said, handing me the cooler. "You're going to be paddling through the Great Meadows and it's going to be hot. There's no more beer, but you'll want those Gatorades."

"But Jim," I said, "what about the cooler? How can we get it back to you?"

"Oh, I'll meet you down at Rocky Hill. That way I can show you the Meadows."

The Great Meadows is formed by three big bends in the river. By car, the distance from Wethersfield Cove to the Rocky Hill landing is about five miles. By canoe, it's a good eight. We didn't need those three extra long, hot, lazy river miles. To make matters worse, Ramsay had fallen back into his old habit of leaving the current to cut the corners. On the first bend, we ran aground. "You know," he said, as I was pulling us free, "this Gatorade is pretty good stuff. I'm actually feeling a kick."

"Well, keep drinking it. You're going to need a kick, we've got a long way to go."

Coming out of the final bend, we saw a young woman with a kayak sitting on a lonely stretch of beach. Ramsay turned the Mad River into shore. "Bugsy," he said, "let's go chat up that girl."

A nervous look came across the woman's face when she realized we were making a beeline right toward her. Disregarding the usual river etiquette, Ramsay guided the Mad River right up next to her kayak. "How you doing?" I said, in my most reassuring voice.

"Fine," she said, eyeing Ramsay's hat, sunglasses, and little girlie vest. I got out, pulled the Mad River up on shore, and waited for Ramsay to start chatting her up, but he didn't. Instead, he got out, walked twenty yards down the beach, sat on a log, and lit up a Carlton, leaving me standing there looking like an idiot. "Is your friend okay?" the woman said.

"Yeah, but the heat's gotten to him. We're paddling the entire river, and I think he's about run out of steam."

This explanation seemed to satisfy her. She told me she'd just taken up kayaking and was toying with the idea of paddling the entire river once she became more proficient. I told her about Chuck and Bob and the Flamingo Kids and how kayaks seemed like the best way to go. Hearing that re-energized her. She got back into her kayak and set off to do another five miles. "Go easy," I said, pointing to Ramsay, "you don't want to end up like him."

Once she was gone, Ramsay came back. "What the hell happened to you?" I said.

"What do you mean?"

"You said you wanted to chat up that girl, then you walk away leaving me standing there like an idiot."

"Bugsy, you did fine. Let's go."

Ramsay got in the canoe and I pushed us off. Maybe it was the heat, maybe it was all the talk about conservation, maybe we'd been together too long, or maybe, like I'd told the girl, he'd just run out of steam. Whatever the reason, Ramsay was becoming noticeably more aloof, morose, and unpredictable.

On the bright side, we only had forty miles to go. Squeak, Squeak, Squeak.

Hal and Joyce Buckingham, our hosts for the evening, were no strangers. I knew them from Kezar Lake in Maine, where they also had a camp. Hal and Joyce were active in conservation, so when Dan Lufkin committed $50,000 to help fund projects we found, I called Hal and asked if he knew of any local trusts that were trying to save land along the river. Hal told me he and Joyce belonged to the Great Meadows Conservation Trust and that GMCT always had a project going in the Meadows. "When you and your friend get here," he said, "I'll fix you up with Jim Woodworth, the president. And plan on spending the night with us."

Hal and Jim were waiting for us when we pulled into Rocky Hill. Once we'd chained the Mad River to a tree of Ramsay's choosing, we sat down at a picnic table and Jim got out a map of the Meadows. On the map he'd marked the thirty-three parcels GMCT owned. Most of them were little tracts of less than five acres. Jim then told us GMCT had just received a bequest of $48,000 from Eleanor Buck Wolfe, one of the founders of GMCT, to acquire additional land within the Meadows. "Do you guys have any ideas on the best way we can use this gift?" he said.

"Just one," I said. "Use it to start a project-revolving fund. That way, you can keep rolling the money over."

"How so?"

"Easy, GMLT borrows the money from the project revolving fund to buy the land, and then starts a fund-raising campaign for each project to get the money back. In essence, you're borrowing from yourself, but this way you're constantly raising new money for new projects, which in turn will keep getting you new members, all of whom would have a direct relationship with a particular piece of land. That's how we built The Nature Conservancy, and with the feds making matching grants for land acquisitions within the Meadows, you've got an even better opportunity. Half of your fund-raising is already done. In fact, here's what we'll do: If you use this bequest to create the Eleanor Buck Wolfe Project Revolving Fund, I'll ask the foundation we're working with to make GMLT a five-thousand-dollar matching grant. That would get you off to a strong start."

Jim liked it and was sure his board would approve it. "Come on," he said, rolling up his map, "I'll take you on a tour of the Meadows."

We'd had our fill of the Meadows. Now we were hot, tired, and ready for a drink. "Jim," I said, "let me tell you something. Fundraising's like robbing a bank. Once you get the money, run. There's nothing more you can say that'll help you, so go home and relax."

The Buckinghams fit our profile of perfect hosts. Their kids were grown and on their own, but Hal and Joyce still maintained their rooms waiting for them to come back with grandchildren. We had the upstairs of their spacious colonial all to ourselves. I was in their son Bucky's room, while Ramsay was in one of their daughter's. After a wonderful dinner of pot roast, mashed potatoes, and garden-fresh vegetables, we adjourned to the family room where I spotted a picture of Hal and Joyce standing with a bunch of other people around a fancy new car in the middle of a baseball field. It was night and the bright lights from the field were shining off the car. Some guy in a coat and tie was in the middle of the group holding a microphone. Everyone looked very happy. In the background, I recognized the Green Monster. "Hal, what are you and Joyce doing standing in the middle of Fenway Park?"

"Oh, that was the night I won the car."

"You won a car? That's unbelievable. You're the second person we've met on this trip who's won a car. How'd you do it?"

"I didn't do anything. I was standing up during the seventh-inning stretch, when they drove this car onto the field and the announcer said whoever was in the lucky seat would win it. He read the section, the row, and the seat, and the next thing I knew, an usher had me by the arm telling me he'd take us down to the field after the game for the presentation."

"How much did you have to pay in taxes?" Ramsay asked.

"Too much. My son-in-law had taken us to the game so I figured since he'd bought the ticket, the car was really his. Plus, with the kids, they needed a bigger car, so I paid the taxes and gave it to them. Then Joyce said if I gave a car to one daughter, I had to do the same for the other, so I had to go buy her a new car." Hal stopped and shook his head. "That game turned out to be a very expensive evening."

"Well," I said, "get to the important part. Did the Sox win?"

"I can't remember," Hal said, then looked at his watch, "but tonight's game is just starting. You guys want to watch a few innings?"

"Sure, that'd be great."

Hal punched the remote and there were the Sox live from Fenway Park playing the Tigers. As we sat back to enjoy the game, Hal said, "Oh, by the way, before I forget, Steve Grant from the *Hartford Courant* called. He wants to do a story on your trip."

Ramsay immediately perked up. "I talked to Steve when I was planning our trip," he said. "Steve did the river in June of 1991. He couldn't believe we were going to be staying with different people every night."

"Well, I told him you'd meet him at the Rocky Hill landing at ten tomorrow morning. Is that alright?"

"Hot damn, you bet it's all right. We've got plenty of stories for Steve."

At that moment, Joyce came in carrying a tray of desserts. "Hal," she said seeing the game, "not baseball again. It's so boring. I thought we agreed you weren't going to watch any more baseball."

"But dear, the boys are big Red Sox fans. They haven't seen a game in nearly a month. They just want to watch a few innings."

First it had been Pete Richardson with his scrambled eggs, then Charlie Cunningham with his ice cream. Now, Hal Buckingham was using us as an excuse to watch the Red Sox. Theresa and Ruth had better watch out. Rookies like Ramsay and me could learn a lot from old pros like Pete, Charlie, and Hal.

25

JUNE 24
GLASTONBURY, CONNECTICUT

Ramsay the Donor

On our way to the river the next morning, Ramsay asked Hal if we could stop at a convenience store for his beer and butts. The day promised to be another scorcher, but our interview with Steve Grant had Ramsay in high spirits. Remarkably, when he came out Ramsay wasn't carrying a six-pack of Bud Light. Instead, he had three quarts of Gatorade: one lemon and lime, one orange, and one fruit punch. "Gatorade?" I said. "What happened to Bud Light?"

"This stuff's better. It gives me a second wind. In fact, I can't wait to try it on my golfing buddies. Having a beer at the turn's been my big mistake. From now on, I'm having Gatorade. I'm betting it'll take four strokes off my game."

"You think so?"

"I know so, and here, I got you one." He handed me the bottle of fruit punch. If nothing else, Ramsay had made two potentially life-changing discoveries during this trip, Port-a-Johns and Gatorade.

As we pulled out of the store, Hal said he had a surprise for us. Instead of going back over the Route 3 bridge, we were going to cross the river on the nation's oldest continuously operating ferry. The ferry had been running between the towns of Rocky Hill and Glastonbury since 1655, and according to a historical marker at the landing, "motive power for the ferry has been supplied at various times by poles, oars, a horse treadmill, and a steam engine."

Power these days came from a diesel engine tucked into the bowels of "Cumberland," a little black tugboat with bright red trim. Capable of holding three to four cars, Cumberland charged $1 for a car and driver, and $.25 for each additional passenger. We offered to pay, but Hal, ever the gracious host, would hear none of it. He handed the captain $1.50, and off we went. The trip took four minutes, just long enough for me to ask the Captain which way the tide was running. "Been coming in all morning," he said, "but it's getting ready to turn."

"Over the next three days we'll be paddling down to the Sound. What do you think; will it be running with us or against us?"

"Depends on what time of day you're paddling, but hang on and we can figure it out." The Captain ducked into the cabin and came out with a computer printout titled, DAILY TIDE AND CURRENT PREDICTIONS—ROCKY HILL—JUNE 23, 2003. "Look at this," he said, tracing his finger over a sinuous curve plotting the ebbs and flows of the tide for a twenty-four-hour period, "I'd say if you're on the river from late morning to late afternoon, you'll be fine." He handed me the printout. "Here, keep it. Just add fifty-four minutes each day."

Steve Grant was an old pro. About our age, he'd seen it all, which was why his interview style lacked Bonnie Obremski's youthful enthusiasm. It wasn't until Ramsay mentioned we'd first conceived the trip twenty years earlier while clinging to a rock in the middle of the Saco River that Steve perked up. "The Saco," he said. "My wife and I used to canoe the Saco. That was back in the seventies before we had kids, and it seemed like we had all the time in the world. We'd float along, drink beer, and swim off the sandy beaches. Those were wonderful times."

"Hell, Steve," Ramsay said, "you don't have to tell us. That's what we do every day."

"Well," Steve said, rising to Ramsay's bait, "what was the worst part of your trip?"

"From the Holyoke Dam through Springfield," I said.

"I remember that stretch from my trip in '91. It was almost dark, and I was wondering where I could camp without getting mugged when a pontoon boat packed with people drinking and having a good time came cruising by. The guy driving recognized me from my articles and invited me aboard. When his wife asked where I was staying, I told her I hadn't found a place so she invited me to their house. It turned out they were from Agawam and lived right on the river. The next thing I knew, my tent was set up on their front lawn and I was eating steak for dinner. It was the best night I had the whole trip."

"Just another day at the office for us," Ramsay said.

"Well, you guys might have had it easy so far, but wait until you hit the tide. If you think the winds up north were bad, let me tell you, the tide will kill you. It was running against me the whole way from here to the Sound. For a while there, I wasn't sure I was going to make it."

"Here, look at this," I said, handing Steve the computer printout the captain had given me. "The guy running the ferry said we might be all right."

Steve studied the printout, tracing his index finger over the tide's sinuous curve. "Damn," he said, "I don't believe it. The tide's going to be with you the whole way. You won't have to paddle a stroke if you don't want to."

"Steve," Ramsay said, "we'll probably have to do some paddling to get to Fenwick Island. That's where our host for the last night lives. He said he'd come get us in his thirty-two-foot cabin cruiser if we got tired, but we don't want to bother him, especially since he's throwing us a big party. You should come, and bring your wife. Katharine Hepburn's going to be there."

When Hal pushed us off, he wasn't saying goodbye. He and Joyce had agreed to pick us up later and take us to a party the Middlesex Land Trust was throwing for us. After consulting the *Guide*, we decided Hurd State Park, seventeen miles downriver from Rocky Hill, would be the best place to meet. That was a long way for us, but Ramsay was on a high after our interview with Steve and thanks to his new drink of choice, Gatorade, he was sure we could make it.

We'd hardly gone a mile when Ramsay started to fall back into his funk. He was gulping Gatorade like a Florida fullback, but was becoming more and more irritable with every stroke. When I mentioned the ferry ride had been fun, he grumped that the ferry was a "waste of taxpayers' money. Why should the state be subsidizing a ferry that serves no purpose and loses money?"

"Tradition?" I ventured. "It's been operating since 1655. Somebody must like it."

"They wouldn't like it if they had to pay what it actually costs to run the damn thing."

"You know, Ramsay, not everything has to make money. Some things are worth the expense just because they make our lives more enjoyable. Those nuts who keep harping on how the national parks should pay for themselves are missing the point. The Pentagon doesn't pay for itself, why should the national parks? One's for our national security, the other's for our national serenity. That's why we pay taxes."

From that point we paddled in silence. I wasn't squeaking mad, I was just too hot to argue with Ramsay. As we passed under the bridge at Middletown, we saw a combination clock/thermometer flashing from one of the downtown buildings. The clock read 12:38, the temperature said 98 degrees. Thanks to the tide, we were making good time, but the heat was taking its toll. There was a main dock running along the waterfront of Middletown, so I told Ramsay to pull over. "I need a break."

Middletown, like Hartford and Springfield, had embraced the river by turning its waterfront into a park. Of the three, Middletown's appeared to be the nicest. There were a number of reasons for that. First and foremost was Middletown didn't have an interstate highway separating its park from the downtown area. Next was the fact that due to the tides, the river was being flushed twice a day, which made it noticeably cleaner. Then, Middletown was a college town, not a big city, so instead of facing an incinerator, waste treatment plant, or even some new condos, Middletown's park looked across the river to the Wesleyan boat house. Finally, the park had an attractive, user-friendly focal point, the America's Cup restaurant.

The restaurant, located just above the main dock, was an upscale establishment. A young yupped-up crowd filled most of the tables on the deck overlooking the river, but it was too hot for us to eat outside. "You want to go inside where it's air-conditioned and grab some lunch?" I asked Ramsay.

"No way I'm going in that place." Like Lou's in Hanover, America's Cup was too upscale for Ramsay. "You go ahead if you want. I'll wait for you out in the park."

There was no way I was going to eat by myself, but I did go in to use the restroom. When I came out, I found Ramsay sitting under a tree having a smoke. He looked terrible. His face was beet red and sweat from his gray T-shirt had soaked through his little girlie vest. I wondered if he was going to make it, so in my most upbeat Major Robert Rogers' voice I said, "Ramsay, come on, get up, we've got to keep going. Your buddy Bill Webster's probably on Fenwick Island right now planning our party with Katharine Hepburn. Hell, we've got to make our meeting with the 'Woman of the Year.'"

For the next eight miles, the tide did most of the work. At Hurd Park, we pulled into a little beach next to some picnic tables, but were surprised to find the park empty. "Bugsy, what the hell's going on? It's a hundred degrees and there's no one here. You'd think this place would be crawling with people?"

"Beats me, maybe we're not in the main part of the park. Watch the bags, I'll go see what I can find out."

I headed down a path that ran next to the river. It connected with a dirt road that wound up to the top of a ridge. I was looking at the road wondering if I had the energy to climb it when an old geezer with a walking stick came hiking out of the woods. I asked him how to get to the headquarters, and he told me to forget about it, the park was closed due to budget cuts. Wouldn't you know it: When things get tight, parks are always one of the first things cut.

"Closed? Well, you can still drive in, right?"

"Hell no. They've locked the main gate. If you want to get in, you have to hike."

"How far's that?"

"Once you get to the top of that ridge, about a mile and a half."

"A mile and a half! You've got to be kidding me." What were we going to do? Even Major Rogers would have a tough time getting his Rangers to walk a mile and half with their bags in this heat. How were Ramsay and I ever going to make it?

I was watching the old geezer peck his way up the ridge wondering what I was going to tell Ramsay when a group of Hispanics came walking up the path. The men were carrying fishing poles. One of them was lugging a big, beautiful striped bass. "Nice fish," I said, hoping he spoke English. "You going to carry it all the way back to the gate?"

"No, we were lucky. Some guy showed us a way to drive in through the woods."

"Say, is there any chance you can give my buddy and me a ride out? We're paddling down the river and we told some people to meet us here, but we didn't know the park was closed."

"We've got two cars. I guess we can squeeze you in."

I sprinted back up the path. "Quick, Ramsay, the park's closed, but I found us a ride to the main gate. Let's chain the Mad River to one of these tables and get the hell out of here."

We were breathing hard by the time we made it to the parking lot at the top of the ridge. I got into one car, Ramsay got into the other. We were so crowded one of the women was practically sitting on my lap. "You know," I said, making small talk, "a good way to cook that fish would be to cut it into steaks and put them on a grill. You could spice them up with some bacon, onions, tomatoes, peppers."

"I'm pregnant. I can't eat fish from the river. Too much mercury."

Of course, she was right. Try as it might, there was no way the river could have purged itself of all the crap we'd seen below Holyoke Dam. If that beautiful fish was in the Connecticut, it had to have chemicals in it. Every species needs two things to exist: clean air and clean water, but as a society we'd rather waste billions ditching, diking, damming, and channelizing our rivers rather than just cleaning them up. How sick is that?

The party the Middlesex Land Trust was throwing for us was being held in a little pavilion overlooking the river at Middletown's River Park. Kätchen Coley, our stranger for the evening, was the first to arrive. Kätchen drove up in a brand new Prius, like the one Chuck Levin had won in the Greenfield Energy Park raffle. Ramsay's notes on Kätchen read, "a delightful older lady," but that description didn't start to do justice to Kätchen. It soon became clear she was the grande dame of conservation in Middletown.

The party was another potluck supper. Before long, the table in the pavilion was groaning under casseroles, pasta salads, cheeses, bratwurst, burgers (regular and veggie), chips, and an endless assortment of dips. The guests were typical conservationists: white, well-educated, inconspicuously affluent, and earnest. Since we were in a public park, there was no keg of beer, but there was plenty of wine, served discreetly from coolers. It promised to be a pleasant evening.

When we'd last checked in with Whitty Sanford, she'd told us Middlesex Land Trust had a project they were hoping we'd help fund. We had $5,000 left from our $50,000 grant, and since Dan Lufkin was from Connecticut and had been the state's director of natural resources, I wanted to make sure we supported at least two projects in the Nutmeg State; the Great Meadows was one, Middlesex Land Trust would be the other.

After we'd eaten and talked with most everybody, Diane Moore and Jane Brawerman, two members of the land trust's board, took me aside. They wanted to discuss a project they were working on. Knowing Ramsay had no interest, I told them to go ahead. Diane and Jane said Middlesex Land Trust was an all-volunteer organization that currently owned and managed forty-five parcels of land totaling 525 acres. That was just what I was hoping to hear. Then they said the project they were working on was a forty-acre parcel they were buying in partnership with The Nature Conservancy. That was just what I didn't want to hear. Like Mary Shanley-Koeber of the Arcadia Wildlife Sanctuary, Diane and Jane made a strong case for the project, but as with Arcadia and Mass Audubon, there was no way we were going to give our last Dumbo's feather to The Nature Conservancy. It was the highest-flying conservation organization in the world.

I was about to wreck the whole evening by saying "no" when to my surprise, Ramsay interrupted. "Bugsy," he said, "can I talk with you for a minute?"

We excused ourselves and walked to the bluff overlooking the river. "What's the matter?" I said.

"We've got to give some money to these people."

"What?" I was amazed that Ramsay was showing interest in anything having to do with conservation. "Why?"

"'Cause Katherine's neat, that's why."

While I'd been talking to Diane and Jane, Ramsay had been entertaining Hal and Joyce Buckingham and some of the younger members of the Middlesex Land Trust with our tales of the river. One of those younger members was Katherine Winslow, a very comely conservationist. As a donor, Ramsay was of the school that believed grants are made to people, not projects, and in this case, he's picked Katherine.

"Well, Katherine might be neat," I said, "but the project they're proposing stinks. It's one of these deals where The Nature Conservancy is using them to help fund-raise for a project, and I'm not making a grant to The Nature Conservancy. Hell, they can raise their own money."

"Bugsy, there's four hundred miles of river. Just tell Middlesex to find another project, but make sure Katherine gets a grant."

With that, Ramsay walked back to the party, but he was right. There was no problem. I'd just tell Diane and Jane they had the grant, but they had to come up with a different project, one that Middlesex could do on their own.

Kätchen Coley's house sat in the bottom of a ravine on the outskirts of Middletown. Frank Lloyd Wright might have designed it. Like Falling Waters it complimented all the natural aspects of the site. Kätchen pulled her Prius into a garage at the edge of the ravine. From there, we crossed a catwalk to the top floor of the house. Inside, each room opened onto a corridor overlooking a center atrium that ran down all four flights to the forest floor below.

Once we were settled, Kätchen opened a bottle of wine and we went out onto a porch at eye level with the canopy. Since technically we were outside, Ramsay asked Kätchen if he could smoke. Kätchen said that was fine, but not on this porch. If he wanted to smoke, he had to go to the porch on the bottom floor. That's where she let Rick, a graduate student who rented a room from her, smoke. "You'll find Rick's ashtray, and you might find Rick. You know, Ramsay, smoking is a disgusting habit. You really should give it up."

Ramsay shrugged off this unsolicited and unappreciated advice. Grandes dames are notorious for being outspoken, that's what makes them grande. Besides, Ramsay had other things on his mind. Tonight he was calling Bill Webster to tell him he wouldn't have to come get us in his thirty-two-foot cabin cruiser; that we'd be paddling into Fenwick Island in two days, and were especially looking forward to meeting Katharine Hepburn at his big party. It was the call Ramsay had been waiting to make the whole trip.

We were enjoying our second bottle when Ramsay came back visibly distraught. His call to Bill Webster had not gone well. Webster wasn't on Fenwick Island planning our party. According to his son, he was off playing in a golf tournament and wouldn't be back for three days. The son knew nothing about our party. We were not going to meet Katharine Hepburn.

I tried to tell Ramsay not to worry, somebody would come along and save us, but it did no good. Bill Webster's big party was to have been the high point of our trip. In Ramsay's dream, fireworks would light up the evening sky as we paddled into a beach where a huge crowd led by Katharine Hepburn was eagerly waiting to meet us. Now, his dream was dead. Both of his tens, John Harrigan and Bill Webster, had turned into zeros. Ramsay excused himself and went to floss his teeth.

26

JUNE 25
MIDDLETOWN, CONNECTICUT

Saved Again

Diane Moore called the first thing the next morning to say she had a new proposal and asked if we could stop by her office at the Department of Tourism in Middletown to pick it up. "In fact, Katherine Winslow's here and we'd be happy to drive you back to Hurd Park," Diane said. "With the park closed, Kätchen's Prius wouldn't be able to get around the gate, but I've got a Ford Explorer with four-wheel drive."

No fool, that Diane. She must have figured having Katherine there would put any proposal in a favorable light. It did, but in fact, the new proposal was perfect. Middlesex Land Trust was going to team up with another little nonprofit, Meshomasic Hiking Club, and start buying odd parcels of land that would link properties already owned by the land trust to the 10,000-plus acre Meshomasic State Forest. One of the ways they planned on matching the foundation's $5,000 grant was by using the deposits on empty bottles and cans. With the parks shut down due to budgetary constraints, Meshomasic Hiking Club had taken on the task of cleaning up trash in the parks. Talk about a grassroots effort. What could be more hands-on than volunteers matching the foundation's $5,000 grant by picking up bottles and cans?

A stack of postcards sat on a table by the door of the tourist center. The card showed an old wooden rowboat sitting on the beach at Lynde Point in Old Saybrook, right where the Connecticut met the Sound. A sign on the table next to the cards read TAKE ONE.

"Diane," I said, "could we have a handful of these cards? We'd like to send one to everybody who put us up and let them know we made it."

"Take as many as you want, that's what they're there for."

Once we had gotten around the gate into Hurd Park and driven to the parking lot, Diane and Katherine insisted on walking us down to the river. Being young and spry, they offered to carry our duffels, but we'd have let our arms fall off before that happened. We might have been old and creaky, but we weren't totally testosteroneless.

Both Katherine and Diane had that I-wish-I-was-going-with-you look in their eyes when they pushed us out into the river. Just before the current caught us, Ramsay said, "We've got room if you want to jump in."

I was proud of the boy. It was a bold, last-ditch effort to salvage what was left of his trip, and for a moment, they looked tempted, but in the end, Diane and Katherine showed they were real pros. They had their grant and were ready to run.

We were spending the night with Richard and Karen Conniff. Ramsay's notes on Richard said, "very nice guy, if we need something just give him a call; journalist." When Ramsay called Richard told him that while they would be happy to have us, both he and Karen had meetings that night and suggested we might want to find someone else. Ramsay had the names of several other people, but after the Bill Webster setback there was no wind left in his sails, so he didn't bother to call anybody else.

There was no way Ramsay could rationally blame Bill Webster for missing us. Ramsay's card on Bill clearly read "wants us on the 3rd." Bill had planned on making our arrival part of his annual Fourth of July party, which, according to friends in Essex, was a very coveted invitation, in part because Katharine Hepburn often did attend. Missing Bill's party was just bad luck. As Ramsay told Bill when they first talked, we had no idea when we were getting there or even if we'd make it at all. So, we were a week early. That was just the luck of the draw, but as we headed downriver, Ramsay became increasingly sullen and withdrawn.

We were meeting Richard at the Deep River town landing. Of all the town landings we'd seen during the trip, Deep River's was the nicest. It had a sandy little beach where we could stash the Mad River, a boat ramp, picnic tables, a gazebo, a nice grassy lawn, and most important, a public phone. While Ramsay called Richard, I stretched out on one of the picnic tables and immediately fell asleep.

The blast from a steam whistle woke me up. There, gliding up to the dock next to the landing, was a steam-powered paddle wheeler. It had no sooner landed than a new and different blast announced the arrival of a steam-powered locomotive. It came chugging right in next to the dock. Waking up to the paddle wheeler on one side and the steam locomotive on the other was like being Rip Van Winkle in reverse. Here I'd gone to sleep in the twenty-first century and woken up in the nineteenth.

"Ramsay, what's happening?"

"Beats me." He pulled out the *Guide*. It said the paddle wheeler and the train were part of a tour run by the Valley Railroad Company. The people on the boat had boarded at the Goodspeed Opera House in East Haddam and paddled down to Deep River. Now, they were going to climb aboard the train and ride back upriver. Sure enough, a wave of tourists started pouring down the gangplank of the paddle wheeler and began climbing up the steps of the old Pullman cars onto the train.

As they were loading, an engineer in bib overalls with a gray-and-white striped engineer's cap and a red bandanna around his neck emerged from the cab carrying a big copper oilcan. He began lubricating the joints of the engine. His efforts weren't just for show. Both the paddle wheeler and the train were the real things. Once the Pullman cars were full, a conductor, looking very hot in his old-time woolen cap and blue serge uniform with shiny brass buttons, pulled out a big gold watch, checked the time, and yelled, "All aboard."

The engineer stopped oiling and climbed back into the cab. He turned the throttle and a white puff of smoke billowed from the stack. It was followed by another, and another, and another. Metal grated on metal as the wheels grabbed the tracks, and with a clank of couplings the train slowly pulled out of the station. As they went by, smiling passengers leaned out the windows and gave us big waves. They all seemed to be enjoying their old-time tour of the Connecticut.

Richard Conniff, his wife, Karen, and their three children, Jamie, Ben, and Claire, lived across the river in Old Lyme. As we were leaving the landing, Richard pointed to an old stone house overlooking the river. "That's where we used to live," he said.

Richard sounded nostalgic, so I asked him, "Do you miss it?"

"It's different. I liked living by the landing. We were there for fifteen years, and the kids grew up on the river, but we're happy in Old Lyme."

Once we got there, it was easy to see why. The Conniffs' new house was open, airy, and looked out over a marsh to the Sound. As Richard had told Ramsay, both he and Karen had meetings that night and couldn't have dinner with us. Richard was on the board of Old Lyme's conservation trust and Karen was a member of the board of education. Before they ran out the door, Richard popped open a very nice bottle of white wine for us, and Karen showed us a pasta salad in the refrigerator.

Jamie, who'd just finished his sophomore year at Yale; Ben, who had just finished his senior year at Old Lyme High and was going to Yale; and Claire, who'd just finished the eighth grade, proved to be excellent hosts. While Claire set a table out on the deck for dinner, Jamie and Ben asked if we'd like to go for a walk. Ramsay said he was going to sit out on the deck and have a smoke, but I told them I'd very much like to take a walk.

Jamie and Ben were tall, smart, good-looking kids, who were easy to be around. Their home was part of a relatively new subdivision consisting of twenty-five wooded lots scattered over what must have been about a hundred acres. Most of the homes looked expensive, but not outrageous. When we did pass a new McMansion under construction, Jamie and Ben didn't seem too thrilled. They weren't enthused about some of their other neighbors either. They pointed to a swath that ran through the woods over what was supposed to be common land. According to them, this "alley" had been cut illegally by the owner of one of the back lots so he could have a better view of the Sound.

We continued down a road that ended at the beach. When I wanted to walk along the shore, they told me we could only go as far as some rocks in front of the house a hundred yards away. "Why's that?" I said.

"We can't get over the rocks. The owner doesn't want people walking along the beach in front of his house so he's cemented pieces of broken glass into the rocks."

"What? You've got to be kidding. Those rocks are below mean high water. He can't restrict public access along the beach. I'll tell you what, if I lived here, I'd get a hammer and pulverize that glass. If the guy didn't like it, I'd tell him to take the shards and shove 'em where the sun doesn't shine."

Big talk from a guy who didn't live there.

We were back on the deck enjoying our pasta salad and wine when a loud roar rattled our fillings. "What the hell is that?" I said.

"A cigarette boat," Ben said, not bothering to look up. "They're out there all the time."

Out there was the Sound. As the roar move repeatedly up and down the shoreline, we had a new winner for the "Most Obnoxious Sound of the Trip." The "Beep-Beep-Beep" of the OSHA-mandated backup signals on heavy machinery and the "Rhee-Rhee-Rhee" of Jet-Skis sounded like choir practice compared to the high-pitched roar of a cigarette boat. To generate speeds that often exceed 100 mph and can go as high as 185 mph, cigarette boats are equipped with huge engines that total two, three, four, and even five thousand horsepower. Engines that size are unbearably loud, but since mufflers restrict power, cigarette boat owners don't use them. They don't care whom they annoy. In fact, annoying people has to be part of the boat's allure. Guys who drive these gas-guzzling behemoths—and they're all guys—are crying for attention.

After dinner, Ramsay and I wrote a postcard to everyone who'd put us up. We said the same thing on each card. "Success!! Thanks to the kindness of strangers, we made it. Your friends, Ramsay and Dave." Doing the cards gave Ramsay a lift. He liked remembering all the people we'd met and the situations we'd gotten into, especially on the upper part of the river. Dinner with the Eatons, being saved by the kids at the Northumberland Dam, meeting Krazy Kate, the view from Riverview Farm. As we worked our way down the list, he kept telling me how he couldn't believe all these people had been so nice to us. When we got to Mark Noonan and the possible love triangle, Ramsay actually laughed out loud. "Hot damn, Bugsy, I'm going to get me one of those henna tattoos."

After Ramsay had signed the Conniffs' card, he said, "You know, I haven't made any plans for tomorrow night. I don't know where we're going to stay."

"Don't worry," I told him, "if worse comes to worst, we can check into the Griswold Inn in Essex. That would make a nice last night. We could have a good meal, and just relax."

"No inns, Bugsy. That would wreck the whole trip. We have to stay with a stranger."

"Well, somebody will show up. They always have. Who knows, maybe Katharine Hepburn will call and ask if we'd like to spend the night with her."

At that moment, Richard came back from his meeting of the conservation trust. When I asked him how it had gone, he said, "Evan Griswold was there. He told me to give you his best, and said if you need a place to stay tomorrow night, he and Emily would be happy to have you."

Evan Griswold had been head of The Nature Conservancy's Connecticut chapter back in the eighties. His roots in Connecticut went back to 1645 when one Matthew Griswold received a land grant from Lord Fenwick consisting of all the property around what is now Old Lyme. The crown jewel of that land was a mile-long peninsula at the end of the river facing the Sound. That peninsula became known as Griswold Point and was still owned by the Griswold family.

Evan and his wife, Emily Fisher, lived on the Point. Forget Fenwick Island. Anyone looking for a place to spend their last night couldn't have asked for a better spot than Griswold Point. Once again, we'd been saved.

27

The View from Griswold Point

We awoke to good news. The front page of the style section of the *Hartford Courant* featured an article entitled "Down a Lazy River" by Steve Grant. Steve had treated us kindly. During the interview, Steve had been somewhat dismissive of our trip. In the article, he sounded almost envious. Steve couldn't get over the fact that we showered, shaved, and put on clean clothes every day. He summed up our idea of roughing it by quoting Ramsay. "We only paddle from 9 to 3. We don't want to miss the cocktail hour."

Ramsay should have been recharged by Steve's article, but he wasn't. He hardly said a word during our breakfast out on the porch with Richard. As it turned out, Richard was a lot more than the "journalist" Ramsay had labeled him in his notes. In fact, Richard had written a number of books and was a regular contributor to major magazines like *Smithsonian, Atlantic Monthly, Time, National Geographic,* and the *New York Times Magazine.*

Richard's new book, *The Ape in the Corner Office,* was about how humans could do better in business if they observed how other species negotiated the tricky balance between conflict and cooperation. "For instance," Richard explained, as he drove back to the Deep River town landing, "the stereotypical Darwinian hard-charger thinks only about accumulating resources, but highly successful apes know it's often smarter to give some things away. Doing favors, sharing food, grooming coworkers with hot gossip are tools for getting ahead that come straight from the natural world."

This unique theory of how to succeed in business should have piqued Ramsay's interest, but it didn't. It wasn't until we were back on the river and passed an old geezer about our age in a rowboat that he perked up. Spying us, the geezer said, "Hey, you're the two guys in the article. Pull over, I've got a story for you."

No matter how dark his mood, Ramsay could not ignore the recognition. He steered the Mad River into a little beach next to a big field. The rowboat came in right behind us. The geezer introduced himself as Dave Warner. Dave said he was sixty-four and claimed to have lived on the water all his life. His great-grandfather had sold fish, produce, and dried meat from the family homestead during the 1850s. "That's it right over there," Dave said, directing our attention to an attractive colonial across the river. "We sold it in the late forties for sixty-three thousand. Now, it's worth two million. Can you believe it? I swear, the growth of people's money has outgrown the growth of their brains."

That was enough for Ramsay. He walked out into the field and lit up a Carlton, leaving me alone to talk with Dave. Dave was a living encyclopedia on this part of the river and we had a good talk, but Ramsay should have stayed, at least for a couple of stories. Walking away was just plain rude.

It was hot and sunny, we had less than ten miles to go, and the tide was pulling us along. We were in no hurry. It should have been a perfect day. My plan was to stop in Essex, a yupped-up, Martha'd-out little town just six miles from the Sound. I had friends who'd lived in Essex, and I knew the town well. The main street ran up from the river and was dotted with small shops and historic homes. They'd be fun to browse and the Griswold Inn was just up from the public landing. A couple of dark ales and a sandwich at the inn's cozy, wood-paneled tap room would be the ideal lunch. Then we could mosey down Main Street to the Connecticut River Museum, which was located on the water right next to the town dock. The museum was where "Source to Seaers" traditionally checked in, and I was interested to find out when Tom and Chuck and the Flamingo Kids had made it. I was sure the Flamingo Kids had left us a note.

I never found out. When Essex came into sight, Ramsay steered us to the opposite side of the river. "Hey, what are you doing?" I said. "Aren't we going to stop in Essex? I want to have lunch and check in at the museum."

"Naw, it's too hot to eat. Plus, I don't want to go over that stretch of open water. There's too much boat traffic."

Now I was boiling. Essex was located along the west side of the river on a peninsula formed by two coves. The open stretch of water Ramsay didn't want to go over was the opening of the North Cove. It was less than a quarter of a mile across, and the boat traffic he was so worried about was nothing more than a few sailboats from the local yacht club. In fact, crossing the cove was less risky than staying in the main channel where we could easily be swamped by the wake from a barge or cigarette boat.

I could feel the canoe shrinking. According to Ramsay's foot-a-day theory, since leaving Vernon Dam the Mad River was now down to six feet and that wasn't long enough for me to put up with any more of this bullshit. The sooner this trip was over, the better. Squeak! Squeak! Squeak!

Evan Griswold's directions were to pull off the Connecticut into Back River, which would be on our left about a mile above the Sound. We were ready to get off the river. Below the Interstate 95 bridge, it had become wide and choppy. Navigating this last stretch was no game for small boats. If we tipped over here, there'd be nobody to save us.

Back River wasn't a river, merely a braid of the Connecticut that ran along the backside of a large marsh known as Great Island. Paddling through the marsh not only was safer than paddling out in the river, it was a lot more interesting. Red-winged black birds flittered through the reeds, great blue herons and snowy egrets fed in the shallows, but by far, the most impressive sight were the osprey. The Department of Natural Resources had placed dozens of platforms on poles throughout the marsh, and an active nest perched on almost every one. The big birds were everywhere, their high-pitched cries a welcome change from the distant drone of traffic crossing the I-95 bridge.

We found Evan's dock and landed. After we got out, we shook hands and Ramsay said, "Well, we made it. Not bad for two coots in a canoe."

"After our ride on the Saco, I can't believe we went four hundred miles without tipping over. That is truly amazing."

We unloaded our bags for the last time and walked up to the house. Evan had left a note on the door: "Make yourselves at home. Be back around 4." It was only two, so while we were waiting, I went inside and called Chris Joyell. Chris was CRWC's steward for the lower part of the river. We'd met him at the Middlesex Land Trust's party, and Chris had impressed me as a smart, down-to-earth young guy who was willing to make material sacrifices to be able to work in conservation. In short, I liked Chris. He wasn't one of these kids who was looking to "do well by doing good." He was happy just doing good. I told him we'd made it, and asked if he could come pick up the Mad River. Chris's office was just across the river in Old Saybrook. He said he'd be right over.

Ramsay declined to go with us to load up the Mad River. Chris, like Earl Bunnell, had a bar over the back of his pickup for holding canoes so Ramsay must have figured his expertise wasn't needed. Or more likely, he no longer cared. He seemed content sitting on the Griswold's deck puffing on a Carlton looking out over the Sound. I couldn't blame him. From the Griswold's deck, you could see all the way to Orient Point, the tip of Long Island. It was the perfect place to sit and reflect on our trip, if Ramsay was reflecting, but being Ramsay, he might have been thinking about doing his laundry.

Once we had the Mad River loaded and strapped down, Chris said, "Well, I guess that's it."

"I guess it is," I said, looking at the goofy caricature of Paul Hamilton on the "Paul's Special Apple Juice" decal Nancy Hamilton had given us at Riverview Farm. By now, I'd expected the Mad River to be covered with decals, like a motor home that had driven across the country, but except for "Paul's Special Apple Juice" and the "I ❤ the Connecticut River" sticker we'd gotten from CRWC, we hadn't seen any. Were window stickers, like fax machines, becoming a thing of the past?

"You want a ride back to the house?" Chris asked.

"Nah, I'll walk. I need the exercise."

"Well, have a good one."

It felt strange watching the Mad River go off without us. It had proven you don't need a fancy canoe to paddle a major river. Having a simple second actually made our trip more enjoyable. We never had to worry about dragging the Mad River over rocks, throwing it on top of a car, or chaining it to a tree. Even my fear of having it stolen wasn't a big deal. If it was, what did we lose? We could have replaced the Mad River for a couple of hundred bucks. There was a good lesson to be learned here: love your equipment, but never let it get in the way of a good time.

Back at Griswold's, Ramsay was still sitting on the deck puffing away. His fair, freckled face was beet red from the heat. He looked exhausted. "While we were getting the canoe," I said, "I saw a trail that winds around the point. I think I'll go for a run."

He nodded at a round thermometer attached to the side of the house, "Bugsy, in case you haven't noticed, it just hit a hundred."

"Good, maybe I can sweat off a few pounds. You want to come?"

Ramsay's look said it all. He wasn't coming.

The trail was a swath mown along the bluff through fields of waving grass that covered the Point. The views were spectacular. The lush, verdant marshes around Great Island laced with a maze of interlocking blue channels; South Cove and Fenwick Island almost hidden in the haze across the mile-wide mouth of the river; Breakwater Lighthouse and Saybrook Beacon rising from the haze to mark the shipping channel; and finally the Sound itself, its sparkling surface stretching all the way to the thin gray line of Long Island.

I stopped to catch my breath at the tip of the point. While watching the Connecticut spill into the Sound, an osprey flew by with a fish in its talons. I wondered if the fish was loaded with mercury and instead of dinner, the osprey was carrying its death warrant. On the surface, our rivers and streams may look beautiful, but nearly forty percent of them are too polluted for fishing, to say nothing of drinking.

One of the great fears of Homeland Security is that terrorists will contaminate our water supply. If clean, potable water is so important to our homeland security, why aren't we aggressively cleaning up our rivers? All Congress has to do is to enact a law that would make it illegal to dump any untreated waste—human, industrial, or agricultural—into a river, but Congress won't do that. As Ramsay reminded me when I was lying on the rock just south of Bellows Falls, cleaning up our rivers is not a national priority. As a society we're too complacent, too shortsighted, too greedy, too arrogant, and too stupid to see what we're doing to ourselves. Forget the terrorists. In the words of Pogo, the possum sage of Okefenokee Swamp, "We've met the enemy, and they are us."

When I got back to the house, Evan Griswold was sitting on the deck talking to Ramsay. He said he and Emily had a long-standing dinner engagement and wouldn't be able to wine us and dine us, but they would try to get home early so we could catch up on old Conservancy doings and hear about our trip.

There was a grill on the deck, so Ramsay told Evan if he could take us to the store, we'd get steak for dinner and cook it right there. I seconded that idea. Steak on the deck would be good and going to town would give me a chance to mail the cards we'd written to all our hosts. Evan drove us to a shopping center with a post office in Old Saybrook. As we got out of the car, I said, "I don't want a big steak. Keep it light. I've got to start dropping some weight."

The line at the post office was long and slow. As it inched forward, I ran through the names on the cards. Counting Claire Porter, we'd spent twenty-seven nights with different strangers. What struck me was how close I felt to every one of them, like I could knock on any door and they'd be glad to see me.

When I finally got to the window, I asked the postmaster if he could hand stamp each of the cards so the postmark would read Old Saybrook. That postmark would be the official confirmation that we'd made it. Outside, I saw a liquor store. Just inside the door stood a big display of Yellow Tail, the Australian wine Jeanne Friedman and C.A. had served us. The 1.5-liter bottles were on sale for $10.95. I grabbed a merlot thinking it would go good with our steaks and be a fine way to celebrate the successful completion of our trip.

After Evan and Emily had left for their dinner, Ramsay fired up the grill. As we watched the coals heat up, I popped open the Yellowtail and poured us each a glass. While we toasted our success, Ramsay showed little enthusiasm. Looking across the river to Fenwick Island was tough for him. He hadn't counted on spending our last night alone. He pictured us celebrating at Bill Webster's big party with Katharine Hepburn.

When the coals were ready, Ramsay went into the kitchen and came back with one steak. "We sharing that?" I said.

"I thought you said you didn't want any."

"I said I didn't want a big steak, but a small one would have been nice."

"I guess I misunderstood."

That said, Ramsay plopped his steak on the grill, but made no mention of sharing it. I grabbed the Yellow Tail and went back into the house while he stayed out on the deck with his steak. That was how Evan and Emily found us when they got home. Me inside drinking my merlot, Ramsay outside having a smoke, savoring the aftertaste of his steak. For the next hour, the four of us talked about our trip. Ramsay was still subdued, like his mind was somewhere else. I did most of the talking. When Evan asked if we'd learned anything new, I said I'd learned *monadnock* was not just the name of a mountain in southern New Hampshire, but applied to any hill or mountain that stood alone. "That's interesting," Evan said. "At dinner tonight I learned the word *meander* comes from the name of a river in Turkey."

By then, the Yellow Tail was gone, and I was seeing double. With no lunch and no dinner, I'd been drinking on an empty stomach. It was time for me to meander to bed.

28

JUNE 27
OLD SAYBROOK, CONNECTICUT

R.I.P. Katharine Hepburn

My train left before Ramsay's. I was taking the 9:16 Amtrak from Old Saybrook south to Newark; Ramsay was on the 9:31 north to Boston. I was going to catch a train from Newark to the Jersey Shore where Ruth was staying with her father. Ramsay was going to take a bus from Boston to New Hampshire where Theresa was at the camp they had rented.

Evan dropped us off at the Old Saybrook station just before nine. As we stood on the southbound platform waiting for my train, we didn't say much. I was still sore about Ramsay not stopping at Essex for lunch. And not offering me any of his steak. I thanked him for organizing the trip. He thanked me for coming along. "You know," he said, "this has been my greatest adventure. Do you think you can get a book out of it?"

"I don't know. I'll have to think about it. It would have been nice if we'd gotten to meet Katharine Hepburn. That would have made for a great ending."

"Maybe next time."

"Yeah, maybe next time."

But there wouldn't be a next time. Two days later, on June 29, death kept its appointment with Katharine Hepburn. Four months later, death unexpectedly met with Ramsay. It came by his own hand.

Epilogue

JUST TAKING UP SPACE

It was November 3 and I was working on this book when the phone rang. It was Ramsay's daughter, Kim. She said her father had an accident, then said, "Actually, it wasn't an accident. A state trooper just came to my door and told me they'd found him dead in his car in Bedford, the town next to us. The trooper said he'd committed suicide, that he'd shot himself in the head."

According to the trooper, Ramsay had left no suicide note. Instead, on the seat next to him, they'd found a hand-printed to-do list. The trooper said they'd never seen anything like it. On the list Ramsay had detailed everything everybody, including the police, was supposed to do to wrap up his life. Kim said Ramsay had designated me to write his obituary, and asked if I'd do it. I said I would.

Ramsay had called Ruth and me in Maine three weeks after we'd finished our trip. He and Theresa were getting ready to leave the camp they rented in New Hampshire and head back to Cincinnati. Before they left, Ramsay wanted to drive over and see us. Ruth suggested they come for lunch. I wasn't so sure. I didn't know if I was ready to see Ramsay. I was still mad about the way he'd acted at the end of the trip, but I'd been working on my notes and figured this would be a good time to get his input.

Ramsay was on a high when he arrived. As soon as we were settled on the porch, the same porch where we'd hatched the idea of canoeing the Connecticut twenty years earlier, Ramsay told Ruth and me how he'd bought a fake tattoo like the one Mark Noonan's friend, Deana, had been wearing at the clambake and completely fooled Theresa.

"I couldn't believe it." Theresa said, still amazed. "I hadn't seen Ramsay for over a month, and here he shows up with this roping chain tattooed around his arm. I thought he'd lost his mind. He didn't tell me it was a fake until it started to wear off two days later."

Ramsay almost fell out of his chair he was laughing so hard. He was as happy as I'd ever seen him. "Bugsy, I've got our next trip all planned," he said, regaining his composure. "We're going fishing for stripers off of Long Island in October."

"Not with me you're not," I said. "I'm mentally and physically exhausted."

"Bugsy, you can't be serious."

"I'm dead serious. Remember that tick I got lying in the grass behind the post office in Orford? I think it gave me Lyme disease."

"You been tested?"

"Not yet, I'm going next week."

Not going fishing took some of the wind out of Ramsay, but he was still on a high. In recounting our adventures, he showed the same enthusiasm he'd had on the upper part of the river. On and on he went, all the while specifying everything I had to put in the book. When he got to Bill Webster, Ramsay said, "Be sure to say when Webster told Katharine Hepburn she wouldn't be meeting us, she died of a broken heart."

Theresa and Ramsay stayed for the better part of the

afternoon. As they were leaving, Ramsay asked me again if I wanted to go fishing for stripers off of Long Island in October. "Get one of your golfing buddies," I told him, "and call me in another twenty years."

The following day Ramsay called to thank Ruth for lunch, and to make sure I got tested for Lyme disease. (I did, and the test was negative. The doctor concluded the reason I felt so crummy was because that's how an old geezer should feel after paddling four hundred miles.) Ramsay also said he'd decided a postcard wasn't enough; he wanted to send a letter to each of our hosts telling them how much we appreciated their kindness. I said that was a great idea and to go right ahead.

Ramsay checked in a couple of more times to see how I was coming with the book. When he called towards the end of October, I told him I hoped to have a preliminary proposal done by Thanksgiving and would like him to go over it. "By the way, did you find anybody to go fishing with you?"

"No," he said, "I gave up on that idea."

About a week later the phone rang. Ramsay said not to send the proposal to his house; he'd just dissolved his marriage to Theresa and was moving to an apartment. I told him he was nuts. "Ramsay, you're too old to be living alone, and you're never going to find anyone to live with you, at least anyone as nice as Theresa. Go back and tell her it was a joke, like the henna tattoo, and pray she takes you back."

"No, it's over. I was going to do it back in December, but when you said you'd canoe the Connecticut with me, I decided to wait. Aren't you proud of me for not mentioning it the whole trip?"

"Proud of you? Hell no, I'm not proud of you. I'm pissed at you. Your planning to get divorced would've been more interesting than most of the things we discussed, plus, if you'd told me, I'd have talked you out of it. This is a big mistake."

"We'll see, but keep working on the book. I'll call you when I get a new address."

That was the last time I ever talked to Ramsay. Two days later, on November 1, he called again and Ruth told him I'd have to call him back, I was outside splitting wood. "Splitting wood? Why isn't he working on the book?"

"Ramsay," Ruth said, "he can't spend all his time working on your book."

"I guess it doesn't matter. I'm never going to see it anyway."

"Of course you are. I just read the proposal. You guys are going to have a fun time writing it."

"Well, tell Bugsy I'm sending him all my stuff: pictures, books, maps, names, addresses, telephone numbers. He should get it in a couple of days. He can do whatever he wants with it."

As the facts surrounding Ramsay's suicide surfaced, it became clear he'd been planning to kill himself for over a year. The trooper who was handling the case told Theresa he'd traced Ramsay's gun back to a dealer in Cincinnati. Ramsay had purchased the gun, a Colt .25 caliber pistol, in June of 2002, right after he'd turned sixty. The "it" he'd never mentioned to me during the trip wasn't that he was going to dissolve his marriage. The "it" was that he was going to blow his brains out.

In letters he mailed to Theresa and Kim just before he shot himself, Ramsay claimed he was bored and didn't want to spend the next twenty years just hanging around taking up space. To people who knew Ramsay, that actually made sense. Business had been his life and when he failed to buy the mail-order swimsuit company, his life was over. Playing golf a couple of times a week, doing his laundry, watching the Weather Channel, waiting for his aunt in Baltimore and his dogs to die was just taking up space. The English poet and critic A. Alvarez, who once tried to kill himself, wrote that suicide is "a closed world with its own irresistible logic. . . . Once a man decides to take his own life he enters a shut-off, impregnable, but wholly convincing world where every detail fits and each incidence reinforces his decision."

That was a perfect description of Ramsay. With his acute analytical skills, I'm sure he was able to construct a compelling case for taking his own life. Once he'd made that decision, he had the ability to make every detail fit and let each incidence reinforce this feeling. I'm sure boredom was the reason for his suicide, but mental health experts tell me that was not the case. They say boredom is just another word for depression, which was the real reason for Ramsay's death.

They might be right. Ramsay could well have been manic-depressive, bipolar, or whatever. His older brother, the one who'd committed suicide at sixty, had been clinically depressed, so the gene was there. Whatever Ramsay's illness, it went undiagnosed. I'd spent twenty-four hours a day for a month with him and can say without hesitation he didn't have phobias, delusions, nightmares, or panic attacks. He never mentioned seeing a shrink, never went to a pharmacy, or as far as I could tell, never took so much as an aspirin. Even his drinking, despite my early concern, was completely controlled. The one diagnosis I can make is that except for our trip, Ramsay's life did seem boring, but I know a lot of guys our age whose lives seem boring and they're not killing themselves.

Howard Corwin, a close friend from Kezar Lake and a very prominent Harvard psychiatrist, told me Ramsay sounded like a compulsive type A. "These are people who've been successful at every level: prep school, college, graduate school, and work," Howard said. "They need to have total control of everything they get into. To them, failure is not acceptable. When one of these people tells me they feel suicidal, I take them very seriously because chances are they're going to do it, and they're not going to fail."

Control over his death would have been especially important to Ramsay. He'd watched both his parents suffer long, painful, expensive illnesses, and he wasn't going through the same thing. And once having decided to kill himself, he wouldn't fail. Thinking back to the French King Bridge I remember how disgusted Ramsay was that his brother screwed up his first attempt at suicide. I can still hear him saying, "I mean, how difficult is it to kill yourself?" That probably was why he used a gun. There's little chance of failing when you put a gun to your head.

Why did Ramsay wait until after our trip? My guess is that he kept a life list of things he wanted to do, and in December of '02, took one last look at it. When he came to our trip down the Connecticut River, he decided to give me a call. I'm sure he never expected me to say yes, but when I did, he decided to postpone his suicide. That would help explain his odd behavior as we approached Long Island Sound. For Ramsay, reaching the Sound wasn't the end of our trip, it was the end of his life.

I read somewhere where people close to someone who commits suicide go through three emotions: the first is shock, the second anger, the third sadness. After getting over the shock of Ramsay's suicide, I told Theresa I was just going to stay mad at him for a while. Mad that Ramsay already had planned to kill himself when he asked me to go on this trip with him. Mad that he'd never talked to me about it. Mad that I never saw it coming. I mean, who'd bother to floss his teeth for twenty minutes every night if he planned to kill himself? Most of all, I was mad that Ramsay would lay such a guilt trip on me, that he still might be alive if only I'd gone striper fishing with him. But as Ruth says, "What were you going to do, spend the rest of your life going on trips with Ramsay?"

My less charitable friends, especially the ones who didn't know Ramsay, say, "Let's get this straight. A guy spends a month with you in a canoe, and then blows his brains out. And this comes as a surprise?"

Granted, I'm not the easiest guy in the world, but I didn't kill Ramsay. In fact, he claimed our trip was his greatest adventure and knowing Ramsay, it probably was. There was no way he could fit our month together into his case for boredom. That's why he planned the fishing trip. The sad part is if he'd just given me a chance to catch my breath, we could have done it again. Two coots mooching their way down a river making grants to little conservation groups was a great idea. Dan Lufkin liked it so much he felt Paddling for Dollars should become a new tool for saving rivers. With Dan's support, we could have spent the next twenty years mooching our way down any number of America's great rivers: the Yellowstone, the Suwannee, the Susquehanna, the Delaware, the Columbia, the Pecos, even the mighty Mississippi. Our trip wasn't over. It was just starting.

Now I'm no longer mad, I'm just sad. How could Ramsay have done this to himself? How could he have been so bored with his life? How could he have not seen all of the opportunities open to him? I'm still wrestling with many of these questions, but there's one that will always haunt me. To get from Cincinnati to Bedford, Massachusetts, where he shot himself, Ramsay had to cross the Connecticut, probably on the Charter Oak Bridge just south of Hartford. As he drove over the river and looked down at the water we had paddled through on that very hot day just a few months earlier, what in this world was he thinking?

Afterword

Luke Eaton graduated from high school in 2007 and went right to work on the farm. Thanks to his extensive collection of Rigid Tools calendars, Luke doesn't mind spending long hours in his shop. With the Auburn Star herd up to 250 milkers, all of the Eatons are keeping plenty busy.

Jeff Wheeler created a comfortable nook in the Village Book Store where customers can buy a cup of coffee and tasty pastries while relaxing with a good book. If you ever get to Littleton, New Hampshire, drop by the store. Tell 'em Bugsy sent you, and you might get a free cup.

Tim McKay waited for the third pitch and blasted not one, but two hits off the Spaceman. And to think Ramsay said, "Bugsy doesn't know his ass from second base."

Carl Demrow is a happy boy. To date, twenty-five landowners have signed conservation easements protecting over 3,500 acres in the Headwaters project. Little Ramsay is no more. After a distinguished barnyard career, he was dispatched by Little Davey, a huge, all-white rooster Carl bought online as a gift for his new wife.

Pete and Keenie Richardson eventually exercised the option they had for the retirement community in Exeter, New Hampshire. While the food is good, there are no eggs on Pete's menu.

The Flamingo Kids are back in California where Kyle remains in a coma. The pink flamingo shows up for birthdays and like all the Derrick family, still hopes for Awaking Dreams.

Mary Hepburn and Ryan Ostebo bought the old cape, and after two years of meticulous restoration, Ryan created another architectural gem. For a while Hayden was a regular visitor, but as he grew older, he gradually drifted away.

Monique Fordham graduated cum laude from Vermont Law School and is now in Washington, D.C., working for the U.S. Forest Service in the Office of Tribal Relations. Rick continues to be a computer geek during the day, but at night morphs into the lead guitarist for a very popular local rock band.

Bob Bissell wrote his novel, liked it, and wrote another. Then, noveled out, he started restoring his old wood and canvas canoe, but quickly concluded he wasn't very handy. With nothing left to do, Bob got recertified and happily returned to his pediatric practice where he feels rejuvenated.

Jeannie Friedman's Mount Holyoke crew continues to dominate the Seven Sisters, and in May 2009, Coach Friedman was inducted into the Philadelphia Jewish Sports Hall of Fame. With Jacob in school, Jeannie and C.A., who formally tied the knot in 2004, are thinking of returning to competitive rowing. When they do, they'll be able to train at Mount Holyoke's new rowing center, scheduled to open in 2010.

Mark Noonan is now the conservation officer for the town of West Springfield. While he doesn't want to rush into anything, Mark is seriously thinking of proposing to his girlfriend of five years.

Bob Glenn, Rachelle Colburn, and Jake are moving back to Texas in fall 2009. Despite the new round of funding, Biocube didn't make it, and after five years with another robotic company in Flagstaff, Arizona, they decided to head home. Jake has set his sights on becoming a pilot, which is not surprising. Ramsay always maintained his little buddy had "the right stuff."

Jim Woodworth finished his five year stint as president and during that time, GMTC completed nine new projects and saw the E.B. Wolfe Land Acquisition Fund triple in size, further proof that volunteers like Jim are the heart and soul of the conservation movement.

Kätchen Coley remains the grande dame of conservation in Middletown, Connecticut, and despite the state's latest round of cuts, Kätchen continues to push for more funding for conservation.

Ramsay could be untying the Mad River (front and back) for his next great adventure while Katherine Hepburn waits to push him off. Life is short, keep paddling.

About the Author

Dave Morine is a native of the greater Boston area. He graduated from Amherst College in 1966 and earned an MBA from the Darden School at the University of Virginia in 1969. From 1972 to 1990, he was the head of land acquisition for The Nature Conservancy, a major conservation organization. Morine left the Conservancy in 1990 and has been writing ever since.

Good Dirt: Confessions of a Conservationist (Globe Pequot Press, 1990; Ballantine paperback, 1993) was his first book, followed by *The Class Choregus* (North Atlantic Books, 1993). Next came *Pit Bull: Lessons from Wall Street's Champion Trader* (with Martin Schwartz and Paul Flint, Harper Business, 1998; Harper Perennial paperback, 1999), then *Vacationland: A Half Century Summering in Maine* (DownEast Books, 2001), and most recently, *Small Claims: My Little Trials in Life* (DownEast Books, June, 2003).

In addition to his books, Morine has contributed stories to *Love of Labs* (Voyageur Press, 1997), *Love of Goldens* (Voyageur Press, 1998), and *Chicken Soup for the Baseball Fan's Soul* (Health Communications, Inc., 2001). Articles, mostly about his work in conservation, have appeared in magazines such as *Sports Illustrated, Reader's Digest, DownEast, Field & Stream, Range,* and *American Forests.* The *New York Times* once described Morine's stories as "embarrassing, hilarious, and unpredictable." These same adjectives could be used to describe *Two Coots,* but with a dark undercurrent; Morine never expected he'd be dealing with his friend's suicide.

Morine resides in Great Falls, Virginia.